The Art of Teaching Speaking:

Research and Pedagogy for the ESL/EFL Classroom

Keith S. Folse
University of Central Florida

THE UNIVERSITY OF MICHIGAN PRESS

KH

8/10/06

Acknowledgments

Someone asked me how long it took me to write this book. The answer is, "It depends." Do you mean the actual writing at the computer? Do you mean the time in the library to locate research? Do you mean the time I spent teaching ESL students in Malaysia and Saudi Arabia? Do you mean the time that I myself spent learning Spanish and Japanese? Actually, this book is the result of more than 30 years of studying and teaching languages in many settings all over the world. For their contributions to my understanding of what teaching speaking is, I thank the many teachers, professors, and thousands of students with whom I have been fortunate enough to work over the years.

Expressing one's ideas accurately on paper is hard work. I thank Kate Brummett, Karen Lyons, and Erica Reynoso for their feedback on early drafts of this work. I am indebted to Charlie Piper, who eagerly and judiciously offered comments on this manuscript. I am particularly thankful to the graduate students in my spring 2006 MATESOL Practicum course at the University of Central Florida, who allowed me to field-test this manuscript with them: Lauren Boone, Nicole Hammond, Rosemeire Johnstone, Karen Lyons, Molvie Simon, and Melissa Weller.

Finally, I am especially grateful to Kelly Sippell, senior ESL acquisitions editor at the University of Michigan Press, for her constant encouragement, steady support, insightful ideas, and extraordinary hard work that ensured the ultimate publication of this book.

Contents

Introduction: An Overview of Teaching Second Language Conversation

Teaching a Conversation Course in Ecuador
Teenagers; Private High School
Mary Goodman

I was an EFL Instructor for more than 20 years in Guayaquil, Ecuador, the most populous and famous port city in the country. During these years, I had a variety of experiences both as teacher and academic director. I worked with many teachers in different schools as I taught a variety of EFL subjects, including Conversation (Listening/Speaking), Grammar, Reading/Writing, Pronunciation, and Video. I know that I am the teacher that I am today because I had the opportunity to teach a range of students in terms of age (Junior High to Adult/Professional), level of English (absolute beginners through TOEFL® Preparation), class size (from 1 to 40), and gender (coeducational versus all-boys' classes).

While I had a variety of experiences teaching Conversation classes, one particular Conversation course will forever remain in my memory. During my time at the all-boys' School of the Espiritu Santo Educational Center, I had to teach 39 very unruly eleventh grade boys after their previous teacher had quit mid-year because she could no longer put up with the discipline issues. Until that time, I had had the luxury of teaching smaller-sized classes with mostly adults where discipline was not really a major issue. Even though the students' level of English ranged from basic to intermediate, I had to make it work; I could not be another teacher who gave up on those boys. I had to quickly analyze what the previous teacher had been doing wrong (in part, following the textbook like a compulsory guidebook—which it was not) so I wouldn't fall into her problems with keeping their attention, which in turn created the discipline problems in her classroom.

One problem was that the students had different levels of interest in English, and few cared for the stale topics that had been used for class discussion. Students—regardless of their age—always do better when they are working on something that is meaningful to them. To gauge their interests, I gave the students an "Interest Inventory" of possible topics of conversation and had them add some additional ones. As a result, I immediately cut out of the syllabus those topics that the students felt were too boring or not appealing.

People need to be doing things. An active learner is a productive learner. In this case, more importantly, an active learner is so engaged that misbehaving or other discipline issues are decreased. How did I accomplish this important goal? I got the students more involved by assigning them research about a particular athlete or singer (or whatever topic they were interested in) and having them present this information to the class in oral reports. Here, I allowed them to use a few index cards with notes on them, but they were not allowed to "read" from a paper. The remaining students had to listen to their classmate's oral report, take notes, make up questions, and grade the oral report (so I was not the only one awarding a grade). This kept the other students involved and focused. I also tried, whenever possible, to make the activities light and fun, keeping in mind that my audience involved eleventh grade boys who would rather be outside playing soccer or flirting with some girl than trying to learn English, the latter seen as a pointless goal at that point in their life.

My general advice to anyone teaching EFL to a large class is to keep the students' discipline issues in check by keeping them busy with active and engaging pair work or small group work (up to three students). Dealing with forty students is tough. Dealing with twenty pairs or thirteen groups of three suddenly made the classroom more manageable. I found that groups of five or more were not effective because one or two students would actually do the work while the others sat around or conversed in Spanish. Thus, grouping does have a limit, and two or three seems to be a good limit. It is important to avoid putting best friends together in pairs; likewise, it is important to try to see that pairings are rotated every so often so learners can work with different people.

Another piece of advice I'd offer is that the type of activity that really engages the students in real, life-like, conversational activities depends very much on their English level. An ESL or EFL teacher shouldn't expect to be able to do debates or commentaries about current events in a classroom where the level of English is basic. Starting out with many visual activities such as Sequence Pictures, Look Again Pictures (find the differences in the pictures), Information Gap and Jigsaw activities, as well as Board Games, Skits, Songs (cloze or fill in the blanks), Games (Taboo, Twenty Questions, "The 10,000 Dollar Pyramid," "Jeopardy," etc.), in addition to teaching about natural disasters (hurricanes, floods, etc.), holidays, proverbs, idioms, phrasal verbs, and discussions about heroes, UFOs, superstitions, customs and traditions all helped to keep my students' interest level high, which in turn helped eliminate many of the discipline problems. The answer for teachers is not any one set of certain activities but rather an eclectic set based on the teacher's and students' personalities and goals.

The last major advice I offer is that it is important to keep in mind that a conversation topic or activity that worked really well with one age group or gender does not necessarily work well with those from another. Many activities that worked well with my adult students just didn't fly with this group. I found that as soon I gave the eleventh-grade boys a Student Interest Inventory and tailored the conversation course more to their interests than to the topics that the book dealt with, I was better able to get the students involved, keep their interest, and maintain discipline.

Why should we be so concerned with the teaching of conversation in an English as a Second Language (ESL) or English as a Foreign Language (EFL) classroom? Though there are clearly many different answers, two big answers are at the forefront. The first focuses on the learner, and the second on the teacher.

Conversation Class from the Learner's Point of View

Knowing a language involves many different things, but when people say, "I know French," first and foremost they mean they can *speak* French. They may be able to read French and they may even have some writing ability in French, but when people—including our learners—refer to "second language ability," their primary goal seems to be speaking. In fact, I cannot imagine the average learner saying, "I want to learn to read Russian" or "I really want to learn to write Turkish." Almost all of my ESL/ EFL students dream of the day when they can finally say, "I *speak* English well."

In a very general usage of the word *speaking,* we can see that speaking a language clearly entails many different aspects. It is important for all teachers of speaking or conversation to remember that the aspects deemed more important depend entirely upon the learner's ultimate purpose in learning to speak English. Thus, you need to know why your learners want to speak English. Is it for business? Business dealings with native speakers? Business dealings with native speakers face to face? Over the phone or via a computer? Is it for conversation? Conversation on the job, as with a tour leader? Is it conversation to be able to communicate at the bank or supermarket?

In conducting this needs assessment of your learners, you will find the answers to these and similar questions that will help you determine what *speaking English* means to your learners. As you consider these answers, you will have a better idea of what to focus on in what you teach or practice with your learners in this English communication class. For example:

- You might focus on *fluency.* Does the speaker stop frequently to search for words? (See Appendix A.) Does the speaker use words that accurately reflect his or her actual social level? (Adults want to sound as intelligent in their second language as they do in their first language.)

- You might focus on *pronunciation.* (See Appendix B.) Does the speaker have a marked accent that inhibits communication?

- You might focus on *language accuracy,* specifically *grammar.* (See Appendix C.) Does the speaker make so many errors or such serious errors that communication is hindered or even impeded?

- You might focus on *listening ability.* The two are inextricably linked. It is not possible to have a conversation without good listening ability. Without a certain level of listening, a conversation would quickly deteriorate into a series of unconnected questions or statements.

Which Name? Conversation or Discussion or Oral Fluency or Speaking?

The fact that conversation can focus on such vastly different aspects as fluency or grammar or listening ability is a clear indication of the broad scope that it encompasses. In fact, most conversation classes will encompass all of these aspects in varying amounts at different times. Thus, it should come as no surprise that even the name for this class can vary. While the most widely used name for this type of language class is probably *conversation*, others tend to refer to it as speaking, discussion, or oral communication. Though there can be certain distinctions, all of these terms are used interchangeably in this work, as they are in most teachers' vocabulary.

Again, it is important to ask yourself (and remind yourself constantly as you plan for this class), "Why are my students coming to this class?" The learners' language needs are the number one driving force behind what you do in this class.

Conversation Class from the Teacher's Point of View

Learners want to learn how to speak a language, and a good program curriculum is based on learners' needs. Therefore, it is only logical that speaking features prominently in almost all language programs, regardless of learner proficiency level, learner age (e.g., children versus adults), or type of course (intensive versus non-intensive). Thus, to be the most effective teacher that you can be, it behooves you to know as much as possible about teaching speaking. Teaching conversation involves much more than merely tossing out a topic to your class for discussion.

In addition to teachers responding to learners' needs, teachers who want to land the best teaching jobs need to show that they can teach speaking classes and teach them well. It is not at all uncommon for teaching job announcements to list "ability to teach conversation" as a major requirement for a position. The ability to teach conversation is especially important in EFL teaching jobs.

Here are four sample job advertisements offered to show employers' desire for teachers who know what they are doing in the teaching of conversation. Notice how—in general—the ESL jobs tend to require all skills, including speaking, while the EFL positions often emphasize conversation over other skills.

> **Position 1 (intensive English program, ESL):**
> Minimum requirements include: (1) M.A. in TESL or related field; (2) at least 3 years ESL teaching experience in intensive English programs, specialized English courses for international professionals, or equivalent; (3) demonstrated ability to teach a variety of ESL courses, levels, and skills; and (4) native fluency/command of standard English
>
> Notes: "a variety of courses" will certainly include conversation, oral communication, or discussion

> **Position 2 (community college, ESL):**
> Duties: Teach lecture and laboratory sections at the intermediate level; evaluate and advise students; develop curricula; serve on committees as assigned.
>
> Notes: "lecture and laboratory sections" is a phrase that most likely refers to a class in which students practice listening (and some speaking) to improve their ability to comprehend lectures on academic topics

> **Position 3 (language school, EFL):**
> Wanted: a British EFL teacher aged 28 at least to give English conversation courses. Our language institute is located in the north of France. It is a town very close to famous cities (such as Reims, Nancy, and Paris). Ability to teach all language skills, with emphasis on speaking.
>
> Notes: "conversation courses" is clearly indicated; many EFL jobs list job information not allowed in the U.S. and other countries (e.g., age, gender)

> **Position 4 (various, EFL):**
> English teaching jobs in Asia and Africa. NO Experience needed! Casual conversational classes held in group discussion type environment. Class sizes can vary from small (3 to 6 students) to large (20 to 30). Teaching hours: usually 4 to 6 hrs a day. Operation hours: 8AM–9PM, must be flexible Mon–Sun.
>
> Notes: "conversation classes" is clearly indicated; the term "casual" means that these students focus more on face-to-face language practice rather than academic English

Most EFL jobs involve a good deal of speaking or conversation classes. Even in programs that work with integrated skills, speaking features prominently. In these cases, you will certainly need to be able to teach a speaking class or the speaking component of that course. While this chapter presents both the learners' and the teacher's viewpoint of what speaking is, in a really good match of learners and teacher, both viewpoints overlap considerably—or at least they should. The rest of the chapters in this book aim to help teachers figure out what learners need and what specific classroom activities can help with those needs in an efficient, effective, and fun manner—because certainly learning a language is supposed to be a fun activity.

The Organization of This Book

First and foremost, this book is designed to be accessible. It is meant to help teachers improve their ability to teach not merely good but rather outstanding conversation or speaking courses. Every chapter has been written with the teacher in mind.

Chapter 1 covers five factors that are fundamental to a successful conversation class: the learner, the curriculum, the topic, the two "languages," and the task. Each of these factors begins with a description or definition. Following this introductory information, there is a section called In the Real World, in which I discuss relevant classroom examples that I have experienced. Finally, I discuss the factor and offer practical application ideas for your teaching.

Chapter 2 presents research on many aspects of conversation or speaking. This chapter explains six key terms through definitions and examples: *fluency, accuracy, interlanguage, comprehensible input, negotiation of meaning,* and *pushed output.* The next section shows teachers how to move from a general topic to a specific speaking task, which is the most important component of a speaking lesson. A substantial part of this chapter is dedicated to research on three key factors in designing an effective task: (1) *the flow of information,* (2) *a planning component,* and (3) *the solution to the task.* This is followed by examples of speaking tasks and an annotated bibliography of selected works.

Conversation classes vary tremendously. In Chapter 3, twenty teachers recount what it was like to teach conversation in different countries. These accounts offer important, meaningful information about the students in these specific teaching contexts. Areas represented include North America (Canada, Mexico, United States), South America (Brazil, Chile), Europe (Germany, Portugal), Asia (China, Japan, Korea, Vietnam), and the Middle East (Qatar, United Arab Emirates). Children's and adult classes as well as academic and general conversation classes are featured.

Chapter 4 includes detailed instructions for using twenty activities that I have used successfully in conversation classes in an ESL setting, an EFL setting, or both. Information for each activity is organized as follows: title, description, materials needed, preparation steps, in-class procedure, caveats and further suggestions, an actual example, and the source. Rather than being a list of potentially good activities, these twenty activities are ones that I myself have taught. I know that they meet the criteria for a successful task and are adaptable to a variety of teaching settings.

While Chapter 4 contains twenty good activities, Chapter 5 details ten activities that did not work well. Most of these unsuccessful tasks took place in classes that I have observed over the years in my position as supervisor, coordinator, or principal. It is important to study both successful and unsuccessful class tasks to help us understand why some tasks are inherently better than others.

Finally, five appendixes offer invaluable information on vocabulary, pronunciation, grammar, lesson plans, and additional teaching resources.

1 Five Fundamental Factors in Planning and Teaching a Conversation Class

It is impossible to dictate what should happen in a typical speaking class because there is no typical speaking class. Perhaps the only common feature in speaking classes in the United States, Brazil, Korea, Egypt, and Spain is that during most of the class time, the students—not the teacher—should be doing the talking. What they will talk about, for how long, and for what purpose will most certainly vary from country to country and even from class to class in the very same school! (Chapter 3 offers twenty teacher accounts from all over the world; you may wish to read some of these accounts before continuing here.)

Regardless of the array of diversity in conversation classes, there are five key factors that every teacher should consider when planning a speaking class:

- The learner, including the learner's age, proficiency level, and goals
- The program or school, since most teachers follow a curriculum with set steps
- The topic being discussed
- The two "languages": (a) *in* the task; (b) *for* the task
- The activity or task that serves as the vehicle for conversation

These five factors are so tightly connected that it is almost impossible to separate only one or two when planning a speaking class. This is not to say that it is impossible to do so. Much to the detriment of language teaching—

FIGURE 1

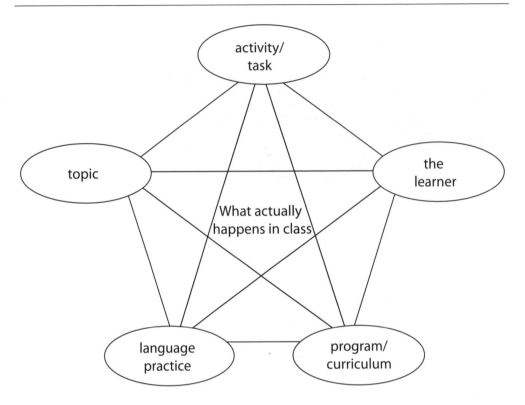

and certainly of student learning—our profession has seen this happen numerous times.

In the 1950s and 1960s, *audiolingualism,* a teaching method that focused heavily on language drills, was the favored method. In the audiolingual method, what mattered most was the activity or task, that is, a drill, not the content, not the learner, and certainly not the topic being discussed. Drills should most definitely be a part of every good language teacher's instruction, but drills should be one of many language tool options, not the only one.

From the 1950s to the mid-1980s, the focus in ESL/EFL teaching (as well as in foreign language teaching in many countries) was exclusively on language, primarily grammar. In this view, it was assumed that mastery of key grammar points would produce great language speakers. Teaching focused heavily on knowing how to form the present perfect tense, for example, or on being able to recite a list of modals. This teaching viewpoint is still strong in many EFL settings, which explains why students who have studied English for ten years cannot even introduce themselves in English.

To be certain, knowing about the English language, including ESL grammar issues, is key to improving speaking ability, but focusing on one aspect such as grammer is not the answer.

In response to this, the ESL world experienced a paradigm shift with the work of Krashen (1985) regarding the importance of what is referred to as "comprehensible input." Reacting to this historic equating of learning grammar with knowing the language, Krashen proposed that the sole ingredient necessary for true language acquisition to take place was comprehensible input for the learners. The teacher's main job, then, became to provide comprehensible input. Unfortunately, this almost cataclysmic upheaval in language teaching has not produced an equally cataclysmic change in learning outcomes or results. ESL (and foreign language) classes have now had two full decades to implement this hypothesis, yet we have not seen an increase in language learning success per se. Again, focusing on one area, here the nature of teacher talk, is not the answer to planning a successful speaking class. To be sure, teacher input is important, but there is no empirical evidence—from research or from now twenty years of actual classroom implementation—to show that "i + 1" is the magical ingredient to learning or acquiring a second language.

The success of what happens in a conversation class depends on these five factors: (1) the learner, (2) the curriculum, (3) the topic, (4) the two "languages," and (5) the task or activity. In the rest of this chapter, we will examine each of these factors to see what the teacher can and should take into account when planning a good discussion class.

Factor 1: The Learner, Especially the Learner's Age, Proficiency Level, and Goals

Learners vary by category and as individuals. In your ESL class, you may find one thing that affects speaking is native country. You have noticed that your Japanese students are generally more reticent than your Mexican students. However, even within this category, you will find many individual differences, with some Japanese being more outspoken than others and some Mexicans knowing more vocabulary than others. However, there are some broad categories that teachers should be aware of as they teach speaking classes.

Conversation classes are different from reading classes or general English classes in several aspects. Because conversation classes tend to be smaller and because the students spend much of the class time talking, you find out much more about each student than you would in other kinds of English classes. Teachers and students often develop a more friendly relationship. The more you know your students, the better you are able to shape the class according to their needs. You need to consider their age, interests, motivation, cultural background, educational background, personality, and (limited) language proficiency (Ernst, 1994; Green, 1993; Lazaraton, 2001; Mulling, 1997; Oliver, 1998, 2000; Peirce, 1995; Perez, 1996; Williams, 2001).

Getting to know your students does not ensure that you can teach the class to the students' needs or wishes, but it is certainly an important step.

In the Real World

My first teaching job was in an intensive English program at a U.S. university. The students had five classes every day: grammar, reading, writing, listening (which included speaking—but not in the way that I emphasize and provide practice for speaking today), and vocabulary. Because most of the books that we used were from the same publisher, the books already had some degree of integration of topics.

This was not only my first time teaching a group of students, it was my first time working with other teachers. I remember sitting in the teachers' lounge one day as the other teachers were discussing problems that another teacher had had with one particular class when, just then, the particular teacher came into the room. Up to that point, I had never seen another teacher so visibly upset. Her students were being disruptive and had refused to do the activities that she had asked them to do!

Even with my limited teaching experience, I knew that this was not a good thing. Other teachers pressed her for more information. She had asked them to sit in a circle—on the floor—and her students thought this was inappropriate. As the discussion continued, I heard the teacher say, "Well, their English is at the same level as my children, so I plan activities that I know my children would like. I never thought they would mind."

Adult ESL students are *not* children. This is perhaps one of the biggest, most insulting mistakes you can make in teaching adults. In fact, the statement that their English is similar to that of children is incorrect on *numerous* levels.

More important, however, children are children and adults are adults. These two groups learn differently.

Unfortunately, in the 25 years of teaching since this incident, I have heard many other teachers say that they treat their adult ESL students as children because of this or that. This is wrong.

If you have given up a year of your life (including a year away from your family, your way of life, your job, and your career advancement opportunities) to go take Bulgarian classes in Bulgaria, would you be happy with a class where you sit on the floor? Sing pointless songs? Create scrapbook projects?

A second example of the importance of taking the learner into account has occurred in every ESL speaking class that I have taught in which there were many nationalities present. Though the class that I'm currently teaching is larger than usual, with 24 learners, the class composition is normal for the state of Florida in that we have about 70 percent Spanish speakers, 10 percent Portuguese speakers, 10 percent Korean speakers, and 10 percent other (including Japanese, Vietnamese, Russian, and Arabic) speakers.

While there are certainly many individual differences, I also know that there are some key interaction differences by group in terms of how they will react to certain teacher actions. For example, if I ask an open-ended question to the entire class—such as "Who knows why the girl in the story did not tell her friend's secret?"—I know that, in general, the Asian speakers in this group (Korean and Japanese) will hesitate to speak up in class. In contrast, I fully expect a Spanish, Portuguese, Russian, or Arabic speaker to volunteer an answer.

I also know—again all things being equal—that certain groups, such as the Koreans and Japanese, have a harder time with listening skills than the other groups. Part of this is due to previous English training; in Japan and Korea, knowing a language is often equated with memorizing grammar or vocabulary, not actually being able to use the language to converse. Thus, I may be the students' first contact with a native speaker who does not translate everything for them. Part of this could also be due to cultural norms in which students have been trained to be quiet in class—whatever kind of class it is—and listen to the master teacher impart information. In other words, participatory or interactive classrooms with communicative activities may be as foreign to them as I am.

A third example of individual learner differences comes from my teaching experience in Japan where one of my classes there was a group of second graders. My educational training was for secondary students, not elementary. At "conversation schools" overseas, however, teachers are often asked to teach the whole gamut of learners—from young toddlers to grandparents and everything in between.

Our school had plenty of materials to help teachers, but what I was not prepared for was second graders' high energy level and short attention span. For my adult learners, I could plan perhaps three activities for the 50-minute class; in stark contrast, my second graders had very short attention spans and had to be doing things almost constantly. When my second graders were doing things, they were focused; when I tried to run an "adult" class in which learners needed to pay attention to me for a prolonged period of time (and I learned that "prolonged" meant more than five minutes), the class faltered. In the end, I had to take my three activities and think of variations to make sure that I had eight or nine or even ten shorter activities planned. These learners—because of their age and cognitive levels—needed to have many activities.

Discussion and Practical Application for Your Teaching

The learner is the most important of the five components to consider in constructing a successful speaking program. Simply put, without the learner, *the class does not exist,* so teachers should consider all pertinent features of the learners with regard to the speaking class.

It would be impossible to create a list of every single feature of ESL/EFL learners that you could consider as you put together your lesson plans, but some of the most relevant characteristics about your learners include: (1) age, (2) reason(s) for wanting to speak English, (3) proficiency level, (4) attitude toward English, (5) time constraints for study, (6) educational background, (7) gender, (8) anxiety level, (9) study skills/habits, (10) personality (introvert versus extrovert), (11) willingness to take risks in speaking, (12) field dependence–field independence, (13) native language–English differences (contrastive analysis), (14) individual learner differences/styles, and (15) opportunities for (real) practice.

The most important thing that you can do as a teacher is to be aware of these characteristics that have the *potential* to impact what happens in your speaking class. I am not saying that all of these—or even most of these—will be relevant in a given teaching situation, but certainly some of these will shape who your learners are as individuals and thereby have a most definite impact on your ability to teach an effective conversation class.

Factor 2: The Curriculum, Program, or School

You are not teaching in a vacuum or on your own private island. If you are teaching a private conversation class, then your class is in fact the "school," so the curriculum that you will follow is most likely an informal one that you have worked out for the student(s) based on particular learner needs. Most teachers, however, are teaching a class within a school or program, and teachers must be aware of (what has been previously decided by someone else as) the curriculum to be covered in the speaking class.

In a language school, the entire class—which may be called conversation, oral communication, speaking, or simply "English"—is most likely dedicated to speaking and listening. In an intensive program with many classes per day, one of two situations may exist. In the first situation, specific classes may be dedicated to specific skills; in this setting, there may be one class dedicated to conversation. In the second situation, all of the classes may be integrated skills. In this situation, certain activities are designated in the teaching plan as communication or speaking activities. It is important for you as teacher to understand clearly the type of program in which you are teaching.

In the Real World

In the 1980s, I taught junior officers of the Saudi National Guard in Saudi Arabia. These students were studying English to reach a certain proficiency level so that they could pass an exam at our school, which would in turn allow them to receive further military training at a military base in the United States. The program consisted of ten levels, and each level took about four weeks to complete.

In this program, the whole curriculum was completely spelled out for me. My "planning" consisted of writing which pages I would cover in the first hour, which pages in the second hour, etc., for each of the five days of the teaching week. This record was kept in my class folder, which was located on a desk in the very back of the classroom. At any time, a Saudi or an American military supervisor—who knew little to nothing about teaching—could come into my classroom to observe my class. When this happened, the supervisor would turn to the appropriate plan for that day, for example, Day

16, Period 3, to see where I was supposed to be in the book and compare that with what we were actually doing. If the two matched, the class was deemed "good." If not, the class was deemed "not on schedule."

I remember a student once asking me about the meaning of the word *encyclopedia* that appeared in our textbook. "Folse," he asked, "encyclopedia same same dictionary?" Having just gotten my master's in TESOL and having had four years of teaching experience, including classes with many Saudis, I answered—quite naively—"Well, yes and no," and I proceeded to explain what a dictionary was and what an encyclopedia was. I gave examples. I used my hands. I tried to draw pictures. I tried to get the students to talk about these words, to use them in a conversation. Now I know how pointless this was! When I finished, the student turned to his classmates and a brief discussion in Arabic ensued. He then looked back at me, smiled, and said, "OK, same same dictionary."

I sighed internally. What I did not know at the time—because I was new to the job and the program—was that the comprehensive examination that the students had to take to exit the program had a vocabulary section on it with multiple-choice questions that consisted of one test word followed by four single-word answer choices, as in this example:

42. pronounce   (A) belong   (B) guess   (C) say   (D) watch

Thus, if there was a question about *encyclopedia*, it might have looked like this:

43. encyclopedia   (A) allowance (B) dictionary (C) helmet   (D) kitchen

The point of this story is that these students did not need a speaking task about encyclopedias. Yes, it might have been good for their overall English proficiency, but their actual purpose was not to become better English speakers. Their goal—as it should have been—was to pass that test as soon as possible to get themselves to the United States for further training and, therefore, job advancement and a higher salary upon their return to the Kingdom. The curriculum—including the textbooks and the tests—was set up to achieve the goals of the program. It was not my job to try to change the curriculum to include a speaking component, and it would have been fruitless to attempt to do so.

My second example is from a conversation school in Japan. It is important to know that English conversation, or *ei-kai-wa,* is actually a sort of hobby for many Japanese. Many adults do not go to English conversation class primarily to improve their English per se. Instead, they go because it is a popular pastime in Japan. They can make friends there. They can learn about a foreign culture. Studying English conversation is seen as a status symbol of sorts.

Before going to this school in Japan, much of my ESL teaching had been in intensive courses in which highly motivated students studied English to pass the TOEFL® (Test of English as a Foreign Language) to get into a U.S. college or university as quickly as possible. These students knew that time was important (and expensive), so they wanted to learn as quickly as possible. In these academic ESL programs, there were usually several proficiency levels, with four being the most common number of levels (e.g., beginning, lower-intermediate, upper-intermediate, advanced).

At the language school where I worked in Japan, we also had proficiency levels. In fact, we had eight levels, from beginning to advanced. Since conversation schools in Japan are at times not as much about learning as attending, I had to readjust my classes to *doing English* instead of the traditional teaching/learning paradigm. Unlike before, I could no longer effectively teach three grammar points in one class. I could not cover twenty vocabulary items. In this program, students were not trying to pass a test; instead, they wanted to practice a little English and do some fun things. I learned very quickly that conversation classes in Japan are ALL about providing opportunities for learners to practice—and the more practice opportunities, the better. Students didn't want to *study* English conversation or *learn* English conversation as much as *do* English conversation.

The curriculum was set up to allow for less material to be covered in a term since more class time was spent on speaking activities. The textbooks that were selected included many speaking activities, with pair work already built into the units. Even teachers unfamiliar with pair work or communicative activities could easily teach according to the school's overall curriculum.

In addition, my Japanese students in each class formed a bond, a bond that was much stronger than anything that I had seen in classes in other countries. This class bond included not only the students, but also the teacher. This espirit de corps was so important that in subsequent semesters, sometimes students would prefer to move down a level if it meant that the group could be with the same teacher again. Our school actually encouraged this since it meant that more students would stay in the program because if students could not be with their language colleagues, they would most likely go to another school or drop their English studies altogether.

This cohesiveness affected our overall curriculum. Students did not worry so much about moving up or down but rather staying with their group. As a teacher in this program, I learned to make allowances for a student who might be a little weaker than the others. This student was going to be in the class, and it was my job to make sure that he or she felt comfortable.

Discussion and Practical Application for Your Teaching

My initial reaction to the curricula at the programs in Saudi Arabia and then in Japan was that they were somehow flawed. The students were not moving quickly enough. The program at the military school in Saudi Arabia focused heavily on language components such as grammar and vocabulary, but the conversation school in Japan seemed to be more about hobbies and culture. To be certain, they had English as their common denominator, but neither seemed exactly right to me.

This initial reaction of mine was incorrect—and actually quite arrogant in retrospect. As Richards (2001) points out, "One of the basic assumptions of curriculum development is that a sound educational program should be based on an analysis of learners' needs" (51).

What were my students' needs? The Saudi students came to our program because they needed to pass a test of basic English proficiency to allow them to go for further military training. This test had no language skills sections (e.g., reading or speaking) per se; it tested primarily knowledge of grammar and vocabulary. Even the listening section relied heavily on grammar and vocabulary questions. My Japanese students came to our program because they wanted to learn a little English, to meet a foreigner, to know something about foreign culture, and to meet other Japanese with similar interests or educational level. My students came to class to *experience* English, not memorize information about the language. In hindsight, it is clear to me now that the curriculum at each school was in line with the *students' needs—and that this alignment is the mark of a good curriculum.*

How does this affect you, the teacher? The school's curriculum or plan of study is important. Almost all schools have an overall curriculum of some sort. (If you are a professional teacher and come across a school without a real curriculum, do not walk—RUN—to the nearest exit.) In some schools, this curriculum is very detailed, even down to what should happen in Week 12 and maybe even Day 3 of Week 12. At the other extreme, we find schools without a real curriculum. Sometimes schools have a "curriculum" that consists of some books on a shelf that teachers can photocopy from, which is not only unprofessional but, more important, copyright infringement and illegal. The curriculum is decided by whatever you want to teach on any given day.

What should you do? It is up to you to be aware of what a curriculum can look like. There is a great deal of variation possible. For example, it is also up to you to know how programs can be set up, for example, individual skills classes or integrated skills classes. In addition, you should know how these different types of programs match or do not match your own philosophy of teaching conversation. If you believe strongly in integrating vocabulary in conversation, for example, then you probably will not be happy in a program that is based on a different method or line of thinking. Finally, as you search for a teaching job, it is completely up to you to know about your new school's program before you get there. Just as you want your students to do their homework before they arrive in class, you should do your homework about your potential place of employment before you go there.

Factor 3: The Topic Being Discussed

Regardless of where you teach or whom you are teaching, a speaking class needs a topic to discuss. Choosing a topic is not hard; on the other hand, choosing a good topic that will create a successful conversation or discussion is a very hard task for many teachers.

Perhaps the most essential planning task is selecting the topic of the discussion activity. Clearly, the topic should be one that the particular learners are interested in because even the best designed activity cannot be successful if the topic is of little or no interest to the students. In a learner-centered syllabus, both teaching and practice materials should center around the needs of the learner (Brown, 2000; Nunan, 1996; Richards, 2001; Yorio, 1986).

When you are selecting the topic, some of the more important factors to consider are the age of the learner, the purpose of learning English, the proficiency level of the learner, and the cultural background of the learner (Barkhuisen, 1998; Mulling, 1997; Oliver, 1998, 2000; Perez, 1996). Can you imagine how each of these four factors could influence or limit your choice of topic for a discussion activity?

Age affects topic choice. Young learners cannot discuss serious topics such as capital punishment or marriage. Older learners do not want to sing children's songs or talk about cartoons. The students' purpose for learning English is critical. Students in a conversation school in Japan want general conversation practice, but academic program students trying to pass the TOEFL® have different speaking needs for the exam. Students' proficiency level impacts the topic choice. Discussing serious topics requires a great deal more language, including vocabulary; thus, beginning students might be able to talk about their family or their pets, while more advanced students could be pushed to talk about serious topics such as nuclear energy or health care problems. Students' cultural backgrounds affect topic choice. Some groups of students can talk about race relations or abortion, but other groups consider these topics taboo, sensitive, or upsetting.

The bottom line is that no one knows your students better than you do, so the ultimate responsibility for choice of topics belongs to you, the teacher.

In the Real World

In some schools, teachers have no say whatsoever in the selection of topics. For example, when I taught at an American military training institute in Saudi Arabia in the 1980s, curriculum planners had produced a list of what to cover, in what order, and approximately how many class meetings this would take. Such planning is not uncommon in large programs that have numerous proficiency levels that students must pass through before graduation or completion. In this particular program, students were expected to complete their course as quickly as possible in order to pass a final exam that would then permit them to receive further military training in the United States. Using two or three class meetings to practice at length ordering from a menu, a topic that was not in the syllabus, was not an option for any teacher. (In addition to displeasing the powers that be, this activity would have frustrated the students because they knew that this topic was unlikely to be on the big test.)

In Japan, part of my teaching duties at the language school were to teach at company classes, which are different from the regular conversation classes. For company classes, I would travel to a company, such as a pharmaceutical company or a bank, and I would teach a group of employees there. These classes could have from one to twenty students, but the exact number that would attend for any given class depended on their workload that day. The learners' proficiency levels ranged from false-beginner (i.e., a learner who has studied the language but cannot function much, if at all) to upper-intermediate—all within the same class.

It was difficult to have topics that would please everyone, so I aimed for the middle. I tried to stick to general topics that would interest Japanese adults of their age range. I never discussed anything controversial. I did not talk about nuclear bombs, abortion, alcohol problems, or women's rights. These topics would have been culturally inappropriate. Also, these workers were still on the clock. They had worked all day. They were in English class from 5:30 PM to 7:00 PM and would then go back to work for a while. In addition to the fact that many adult learners wanted to *do* English rather than learn more grammar, these Japanese were tired and needed a break from their work. All of these factors came into my decision to play language games or discuss light topics.

Another class that I had in Japan was a group of junior tennis players. This group of six young people, ages eleven to fourteen, included some amazing tennis players. During their after-school tennis practice one day a week, I had English conversation class with them. We met in the pro shop right next to the courts. When we did the textbook activities about families, colors, or clothing, the students were polite but certainly less than interested. However, when I brought in activities that involved famous tennis players, the students were incredibly enthusiastic. This was obviously a topic that they were interested in.

Discussion and Practical Application for Your Teaching

Every speaking class needs something to discuss, the topic. The choice of topic is crucial. As teacher, you may not be able to control your students' age or study time availability or personality, but you most certainly can and should exert your role as teacher to make sure that the topics covered are ones that are most conducive to a successful discussion class. The topics should match your needs analysis of your students.

It is up to you to become familiar with some possible topics. One good way to do this is to look at not one or two but ten different conversation books to see what kinds of topics are covered. Pay attention to which topics are included for which proficiency levels. Once you have the ability to create a list of at least twenty topics off the top of your head, then you are ready to match topics with your students' needs.

While teachers have an idea of what will work and what will not work as a viable topic, it is also wise to let students have some say in this. This is especially prudent when dealing with controversial issues such as same-sex marriage or the death penalty. When I teach from my book *Discussion Starters: Speaking Fluency for Advanced ESL/EFL Students* (Folse, 1996), which includes both light and serious topics, I begin with Unit 2, Smoker's Rights, because I know this is a "safe" topic in that the topic and the tasks in the unit are unlikely to upset anyone. At the same time, I go over the table of contents with all of the students. One of their first small group speaking tasks is to go through the list of unit topics in the book and decide as a group which five they would like to talk about. As students are presenting their ideas to the class the next day, you should keep a tally of the topics that receive the most votes to help formulate your speaking curriculum for that course. At the same time, you should listen to your students' English proficiency to gauge not only the overall group speaking level but also who the stronger and weaker students are.

If you are not using a textbook, perhaps you could give your students a list of 20 to 50 topics and have them work in groups to choose, say, five topics that they would like to talk about in English.

Factor 4: The Two "Languages"—*IN* the Task versus *FOR* the Task

Historically, learning a language has meant learning the parts of the language, that is, its grammar, vocabulary, sound system, spelling, etc. Perhaps this tradition came about because "educated" people studied Latin, and they tended to study it in the grammar-translation method, which emphasized translating the pieces (words) of the language. With the enormous emphasis on communication these days, however, people tend to focus on the ability to speak a language, not just read it or write it or know its grammar rules.

I am not saying that grammar or vocabulary or writing skills are not important. The truth is that a good conversation teacher knows the components of the target language and has the ability to (1) construct a lesson around an important language component (e.g., a list of fifteen family words), (2) point out important language components within a dialogue (e.g., the negative of *I go* is *I don't go* but the negative of *I went* is not *I don't went* but rather *I didn't go*), or (3) do both 1 and 2. Without a solid grasp of this knowledge, it is doubtful that the teacher can design activities that will stretch their learners' current level of English. This knowledge is so important, in fact, that I would argue that an unknowledgeable teacher will find it extremely difficult, if not impossible, to be an efficient language teacher.

In doing any speaking task, the teacher must be aware that there are two languages required. One language is the language in the actual task. The second language is the language that students need to complete the task. Before we go on, let's consider an example speaking activity.

Speaking Activity
Test Your Geography about South America

STEP 1. Rank these from smallest (1) to biggest (6) in terms of population.

____ The population of Argentina

____ The population of Bolivia

____ The population of Chile

____ The population of Colombia

____ The population of Ecuador

____ The population of Peru

STEP 2. Work with a partner to compare your answers. Discuss any differences and try to arrive at a common set of answers. DO NOT SHOW YOUR PAPER TO ANYONE.

A good teacher never goes into class and says, "Do the activity on page 80" or "Work on this handout." A good teacher piques students' curiosity by saying, "Has anyone been to Peru?" or "Can you name ten countries in South America? Let's see who can name the most countries." Issue a challenge to your students. After this brief introduction to the topic of the task, then and only then should you begin the task.

As you look at this speaking task, which language or types of phrases would you choose—if any—to teach or review before doing the task? The answer would of course depend on your students, but most teachers would highlight the words *geography, rank,* and *population.* A teacher who is familiar with ESL grammar issues would probably pick up on the superlative forms *the smallest* and *the biggest.*

This list is indeed a good list of language, but it is only half the language for this task. What is the purpose of this task? Remember that it is a speaking task. In Step 1, students work individually to rank the countries. It is true that students will need the language just listed. However, this list includes the language *in* the task, but it does not include the language that students need *for* the task.

Imagine that Student A has now filled in his numbers and is about to talk with a partner. Student A has Argentina as 1, Bolivia as 2, and Colombia as 3, but Student B has Argentina as 3, Bolivia as 2, and Colombia as 1. What would they say to each other? Here is one possible scenario.

A: I think Argentina is number one, Bolivia is number two, and Colombia is number three.

B: Wait. Say again.

A: Okay. Argentina is number one, Bolivia is number—

B: You think that Argentina is the big one?

A: Yes. I think is very big the people in Argentina. Sure is number one.

B: Really? I am not agree with—

A: What were you write for Argentina?

B: Argentina is number four? [for vs. four]

A: No. Argentina is number one. Is the biggest.

B: I think Colombia is number one. I went Colombia one time. Has many people. Really a lot.

A: I'm not sure. I still think that Argentina population is more big than Colombia.

As you can see, the students need a different set of language. To be sure, there is some overlap, but most of the learners' needs *for* the speaking activity are different from the language needed *in* the activity. Here is a comparison of the two possible languages regarding this task. Remember that this list will vary considerably depending on your students' proficiency, age, etc.

Language IN the task:	Language FOR the task:
geography, rank, population	*I think that _____.*
the smallest / biggest: the _____ est	*I'm sure _____.*
	Are you sure that _____?
	What did you put for _____?
	I don't agree with you/your answer.
	The population of _____ is bigger than the population of _____.
	Could you repeat, please?
	Wait a minute.
	I still think that _____.

If you want students to succeed in a speaking task, you must give very careful thought to the language **in** the task as well as the language needed **for** the task. Most teachers are very good at the former. In fact, they almost never give much thought to the language needed for the task. Because they lack the vocabulary **for** the task, students may either be very quiet or use their native language to accomplish the task.

In the Real World

In Japan, how many times did I hear teachers at my school or at teacher meetings and conferences lament the fact that their students just did not speak much during class? These teachers' speaking activities were not succeeding for a number of reasons—for example, the foreign teachers were not familiar with Japanese students' reticence, the teachers were not familiar with the perceived powerful role of a teacher in a Japanese classroom, the topic was not interesting to the students—but one reason for the silence in class could be that the students just did not know what to say or lacked confidence in using the phrases that they had been taught. I think this may be the most common mistake made in speaking classes. I am not saying that teaching the two languages for a task will make the task successful. Certainly no *one* factor ensures the success of a task. However, if students do not know what to say and it is teachable but you have not taught it, then you cannot be surprised or annoyed when they do not speak.

Discussion and Practical Application for Your Teaching

Look at the language in the activity that you plan to use—whether the activity is in the book, on a handout, or said by you. In targeting the language *in* the activity, you will need to be familiar with the vocabulary and grammar that is within your students' English proficiency level. This of course presupposes that you are familiar with ESL/EFL grammar and vocabulary issues. (See Appendix A and Appendix C for more on these two important components of speaking proficiency.) The actual list that you compile depends on your students' level of English.

Consider the language need for the task. If two (or more) native speakers were doing this task, what would they say to each other? Try to imagine this conversation—or have two of your native-speaking (or very advanced non-native) friends do the activity so you can see what two natives would *really* say.

The teaching point is clear: For a speaking activity, teach both languages.

Factor 5: The Task that Serves as the Vehicle for Conversation

After being a teacher in my own conversation classes and then a mentor-teacher in (observing) other teachers' classes, I have seen the crucial role that the task or activity plays in the success of conversation classes. Classes that are assigned specific tasks *always* do better than classes that are given more general assignments. A concrete task such as "rank these ten boys' names in popularity for new babies last year" will involve students more than a less specific task such as "make a list of good names for baby boys" or a "non-task" such as a supposed "class discussion" in which the teacher ends up talking most of the time.

At times, I have observed novice and even experienced teachers who dominated the discussions. To provide objective data, I timed teacher-talk and student-talk. Those who talk too much in the discussion class rarely realized that they were doing so much of the talking, at times up to 80 percent of the class time. If the students had been given a finite task, the teacher would have had a different role: to quietly observe the students as *they* talked. In a good speaking task, the teacher has for the most part no speaking role.

A great deal of information and examples will be given on task type in Chapter 2, pp. 45–53.

In the Real World

Even early in my teaching career, I was always good at teaching grammar or composition or vocabulary classes. I was good at concrete areas of language. In the grammar class, I knew how to present the grammar points in several different ways. I knew how to do oral drills, then assign graded fill-in-the-blank exercises, and finally work with production exercises. This meant drill followed by completion or multiple-choice activities followed by more creative activities.

My problem was that I did not have any parallel set of activities for teaching speaking. To put it mildly, I was pretty useless in anything but reading, writing, lab, or grammar classes. I was less skilled at teaching conversation classes because I didn't know what to say to ensure that conversation would start and then be maintained. This inability to lead a conversation or discussion class was due partly to my own rather shy personality (when I started teaching) and partly to my own lack of teaching skills for this kind of class.

There are many skills that a good speaking teacher needs, but one of the more important ones is the ability to choose a topic, narrow it down to a more specific subtopic, and then select or design the right kind of task. A mediocre topic with well-designed tasks will probably produce a better class than a really good topic with mediocre tasks. To be sure, some students will talk, but your goal is to ensure that *everyone* talks, not just those who already speak up. The right kind of task can do that.

Discussion and Practical Application for Your Teaching

Good teachers think in terms of tasks or activities. When grammar teachers think about teaching the difference between simple present and simple past tenses, their minds almost immediately turn to what the students will do in class after the initial presentation. In a similar way, when conversation teachers think about covering the difference between tipping customers in the United States and tipping in the students' countries, their minds almost immediately turn to what the students will do after the initial presentation.

As will be discussed in great depth in Chapter 2, three features that research shows that contribute toward the likelihood that a task will be successful are that:

- the task should require information exchange
- the learners should have time to plan their language
- the task should have one or a finite set of answers

Some teachers have such great outgoing personalities that they are seemingly always able to pull off a great speaking class, but for most teachers, teaching conversation is difficult. Using specific tasks that meet these criteria will make your job much easier and more enjoyable.

Conclusion

There are many factors that contribute to the success of a task, but five key factors have been discussed. While none of these factors can guarantee that a task or activity will be successful with a certain group of learners, together they play an integral role in whether or not the conversation class is full of students' voices or mostly silent.

2 Research on the Teaching of Conversation

Traditionally, it has been incorrectly assumed that being able to speak a language equates with being able to teach the language, especially for a class as "easy" as a conversation class. The truth is that for many teachers, the speaking class is actually one of the most difficult to teach well. After reading the Introduction and Chapter 1, it should be clear to you that effective conversation teachers must be able to do much more than just speak the language well. In fact, most of what good conversation teachers do is not as related to their language ability as to their knowledge of students' cultures, first languages (compared to English), and materials design or selection. (It should go without saying that good teachers—regardless of what they are teaching—also have good classroom management skills and explaining skills.)

Of all these factors, perhaps the most important for conversation teachers is their knowledge of materials design or selection, that is, their ability to put together a series of good tasks. Your success as a conversation teacher is directly related to your ability to plan a good lesson, and a good lesson consists of and actually depends on high-quality tasks.

Think about this for a moment. Your lesson consists of a series of activities or tasks, and most teachers tend to conceptualize any given lesson in concrete terms of the tasks in that lesson. As the teacher, you are the person responsible for selecting or modifying existing tasks or putting together your own original activities. Thus, this chapter will present research findings on the design of speaking tasks, findings that can help you put together the best conversation class possible.

Key Terms in Research on Second Language Speaking

Before we go further, it is important to have a common base of familiarity with six key terms in second language research and pedagogy regarding speaking skills: *fluency* versus *accuracy, interlanguage, comprehensible input, pushed output,* and *negotiation of meaning.*

Fluency versus Accuracy

A speaking activity can be categorized as either a *fluency activity* or an *accuracy activity.* Simply put, *fluency* here refers to the amount of language produced in the task, while *accuracy* refers to the linguistic correctness of what is said in the task. In a conversation class, we are much more concerned with getting students to talk. While accuracy is certainly important, teachers really want activities that focus on fluency. Ideally, we want fluency activities that do not simply allow or even encourage students to talk but rather fluency activities that *require* learners to speak.

I often relate teaching conversation class to teaching tennis, my second pastime after languages. In an ideal world, I would be able to help my tennis students become better tennis players by teaching them to make more accurate shots. In an ideal world, students would practice lots and lots outside of class so that the teacher could use the little amount of class time we have to hone certain skills. In other words, the teacher could help the students by working hard on accuracy.

If I think about the conversation classes that I have taught to adults in the United States or to children in Japan, my students were extremely busy. In many of my conversation teaching jobs, the students worked all day and came to conversation class at night. This is the reality that most conversation teachers deal with. Therefore, the unfortunate truth was that most of my students were really busy—as most people are today—and rarely practiced outside of class. (Doesn't this sound familiar already?)

During tennis class, I could not work on their errors because my students weren't making any errors—because they weren't hitting tennis balls. I couldn't talk about different ways of directing a backhand or a strategy when the score was 30–15 versus 15–30 because very few students had been practicing. In class, I had to do activities that would allow the students to hit as many tennis balls as possible. My concern was not on whether the ball went in or out of the court (i.e., no focus on *accuracy*) but rather on how many tennis balls they hit (i.e., *fluency*). As they hit more and more, I could then focus my teaching—at times—on specific shots or tennis tips, but I still had to spend the majority of class time just letting the students hit as many tennis balls as possible.

For a tennis fanatic like me, this kind of teaching was almost painful in the beginning. I was totally committed to tennis, and I expected the students to be the same way. I had to accept the fact that my students were extremely interested in improving their English, but their work and family commitments left relatively little time to do much work on their tennis outside of class. Thus, my class had to move away from a focus on *instruction plus practice* to one of *practice with some instruction*. My students needed to hit some tennis balls under the guidance of a knowledgeable coach who could keep everyone on task during the hour, set up interesting and varied practice drills that would require everyone to hit lots of tennis balls, and offer judicious feedback.

As you plan your speaking class, think about tennis balls. Your number one goal in a speaking class is get your students to hit as many tennis balls as possible—that is, to get each of them to talk as much as possible. While this holds true in all speaking classes, this heavy focus on fluency activities is extremely important in an EFL setting (or in an ESL setting where students speak their native language most of the day—which is very common) because the only opportunity that your learners may have to hear or speak English could be your class. It is one thing not to take advantage of English-speaking opportunities outside of class, but it is another to be in an EFL setting where there is little or no English outside of class (e.g., rural Japan or the middle of Brazil).

An obvious way to improve students' speaking skills is through actual speaking, and this can be done through well-designed fluency tasks. Yes, they need structures, vocabulary, pronunciation insight, and even culture information, but they need to spend their time speaking, as much as is feasible. Thus, one of the teacher's main jobs is to ensure that students are talking. How can you do this? The answer has many aspects, but perhaps the most important piece of the answer is the task or tasks that you choose for the class. Fortunately, researchers in our field have studied extensively the effect that the design of a speaking task has on student output, or fluency.

Interlanguage

Learners' progress in their new language is hardly ever linear. It is important for all language teachers of all types of students—from children to adults—to fully comprehend this statement. Errors are not bad; they are a sign of language development (Corder, 1967, 1981).

When students learn something new about the target language (here, English), their ability to produce that new structure in English may increase at that particular moment, but very shortly afterward, this ability may decrease. For example, when a student finds out how to make a negative command (i.e., *Please don't* + [Verb]) or how to differentiate between something happening now versus something happening every day (e.g., *he is cooking* versus *he cooks*), there is often a sharp spike in the learner's ability to produce this structure well (as well as a sharp spike in teacher job satisfaction!). If this learning occurs in a typical classroom setting (as opposed to natural acquisition outside of a classroom), the teacher might then follow up this instruction with standard completion exercises (e.g., *Every day John [is running, runs] around the lake three times.*) on the board, in a drill, on a worksheet, in the textbook, or on a computer program. Once again, the learner's apparent accuracy will be high.

Without remedial work in the next few days, however, the learner's ability with this new feature will most likely diminish again, and he may make errors with the structure (e.g., *Every day John is run around the lake three times.*). A few days later, with or without any further instruction or practice, the same learner may then get the structure right. This sort of "jagged growth" highlights the learner's *interlanguage.*

Interlanguage, a term coined by Selinker (1972), refers to the learner's current level of English proficiency (if he or she is an ESL/EFL learner). This current level ranges from no ability in the second language (i.e., the ability to express something only in the first language) to the ability to express that same thing in both the first and second language. Prior to the early 1980s, most linguists viewed learners' errors as something negative to be wiped out as soon as possible. However, in the early '80s, a very important paradigm shift regarding the nature of errors occurred in our field.

In a seminal article, Corder (1981) pointed out that learners' errors tend to be quite systematic, so that we conclude that second language learners'

---

*indicates a non-grammatical structure

errors follow a fairly predictable pattern in which these errors are deemed a normal and necessary part of the language acquisition process. At first, their English is full of errors, which often mimic their native language structures. At other times, the errors are due to an incomplete understanding of the rules in the target language. Gradually, this understanding changes as the learners' structures become more and more like English. This "language" that is in between the native language and the target language (English) is called interlanguage.

Because the ability to negate an utterance is so important in conversation (e.g., *No, I don't have any coins* or *I haven't ever gone to France*), let's look at the complexity of negation in English and its interlanguage stage.

Negating in English is very complex. Consider these general rules for negation in English:

1. *be: not* after   I am not here. She wasn't there.

2. modals: *not* after   I can't go. She could not have taken the money.

3. auxiliary *have: not* after   I have not used the money. She hadn't seen me.

4. verbs: *do / does / did + not*   I don't see you. He doesn't say much. We didn't go.

    a. For third person singular present, the verb loses its *-s:* *He does not cooks eggs.

    b. For past tense, the verb loses its past tense: *He did not cooked eggs.

Summarizing the research on the developmental stages of negation in English, Ellis (1991) lists the four stages:

1	External Negation	*No you eating here.
2	Internal Negation	Keith is not coming today. *We no can speak English. *I don't was home yesterday.
3	Negating Modals	*He can't to play tennis. You shouldn't do that.
4	Negation follows English rule of auxiliary + *not*	They didn't want the money. *He doesn't needs a new car.

In Stage 1, the learner negates with *no* or *not* but outside the utterance. In Stage 2, the learner negates within the utterance, but *no, not,* or even *don't* appear somewhere inside the utterance. Even when *don't* is used, it is not analyzed as auxiliary + *not* but rather as one single item *don't.* In Stage 3, the learner consistently negates modals correctly. However, it is possible that the learner does not understand the auxiliary + *not* aspect of the negation. Finally, in Stage 4, the learner uses auxiliary + *not* before the verb. Errors may continue, but the errors are with additional *-s* (e.g., *He doesn't likes tennis.*), *-ed* (e.g., *She didn't worked last week.*), or irregular verb (e.g., *The class didn't began on time.*)

An obvious goal of an effective speaking activity is that it will allow students to discuss a certain topic. However, a less apparent but potentially more important goal is that all participants stretch their interlanguage. A mediocre speaking activity will allow students to get by with the language that they already know. We see this in class all the time; in fact, we see learners whose English level seems to have "fossilized" at a certain level beyond which they cannot progress. In contrast, a well-designed speaking activity will push learners to go beyond their safety zone in English and thereby stretch their interlanguage (Pica, 1996a, 1996b; Polio & Gass, 1998).

Comprehensible Input

Prior to the 1980s, the main emphasis in language classes was usually on learning the components of a language. Course curricula had final goals such as "students will learn the 49 most common prepositions in English" or "students will be able to differentiate a regular past tense verb from an irregular past tense verb." Students who could demonstrate such rote or mechanical knowledge well received high marks and were considered successful language students.

While these language goals focus on important aspects of English, curricula at that time had goals that measured *knowledge of language* instead of *use of language for communication purposes.* Around the early '80s, however, linguists began to look at the language learning process differently. For example, errors, as just explained, were no longer viewed as detrimental but rather as a natural part of the language process.

Around this time, the focus in second language courses shifted from language components such as grammar or even errors to communicative ability. This was the birth of the so-called *communicative approach.* One of the most influential ideas to come out at this time was the notion of the importance of "comprehensible input" (Krashen, 1985). For Krashen, there was a distinction between learning and acquiring a language, with the latter being the only true indication of second language attainment. According to Krashen's hypothesis, the sole necessary ingredient was not a grammar exercise or a language classroom but rather comprehensible input, which is referred to as $i + 1$, where i represents the learner's level and the $+ 1$ represents language that is just beyond the learner's grasp.

Many second language experts disagree that comprehensible input is the sole ingredient necessary for second language acquisition. On the other hand, few would argue against the value of using language and activities at a level that is just beyond the learner's current proficiency level. Thus, an effective speaking activity should encourage learners to aim for the $+ 1$ in $i + 1$, because simply maintaining the student's i without the $+ 1$ is obviously insufficient for proficiency growth. In fact, without the $+ 1$, the student is simply maintaining his or her current interlanguage, which is certainly not the goal of a speaking class.

The question for you as a conversation teacher is how to form comprehensible input. Simply speaking more loudly does not make language comprehensible. (It just makes you look silly to your learners.) Slowing down speech rate, on the other hand, can be very helpful in making language more comprehensible to non-native speakers, but the teacher needs to know which aspects of English are problematic.

Comprehensible input is easy to define in general terms, but extremely difficult, if not impossible, to operationalize in specific teacher actions. (In fact, this has been one of the major criticisms against Krashen's views. See Gregg, 1984; Long, 1989.) The general suggestions that follow can help make native English more comprehensible for ESL/EFL learners.

1. Enunciate more carefully, particularly avoiding assimilating adjacent sounds and words. For example, native speakers in informal settings might use /waja/ instead of *What did you* in "What did you think of the movie?" or /duyawana/ instead of *Do you want to* in "Do you want to hear this again?"

   These assimilations are perfectly normal in informal conversations among native speakers; that is, these assimilations are correct English. However, these assimilations make the language difficult to grasp and therefore nowhere near the level of $i +1$ for most ESL/EFL students. At some point, your learners will be able to catch these assimilated sounds in phrases when you speak normally, but you should be aware of these assimilations and try to avoid the confusing ones most of the time, especially with lower levels of proficiency.

2. Be aware of common ESL student mispronunciations, which are often based on interference from either a student's native language or English spelling. (See Appendix B.) An example of native language interference is when Spanish speakers tend to pronounce /ɛ/ in front of English words that begin with *s* + consonant, so that school and speak come out *eschool*** and *espeak***. English spelling causes numerous pronunciation problems. The past tense of regular verbs in English is formed by adding *–ed* to the verb, but this *–ed* can be pronounced three ways: /t/ in *missed*, /d/ in *robbed*, and /ɪd/ in *needed*.

How can the students' mispronunciations affect whether your input is comprehensible? If a student thinks that the building where you study is called an *eschool*** but you say *school*, then the student might be initially confused by what you are saying. Likewise, if students think that *missed* is pronounced /mɪs-ɪd/ (i.e., two syllables), then when you say, "Some of the students missed the bus," they may not understand what the students did because they will not associate your /mɪst/ with their rendering of /mɪs-ɪd/.

The good news for you is that pronunciation errors tend to be systematic, so once you figure out some of the most common errors that your students make, you can incorporate them in your lesson plans.

3. Be aware of grammatical structures that are either confusing or unknown to your learners. (See Appendix C.) If you cannot name ten ESL grammar points right now, then it behooves you to get an ESL grammar book or workbook for ESL students—not teachers—and work through it. (We require this of all students in the grammar course in the MATESOL program where I teach.)

Knowing ESL grammatical points or structures is a necessity for *every* ESL teacher whether teaching reading, conversation, or writing. To ensure that your language is comprehensible input for your students, you must have enough experience with ESL to recognize which structures are known by beginning, intermediate, and advanced learners. For example, past modals such as *must have eaten* or *should have exploded* are not comprehensible to beginning or intermediate students. Lower-proficiency learners will believe that *The house should have exploded* means that the house actually exploded because they will catch *house* and *explode*, the two main content words, but will not know that *should have + past participle* means that an action did not actually happen.

In a construction such as *He wants me to visit her,* the learner will probably understand *He is visiting her,* which is not the message at all. In English, we use the grammar structure of *person A + want + person B + to + VERB* when one person wants a second person to do something. In contrast, Romance languages such as Spanish, French, and Italian use the construction *person A + want + that + person B + VERB* (subjunctive, i.e., a special verb form).

4. Perhaps the biggest aid in making language comprehensible involves monitoring vocabulary use. (See Appendix A.) It takes time for you—especially if you are a novice teacher—to come to know which words are understood by which students at which level. For example, one seemingly obvious factor in difficulty is word size, with many people mistakenly believing that bigger words are harder. Actually, your students are much more likely to know big words such as *dictionary* and *introduction* rather than smaller words such as *hem* or *dig.*

Perhaps the fastest way for you to learn the extent of your learners' English vocabulary is to look at a reading skills book that (other teachers or publishers have indicated) is appropriate for the current level of your students. Get that book—and the one at the level just below it. You should study these two books as if you were using them to learn French 1 or Finnish 1. The words in these books, especially the lower of the two, represent the vocabulary that your learners most likely know. This is roughly *i* in the *i + 1* formula.

All languages have idioms. English features its share of idioms, including idioms with colors *(to be in the red),* animals *(a bird in the hand),* numbers *(to be on cloud nine),* body parts *(rule of thumb),* and fruit *(the apple of my eye).* While these idioms are colorful and interesting, they are not the most common idioms in English. Most materials on English idioms are intuition based and therefore often include seldom-used idioms, which in turn limits their effectiveness for ESL/EFL students.

With the aid of modern computer technology, we can now compile frequency lists from actual corpora, including newspapers, textbooks, and college lecture transcripts. A ground-breaking linguistics project begun in 1997, the Michigan Corpus of Academic Spoken English (MICASE), entailed the recording and transcription of nearly 200 hours of university academic discourse, which included 1.7 million words. (Further information is available at www.hti.umich.edu/m/micase). In a seminal study, Biber et al. (1999) used a corpus of ten million words of natural, spontaneous conversations in the United States and United Kingdom to compare spoken English with written English. For teachers and learners, the good news is that these large-scale studies have had a tremendous impact on ESL/EFL materials.

Research studies (Liu, 2003; Simpson & Mendis, 2003) have shown that vocabulary will vary according to the nature of the corpus. Certainly we would not expect history textbooks, business documents, daily conversations at a bank, and television news programs to have the same set of vocabulary. Table 1 illustrates this point simply through a comparative listing of the fourteen most commonly used idioms in two corpus projects. Studying academic discourse data, Simpson and Mendis (2003) examined the MICASE. Looking at spoken English, Liu (2003) combined material from three corpora (i.e., a professional corpus, a media corpus, and MICASE) totaling six million words. (Though there is divergence between these two lists, which no doubt reflects actual differences of occurrences, some of the divergence can also be due to differences in how the term *idiom* is operationalized.)

Table 1
Most Common Idioms from Two Different Corpus Studies

Academic Discourse (Simpson and Mendis, 2003)	*Spoken English (Liu, 2003)*
the bottom line	kind of
the big picture	sort of
come into play	of course
what the hell	in terms of
down the line	in fact
what the heck	deal with
flip a coin (flip side of a/the same coin)	at all
on (the right) track	as well
knee-jerk	make sure
hand in hand	go through
right (straight) off the bat	come up
carrot(s) and stick(s)	look for
draw a/the line (between)	find out
on target	go on

Finally, one aspect of English, particularly spoken English, that hinders comprehensibility is *phrasal verbs*. Phrasal verbs, which occur in Germanic languages but not in Romance languages, are two- or three-word combinations of a verb and a preposition or particle. Examples include *put up with, put off, put on,* and *put away*. Phrasal verbs are rarely transparent in meaning, so in *She put up with her neighbor's noise for years,* no one *put* anything and there is no connection to *up* or *with*. In addition to not being transparent in meaning, phrasal verbs often have multiple meanings, for example, *he took off his shoes, the plane took off, that song took off in 1999.*

If meaning were not enough of a problem, there is the issue of actually catching the phrasal verb in native speech spoken at normal speed. Indeed, in spoken English, phrasal verbs are a *major* impediment to listening comprehension. Phrasal verbs occur frequently, with the particle or preposition not stressed, so that a student who hears "They've decided to put off the meeting for the time being" would not understand the statement but would probably catch *they, decide, put, meeting,* and *being.* In fact, a lower-proficiency student might turn to you and ask, "Teacher, what is *meet in being* or *meet in time being*?"

What can you do? To help your learners you need to realize how often you use phrasal verbs in your speech. When talking to beginning-level or intermediate-level students, you should limit your use of phrasal verbs and other idioms.

5. Your natural inclination, especially when your students do not understand something that you have just said, is to paraphrase immediately. However, you should avoid paraphrasing in your second attempt at explaining something. Wait until the third attempt.

   Why? The first time that you say something, the language is just entering the learners' ears and mind. Students are still processing what they have just heard or what they *think* they have heard. They would like to hear the same or very similar line one more time. Try to repeat yourself on the second attempt. On the third attempt, you can paraphrase some of the words or phrases that you think are preventing what you are saying from being comprehensible and therefore comprehensible input.

Consider this brief excerpt from a teacher talking to a group of lower-proficiency ESL students.

Teacher: Ok, I'd like you to open your books now (pause) to page one hundred sixty-one (pause) one hundred sixty-one.

Class: (Some students touch their books.)

Teacher: Ok, everyone. Right now I'd like you to open your books to page (pause) one hundred sixty-one.

Class: (more students are opening their books)

Teacher: Good. Yes, page one-sixty-one. (Teacher holds up his book open to pages 160 and 161.)

Teacher: Ok, now that you have your book open to page one hundred sixty-one, what do you see on this page?

Student A: Some cat. And. . . . two house.

Student B: Yes, there are cats and houses.

Teacher: Ok, what do we see on page one hundred sixty-one? We can see . . .

Class: Cats

Teacher: Yes, some cats . . . and? (begins to write *cats* on board) How do you spell *cats*?

Class: C . . .

Teacher: (writes C) Yes, how do you spell the word *cats*?

NOTE: The first three utterances of the teacher, which form the example of this excerpt, were two seconds from each other.

Negotiation of Meaning

Ironically, one goal of an effective discussion activity is misunderstanding and uncertainty—that is, there should be an element of confusion that causes breakdown in communication. When this confusion or miscommunication between speakers arises, they must negotiate until meaning is clear. This repair is often referred to as *negotiation of meaning*. In this process, the speakers attempt to successfully convey information to one another; they reach mutual comprehension through restating, clarifying, and confirming information.

Consider this excerpt of a discussion between two students in a pair work activity called Find the Differences. In this activity, both students have a slightly different version of the same picture. Without showing their pictures to each other, the students have to work together to talk about what is and is not in their pictures in order to identify the eight differences.

Example of Negotiation of Meaning between Two ESL Learners in a "Find the Differences" Task

A: In my picture, there is house with one big tree and two small trees.

B: Yes, me, too. I have three trees.

A: Are the trees the same?

B: Yes, I have three trees.

A: But are your trees big?

B: Yes, two tree are very big.

A: My picture has two little trees.

B: What? What is "tooleedle"?

A: Two is number. "leedle" is small. (Uses hands to mimic "small.")

B: Oh, Ok. You mean little.

A: Yes, no big. Not big.

B: Ok, I have a good idea for something different maybe. My house number is 13. What is your house number?

A: Please repeat the number. You mean 13? Or 30?

B: 13.

A: (laughs) I don't know which is correct. Ok, I have a question. Is your number more than 29 or less than 29?

B: Less than. (laughs, too)

A: Oh, Ok. I understand now. My house number is the same.

B: Ok. For me is also difficult 13 and 30.

Now why would you as a good teacher hope that communication in the communication classroom breaks down? Negotiation of meaning can lead to a repair in the language of the conversation. This negotiation and repair process results in comprehensible input that can be beneficial in second language acquisition (Dolly, 1990; Ellis & He, 1999; Lyster & Ranta, 1997). In other words, we want a communication problem to occur so that learners will have to speak to each other in order to repair it. Thus, in ideal speaking activities, differences in pictures, opinions, or answers are good because these differences provide something to talk about, and the more talking there is, the more likely a communication breakdown is, which then requires negotiation of meaning. This negotiation of meaning pushes learners to practice the target language as much as possible, inevitably providing both positive and negative input (Mackey, 1999; Mackey & Philip, 1998). In addition, the learner's vocabulary ability, an especially important part of second language proficiency, is reinforced (Folse, 2004; Nakahama, Tyler, & Van Lier, 2001) through the negotiation of meaning facilitated by well-constructed discussion activities (Folse, 2003). Even in a seemingly simple situation, negotiating with another student in pair or group work requires students to stretch their interlanguage as they force themselves to repair their communication to make themselves be understood.

Pushed Output

While Krashen believes that comprehensible input is the causal factor in language acquisition, Swain (1985, 1995, 2005) promotes the value of *pushed output* in addition to comprehensible input. Through pushed output, language learners use their output as a means to test their hypotheses about the language in communicative situations. When they are unable to communicate effectively, they must rethink their utterances and modify the relevant parts. In this process of modifying their interlanguage utterances to express exactly what they want to say, the learners carry out some restructuring that impacts, or pushes, their interlanguage (Swain & Lapkin, 1995). Language educators believe that opportunities for both comprehensible input and output are important in language learning (Swain 1985, 1995; Swain & Lapkin, 1995; Pica, Holliday, Lewis, & Morgenthaler, 1989; Pica, Kanagy, & Falodun, 1993; Pica, Lincoln-Porter, Paninos, & Linnell, 1996).

Modifying an activity so that it has not just output but pushed output is easy if you know about your learners' current i in the $i + 1$ formula. Again, you need to know about your students' current level of grammar knowledge and vocabulary knowledge. Consider these two tasks. Both require output, but the second one requires students to struggle more as they have to say something that they want to say but do not necessarily know how to say. In other words, Version B forces or pushes students to express things that they may not know how to say exactly.

Activity 1, Version A

Directions: Here is a list of six items that you can buy at the school bookstore.† For each item, decide if it costs more than or less than $1. If it is less than $1, write –. If it is more than $1, write +.

____ a can of Coke®

____ a newspaper

____ a banana

____ a tuna sandwich

____ a pack of cigarettes

____ a bag of potato chips

†Teacher: Use a store that everyone in the class knows. This activity should focus on real prices, not imaginary ones. The store should be one that is meaningful to everyone in the class.

Now let's analyze Version A. In this activity, students can work alone and then in pairs. Tell them that they must agree on their answers.

In Version A of Activity 1, students will practice three grammatical patterns. The first one is the comparative form of *X is more than Y*. Students may also practice embedded clauses as in *I think [that] X is more than Y*. The third ESL grammar point is third person singular of *cost* and *be*, as in "A bag of chips costs more than $1." Students will also practice the difficult pronunciation of the consonant cluster /sts/ in *costs*. Most of the vocabulary in the task will be easy, and most of the vocabulary that students need to do the task is easy (e.g., *I think, I'm not sure, I bought, I don't remember*).

Activity 1, Version B

Directions: Here is a list of six items that you can buy at the school bookstore.‡ Rank these items from 1 to 6, with 1 being the cheapest and 6 being the most expensive.

____ a can of Coke®

____ a newspaper

____ a banana

____ a tuna sandwich

____ a pack of cigarettes

____ a bag of potato chips

‡Teacher: Use a store that everyone in the class knows. This activity should focus on real prices, not imaginary ones. The store should be one that is meaningful to everyone in the class.

Now let's analyze Version B. In this activity, students can work alone and then in pairs. Tell them that they must agree on their answers.

In Version B of Activity 1, students will probably need the same three grammar structures. However, there will be much more discussion in this task because students have to rank the items, which requires them to consider the price of each item against the other five items each time, not just against the base figure of $1 as in Version A. Suddenly students need to disagree, and they need to explain <u>why</u> they disagree. This could entail expressing surprise at someone's answer *(How can you say that?)* or explaining a specific past action *(The last time that I bought a can of Coke, I think it cost* [note past tense] *eighty-five cents)* and then making a comparison with another action *(but when I bought a newspaper, I'm sure it was only 50 cents).*

The ideas that students need to express in Task B are more complex than in Task A. Students cannot get by with simple phrases such as *I think ___ is more than $1.* Students have to dig deep to express notions that they would normally avoid expressing in English. If you plan well and if you know your students' grammar and vocabulary level, then you can pre-teach any phrases that students may need. This will allow them to go beyond their normal comfort zone.

When I lived in Japan, I had a basic knowledge of Japanese from some coursework in a Japanese intensive language course. One of the structures that I never learned well was reported speech. Direct speech is the actual quotation as in *John said, "Keith, I'm ready."* Reported speech would be *John told Keith that he was ready* or *John told me that he was ready* or *John said that he was ready*. I never learned how to say this structure in Japanese, but I understood it to some degree. For this reason, the bane of my existence at the school office in Japan was the telephone. When the telephone rang for Mr. Yamaga, one of my colleagues, I had to take the call if he was not there. I was able to respond to the caller in Japanese, and much—but not all—of the time, I could understand the message that I was supposed to give Mr. Yamaga. However, when Mr. Yamaga returned to the office, I did not know how to do reported speech in Japanese with *"Mr. Yamaga, Mr. Suzuki called and asked me to tell you that your meeting is canceled."* Instead, I always reverted to my compensatory communication strategies and to my basic Japanese of *"Mr. Yamaga, there was a call. You know Mr. Suzuki, right? He called you. You have a meeting today, right? Today's meeting is canceled. You understand, right?"*

I was able to get the message across, but I never moved beyond this Tarzan-like rendition of reported speech. I needed some instruction followed by a good practice task with this structure of reported speech in my Japanese class. Again, this requires the Japanese teacher to know Japanese grammar points for non-native speakers.

Moving from General Topic to Specific Task

To plan your specific task, the first order of business is to choose a topic. The importance of the topic as well as the issues that can influence your choices of possible topics have been discussed earlier (see Chapter 1, pp. 19–20).

A conversation class cannot function on topics; it must function on *tasks*. A good conversation teacher thinks in terms of tasks, not topics. The next step for the teacher is to develop various tasks that emanate from your topic.

In order to do this, it is important to be familiar with the features of effective speaking activities in general and with an array of common activity types (see Chapter 4).

Holidays and festivals are good safe topics for any class. If you are new to an EFL setting, you could have students explain customs associated with a certain holiday. Since you really do not know the customs, this is a true communicative activity.

If you are in an ESL situation, then you could discuss holidays in the host country that are different from those in most of your students' countries. (Again, this assumes that you know this information or at least something about it, which you most definitely should if you are an ESL teacher.) Another possibility would be to compare holidays that you know are the same— for example, Christmas in the host country with Christmas in Mexico. In both countries, people celebrate this holiday, but some of the traditions are different. Thus, your subtopic then is the Christmas holiday, but your more specific topic will be on similarities and differences of Christmas celebrations between the ESL students' native countries and the United States.

Many teachers make the unfortunate mistake of assuming that they now have a *task*, i.e., compare holidays. The teacher goes to class, looks at the students, and says, "Today we're going to talk about Christmas here and in your country. What do you know?" The teacher might even stand at the blackboard, chalk in hand ready to write, and say, "Let's make a list." Now with some groups, this might generate some discussion; however, any speaking that is produced is likely to come from students who are outgoing and have good speaking skills already, or the students who do not necessarily need practice. Just as you would never allow only one-third of the students in your class to open their books to read when you expect the whole class to read, you should not give a pseudo-task that is not likely to be done by most people in the class.

The "now talk to each other" pseudo-task is not acceptable. This is one of the most common "lazy" excuses for a real speaking task. The group will not react to this although some individuals may. You need to think in terms of a specific activity that students must do. Remember that the base of the word *activity* is *act*. What specific *action* do students have to do?

Let's review our speaking class plan so far. Your subtopic is the Christmas holiday, but your more specific topic is the similarities and differences of

Christmas celebrations between the ESL students' native countries and the United States.

This last subtopic is certainly more specific, but it is not a task yet. Using mostly words that your students will probably know, you should make a list of things associated with Christmas in the United States, such as (1) a tree, (2) big family dinner, (3) opening presents, (4) midnight church, (5) sending Christmas cards, (6) drawing names at school for a gift exchange, (7) giving a gift to a child in need, (8) snow, (9) children getting their picture taken with Santa Claus at the mall, and (10) hanging stockings (new word you must explain). Write this list on the board and have students get into groups to discuss whether or not they do these things in their country. (Alternatively, they could identify three things that are similar and three things that are different between the countries. Again, this is a specific task.) When they finish their *similar* or *different* list, ask students to come up with five additional things that people in their country do for this holiday.

Designing an Effective Task

After you have chosen the topic for the activity, then you can create the actual design. The three main design factors that research (Doughty & Pica, 1986; Pica & Doughty, 1985a, 1985b) shows can influence the ultimate effectiveness of the activity are:

1. whether the task is a *one-way task* in which information exchange is optional or a *two-way task* in which information exchange is required

2. whether learners are given *time to plan* what they might say in the task

3. whether the solution to the task is *open-ended*, i.e., with several possible solutions, or *restricted* to one or a finite set of answers

The answers to these questions can play a significant role in the successful design and implementation of speaking activities in ESL/EFL conversation classes.

The Flow of Information: One-Way versus Two-Way Tasks

The first issue concerns the flow of information between the participants. In a one-way task, one student has all the information and the other student (or students) have to get the information. In a one-way task, the information flows in one direction only. In a two-way task, the information must be exchanged by all involved in order for the task to succeed. Because different participants have different pieces of the task, two-way tasks are also referred to as jigsaw tasks since they are similar to assembling a (jigsaw) puzzle.

To compare the two types of tasks, imagine a scenario in which Student A has the facts, but Student B does not. If A passes enough of the information to B, the task has been successfully completed. Student B does not have to share any information for the successful completion of this task; thus, the probability of equal negotiation of meaning is low. Even if the roles are reversed and now B tells information to A, the flow is still one way.

An example of a one-way task is telling a real story. The teacher provides some limiting framework such as, "Tell your partner about the first trip you ever took on an airplane." A tells her story to B. Even if B then tells his story to A, the information flow is still one way. There is no required information exchange at all; in fact, there is no real reason for either student to listen carefully to the other because the listeners are not required to do anything specific with the information. There is no real task except to listen.

Most one-way tasks can easily be modified so that they become two-way tasks. The previous one-way task involving students who had to recount their first airplane trips could be modified to a two-way task by requiring the partner to write down three specific facts for the speaker's story (e.g., the year of the trip, the purpose of the trip, the name of the airline, etc.). Since the listener is unlikely to get the information the first time he or she hears it, he or she will have to ask for repetition and modification of the input. This repetition results in modified negotiation or negotiation of meaning between the speakers. The essential difference between a one-way task and a two-way task is in who holds the information and whether the information exchange is optional or required to complete the fluency task. All things considered, a two-way task is better than a one-way task.

What is the impact of a two-way design on negotiation of meaning? Pica and Doughty (1985a; 1985b) found no difference in quantity of negotiation of meaning in a one-way task, but when they used two-way tasks, in which information exchange was required, they did find statistically significant differences. Thus, conversation work can result in more negotiation of meaning provided that the task is a two-way task requiring exchange of information.

Other studies (Doughty & Pica, 1986; Long, 1989; Newton, 1991) have found that two-way tasks result in more negotiation of meaning—or more hits to tennis balls to use our tennis analogy. While quantity of examples is important, Long (1989) suggests that two-way tasks produce not only more negotiation work but also more useful negotiation work.

Stretching Interlanguage: Planned versus Unplanned Tasks

How often have I observed an inexperienced teacher begin a conversation class with a very general question such as, "What do you think about getting married before age 20?" The few students whose English (and personalities) will allow the spontaneous, unplanned talking that is required to answer this question tend to speak up and dominate the discussion, but these are the very students who least need this class. One way to put all students—the outgoing as well as the reticent—on equal footing is to allow a planning phase before completing the speaking task.

Activities that include a planning phase promote more successful student output. Simply requiring students, for example, to write out a response in a task pushes learners to go beyond their current interlanguage (Long, 1989). Again, including this planning component is desirable because the teacher's objective is to encourage and even require all students to speak. In my experience, even the most quiet students will at least read their answers, which is certainly a good starting point on the continuum from totally quiet to very talkative.

Ask your students to write out what they think before they come to class (or in class if you have sufficient class time for this). This very important but too often overlooked aspect of a successful discussion activity is perhaps the easiest for the teacher to incorporate. For example, if the activity is to discuss marriage before age 20, students should be allowed time to explain their opinion in writing. Teachers should set clear minimum and maximum length requirements. A minimum length is important to make sure that everyone spends a certain amount of time thinking about the issue beforehand. A maximum length is also suggested because it will force more verbose students to concentrate on the points that they think are most salient. In both cases, a length requirement serves as a framework that can better help speakers organize their thoughts. Depending on the task, teachers might ask students to write between 50 and 100 words.

Long (1989) found that planning is important because learners tend to produce language that is more complex and more target-like. Planning allows learners to have time to find any language necessary to explain their ideas. Teachers should encourage students to incorporate recently studied vocabulary and grammar constructions in their output. In essence, you are indirectly encouraging pushed output. Research on second language vocabulary, for example, shows the value of repetition and recycling of vocabulary to acquisition (Elley, 1989; Folse, 2006; Hulstijn & Laufer, 2001; Joe, 1998).

Note that "target-like" does not mean that the language is more accurate. Instead, it means that learners are more likely to take a chance to practice structures that they have studied but are not so comfortable with yet. Instead of overusing the word *maybe,* as most ESL learners do, they may actually use the modal *might* in their sentences, which is what normally happens in English, the target language here.

In sum, including a planning component into a discussion activity can improve the language and clarity of meaning of a speaking activity. However, it is neither necessary nor desirable for all speaking activities to be planned ones, just as learners do more than complete fill-in-the-blank activities in a grammar class or copy model sentences in a composition class.

The Solution to the Task: Open versus Closed Tasks

The third essential factor in the design of an effective speaking activity entails the final solution or answer of the task. An open task has several possible solutions. A closed task has one or a finite set of possible solutions. (Open tasks are often called *divergent* tasks, while closed tasks are called *convergent* tasks.) All things considered, research shows that adult learners tend to produce more language when there is only one finite solution to the task. Again, this means that students are hitting many more tennis balls.

Examples of open tasks include free discussion (e.g., What kind of car do you think is best for a university student?) and *what if* discussions (e.g., What would you do if you had ten children?). In an open task, the teacher should inform the learners that there is not any one single answer or even a limited set of solutions.

A very good example of a closed task involves using letters to advice columns in newspapers. Two of the most well-known advice experts in the United States were Abigail Van Buren ("Dear Abby") and Ann Landers. After the teacher has taught any unknown vocabulary in the advice-seeker's letter, students read the letter and then individually write their short response to the writer. At the next class meeting, students work in small groups (three to four members) to discuss their solutions and to come up with what they believe is the best answer, that is, the one they believe will be the response that Dear Abby or Ann Landers actually gave. At the end of the activity, students can compare their individual and group answers with the expert's actual reply. In a closed task, participants must converge on a single solution or one of a limited set of solutions.

Research shows that the fact that the participants in a closed task know from the start that they are working on an activity with a finite solution affects adult participants' interactions and language. Long (1989) found that student speech in closed tasks features more topic and language recycling, more feedback from the other participants, more incorporation of feedback, and more rephrasing of language. Obviously, closed tasks generate more negotiation work than open tasks do.

Examples of Effective Speaking Activities

The likelihood that a speaking activity will go over well in class, which means that the task will produce a great deal of student talking, is improved when that task features two-way interaction, allows learners to plan what they might say, and has a closed solution. This is not to say, however, that an activity must have these three attributes to be successful, only that it is more likely to produce a large amount of student talking—even if the teacher is not naturally good at drawing out student talk.

Many teachers have successful speaking classes because their activities already meet these three criteria. Other commonly used classroom activities can be easily adjusted to include these three criteria. Some teachers have the right personality to make even mediocre tasks work well; likewise, some groups of students are so motivated and energetic that they will seemingly talk about any topic with just the slightest of conversation prompts.

One of the best activities for a conversation course is the use of real court cases. (See Activity 9, Chapter 5.) If the lesson is designed well, then the task can include the three features explained in this chapter: two-way interaction, student planning, a closed task with one answer.

In Folse and Ivone (2002), we designed a unit called You Can Be the Judge: Who Is the Real Owner? in which students read a brief description of a real-life court case and must then work together to decide what they would do if they were the judge in this case and why they have arrived at this decision. A worker drank a soft drink that her coworker had left overnight in the office refrigerator. Upon opening the drink, the worker discovered that the bottle cap had a million-dollar prize as part of the soft drink company's promotion. The worker claimed the "finders keepers, losers weepers" justification and the lack of any name of the owner on the bottle as her right to the prize. The coworker did not have any proof of payment for the drink but testified in court that the bottle was really hers.

In the task, students must write out in approximately 75 words what they would do if they were the judge and then offer two or three supporting reasons for their decision. Students then work in small groups to discuss their decisions and reasons and attempt to arrive at a group consensus on the question of the ownership of the million-dollar prize.

Solving a problem such as this in small groups can lead to a great deal of speaking in English. Because all the members of the group (three to four members is a good number) must contribute their ideas to come up with the best decision, these activities are two-way tasks. There is a planning stage in which students are required to plan (and write out) their thoughts. This factor allows time for thinking and for searching for appropriate vocabulary. Finally, this is a closed task because there is only one judge's decision. Activities that require a two-way exchange of information, feature a writing and planning stage, and have a finite answer (i.e., closed task) are more likely to promote discussion by all group members and thereby promote speaking fluency.

Conclusion

Though the general public often mistakenly believes that the sole qualification for teaching a good conversation class is that the teacher speak the language, students certainly expect more. They expect the teacher to put together a class with good speaking activities. Teachers cannot simply toss out a topic to the class for "group discussion."

According to second language research findings, the type of activities that are more likely to promote discussion by all students—whether in pairs or small groups—and at the same time stretch learners' interlanguage are those that require a two-way exchange of information, feature a planning stage, and require a finite answer (i.e., closed task). Careful attention to these three factors in any speaking fluency activity can increase the potential for a successful speaking activity.

In Chapter 4, we will see twenty activities that have worked well in conversation classes in both ESL and EFL settings. As you read about these activities, consider the three factors highlighted in this chapter.

Annotated Bibliography of Selected Works

The following seven articles have made an important contribution to research and pedagogy on teaching speaking or conversation. Instead of grouping the articles by similar research questions, for example, *What is the effect of task type on total output?* I have decided to list the works alphabetically by authors' last names. Many articles deal with more than one variable, such as learner proficiency level, first language interference, or pre-teaching vocabulary, so that listing them by topics would require multiple listings of each article.

Doughty, C., & Pica, T. (1986). Information gap tasks: Do they facilitate second language acquisition? *TESOL Quarterly, 20,* 305–325.

A must-read for anyone interested in research in speaking interaction, this study examined the effect of task type (closed or open) in pair work, group work, and teacher-fronted (i.e., whole class) work. Doughty and Pica found that pair work and group work resulted in more interaction than did teacher-fronted work. More important, they found that closed tasks produced more negotiation of meaning than open tasks.

Implications: Teachers should build in a good amount of pair work and group work, but the work should include closed tasks. However, this is not to say that the teacher's role is unimportant. Doughty and Pica point out that (1) the teacher is often the main source of correctly modeled grammatical input and (2) the teacher is responsible for setting up pair work and group work of the correct type.

Duff, P. (1986). Another look at interlanguage talk: Taking task to task. In R. Day (Ed.), *Talking to learn* (pp. 147–181). Rowley, MA: Newbury House.

Four Japanese and four (Mandarin) Chinese ESL students were paired to complete four tasks: two problem-solving (convergent or closed tasks) and two debates (divergent or open tasks). Task type and ethnicity were significant. Problem-solving tasks featured significantly more negotiation of meaning. Chinese speakers—whether in Chinese/Japanese or Chinese/Chinese dyads—produced more words and asked more questions than their Japanese counterparts.

Implications: Teachers should use closed tasks more than open tasks. Both take the same amount of teacher time and effort to prepare for class, but closed tasks produce more negotiation of meaning among students. In addition, some groups are more accustomed to speaking out in classroom tasks.

Panova, I., & Lyster, R. (2002). Patterns of corrective feedback and uptake in an adult ESL classroom. *TESOL Quarterly, 36*, 573–595.

In their study of adult ESL classrooms, Panova and Lyster examined ten hours of classroom interaction consisting of more than 1,700 teacher turns and 1,600 student turns. Most teacher feedback on student errors was in the form of implicit types of feedback such as recasts (for example, Student: "Yesterday I go to the park. I had good time." Teacher: "Ok. You went to the park yesterday and you had a good time. What did you do there?"). The fact that this teacher rarely used feedback that required learner-generated correction may account for the low rate of learner uptake or repair of errors.

Implications: This is but one of several studies that show that adult learners are not quick to pick up on their errors when teacher feedback is a reformulation or correction of the learners' errors. This would seem to imply that teachers should not correct their students' mistakes in speaking. However, this is not the teaching point from this article. The teaching point is that just reformulating students' errors, which is in essence just supplying comprehensible input, will not result in uptake or reformulation of the correct form. Teachers may need to bring certain errors to learners' attention at the end of the activity because doing this during a conversation or discussion can do more harm than good. (See pp. 210–211 in Chapter 6, Assessment.)

Pica, T., & Doughty, C. (1985). The role of group work in classroom second language acquisition. *Studies in Second Language Acquisition, 7*, 233–248.

This was one of the original works to examine empirically what actually happens in teacher-fronted versus group work classes in terms of negotiation of meaning. Results favor group work but only when the task is a two-way task, i.e., it requires information exchange from all participants. Only this type of two-way convergent task resulted in substantial negotiation of meaning.

Implications: Students working in groups produce more language than when working as the whole class with just the teacher. Although group work can be better than teacher-class work because group work produces more language, only closed tasks produced more negotiation of meaning. Thus, teachers should incorporate closed tasks to be done in group work.

Pica, T., & Long, M. (1986). The linguistic and conversational performance
of experienced and inexperienced teachers. In R. Day (Ed.), *Talking
to learn* (pp. 85–98). Rowley, MA: Newbury House.

In two studies, Pica and Long examined the amount of negotiation of
meaning. A comparison between ten teacher-fronted classes and informal
native speaker–non-native speaker interactions found that informal
interactions produced more negotiation of meaning than teacher-fronted
classes. A second study found that experienced and novice teachers are
equally likely to dominate the classroom discussion.

Implications: When the teacher participates in the speaking arrangement
(i.e., a teacher-fronted class), teachers tend to dominate the classroom
discussion. This study found that a teacher's amount of teaching
experience did not make a difference: Teachers in general tend to dominate
a discussion when involved in the speaking arrangement. Teachers should
put students in groups and limit their own participation.

Porter, P. (1986). How learners talk to each other: Input and interaction
in task-centered discussions. In R. Day (Ed.), *Talking to learn* (pp.
200–222). Rowley, MA: Newbury House.

In this seminal study of real speaking tasks, eighteen participants (six
intermediate ESL, six advanced ESL, six native speakers) completed three
different ranking tasks with three different partners, one from each of
the three groups. The 27 discussions averaged 22 minutes in length and
produced ten hours of data. Learners rarely picked up student errors or
miscorrected. Learners got better-quality input from advanced learners,
so teachers might wish to pair students of different proficiency levels.

Implications: Teachers and students often express concern that some
students will pick up the mistakes that their partners or group members are
making when they speak with each other. This study showed empirically
that very few student errors can be attributed to other students' mistakes.
This study also found that putting students in pairs of mixed abilities
results in better-quality input for the weaker of the two students.

Storch, N. (1999). Are two heads better than one? Pair work and grammatical accuracy. *System, 27*, 363–374.

Noting that much of the extant research showed that student negotiation of meaning dealt with vocabulary, Storch examined to what extent grammar-based tasks such as gap-filling and error editing would result in negotiation of grammar. Storch found collaboration had a positive effect on overall grammatical accuracy, but this effect varied according to the specific grammatical item.

Implications: Having students discuss grammar issues in small groups can result in negotiation of meaning, but the particular grammar point—and not grammar in general—needs to be highlighted by the instructor.

3 What Does a Conversation Class Look Like?

Before we examine approaches to conversation and speaking, teaching techniques, or even specific classroom activities, it is important for us to have a good picture of what a conversation class looks like. Unfortunately (or fortunately), there is no one answer here. Conversation classes will vary by country, by student proficiency level, and even by the nature of a given group of students. Hence, a speaking class for beginning-level Moroccan students at a language institute who do not know each other at all would be completely different from a speaking class for intermediate-level mixed nationality (ESL) students at a community college in California who were together the previous semester in a beginning class—even though the Moroccan students and the California students might be using Book 1 and Book 2 of the same publisher's speaking series.

Here is a description of a conversation class that I taught in Japan.

Teaching Conversation in Japan
Adults; Language School
Keith Folse

I taught at a conversation school in Maebashi, Japan, a medium-sized city of 400,000 residents, for five years. Our school had more than 1,000 students who came once a week for *ei-kai-wa*, or English conversation. I had separate classes for young children, for junior high students, and for adults. We taught all levels from beginners to adults.

About 90 percent of my classes were with adults. Class size tended to be around ten. Once a group formed, it tended to stay together with that teacher over time, which created a certain kind of group feeling that I have not experienced nearly as much when teaching in other countries.

In class, we spent very little time on grammar rules. Most of our time was spent on speaking and listening activities. My goal was to get each student to talk, which is quite a feat when teaching Japanese students because they tend to be very quiet. In many ways, my students were more interested in U.S. culture and what American daily life is like than in English. I found that any discussion comparing the two cultures often engaged my students more than centering a lesson around a topic such as clothing or around a language feature such as present perfect verb tense.

My best class was a small group of mostly older students, who were not able to study English or any Western languages during World War II. For them, English was some sort of elusive goal, and I was always impressed with their persistence in trying to learn to speak English.

I never had a discipline problem with my Japanese students. Classroom management was easy. One thing I did learn was that the teacher needs to take control and make things happen. For example, instead of saying, "Should we work in pairs or in groups?" a better way to manage the class is to say "Okay, let's get in pairs for this activity." If not, a lot of time can be wasted.

If I had to give one piece of advice, it would be to be patient. Ask questions and be prepared to wait. I saw too many inexperienced teachers (but with very good credentials) get frustrated at the silence that would occur when they asked the entire class an open-ended question, such as "What is your favorite food?" Ask the question and wait for an answer. Allowing students, especially persistently quiet Japanese students, enough time to consider and then respond is a skill that takes time to develop.

In this description of my conversation classes in Japan, several key points stand out. The **issues for reflection** include:

1. Japanese students can be very quiet, which is likely to be unnerving to a teacher who is trying to get them to speak and even more so to a teacher who does not have much experience with reticent groups.

2. My students were more interested in American culture than they were in the English language, something that I had almost never encountered in my earlier teaching, so I tried to use culture topics to pique their curiosity. Tailoring the class to their needs was successful.

3. I found it necessary to rethink my way of approaching teaching ESL/EFL. I had to put aside my earlier teacher training that emphasized the teaching of grammatical structures and make my classes as communicative and student-centered as possible. Instead of assessing a class that I had taught in terms of how many language items (e.g., grammar structures or new idioms) I had taught, I learned to evaluate my own classes in terms of how much student speaking I was able to elicit.

I have described my experiences teaching conversation classes in Japan, but to understand the teaching of speaking or conversation, we need to consider many different settings and classroom environments. Perhaps the very best way to accomplish this is to read the first-hand accounts of other teachers who have actually taught ESL/EFL speaking in different settings. You need to hear about their students, including their language goals, their concepts of what a conversation class should be, and their classroom norms. In this chapter, you will read twenty descriptions of speaking classes at locations all over the world. These descriptions are from:

- North America (Canada, Mexico, United States)
- South America (Brazil, Chile)
- Europe (Germany, Portugal)
- Asia (China, Japan, Korea, Vietnam)
- Middle East (Qatar, United Arab Emirates)

Why are these teaching vignettes important? In Chapter 1, we discussed the five fundamental factors that affect what actually happens in a conversation class—that is, the activity or task, the learner, the program or curriculum, the topic being discussed, and the language practice. As you read these teachers' personal accounts, consider how these five factors promoted or limited the resultant class. Think about how the teacher did or did not take into account the age of the learners (children, adults), their purpose in learning

English (academic, survival, work-related), the nature of the course (daily, weekly, intensive), and the cultural norms of the students. We don't teach in a vacuum. No matter how much training you have had from workshops or textbooks, only a real teaching situation can make you see how hard it is for all the necessary factors to come together to produce a good class. These brief teaching stories offer a window into such real situations.

Following each story, a list of teaching issues for further reflection is presented. The items in these lists can help focus your attention regarding teaching conversation.

CASE #1

Teaching Conversation in Chile
Adults; Language School
Wells Rutland

After I received my M.A. in TESOL and had two years of ESL teaching experience in both an intensive program for adults and at a community college, I had my first experience teaching English overseas (EFL) in Santiago, Chile. I had taught many different nationalities, especially Latin Americans, so I thought I had a good idea of what to expect of Chileans since they are Latin Americans. However, Chile may be *in* South America technically, but somehow it is not really *of* South America.

Chile is a narrow strip of coast along the western border of the continent and is geographically isolated to the point that it is much like an island. To the extreme north sits the Atacama Desert, the driest desert on earth. To the south lies frozen Antarctica. To the east stretches the world's longest mountain range, the Andes, and to the west lies the great Pacific, the world's vastest ocean. I guess you could say that Chile is to South America what Great Britain is to the European Union. You might find this little geography lesson handy one day in a game of Trivial Pursuit®, but for an ESL teacher giving his first shot at EFL, prior knowledge of the facts that I have revealed to you would have proved priceless. Honestly, for a young *gringo* who grew up a stone's throw from Havana, "Latin" has always meant one thing: boisterous, verbal, outgoing interaction in class. For a young teacher standing in front of his first EFL class, I discovered that my concept of "Latin" did not apply to Chileans.

My first class started the day after my plane arrived. It was August, and it was very cold. The class was a three-night-a-week conversation class that consisted of eight overworked adults. It started at 7:30 PM and finished at 9:00 PM. On the night of the first class, I found my way to the room a minute or two before class time and found all eight students seated in a tight semi-circle at their desks. Punctual. A few of them were chatting quietly in Spanish but stopped immediately as I entered. One gentleman stood up. Polite. I smiled and introduced myself. Afterward, I asked if anyone from the class would like to volunteer to introduce himself or herself. Quiet. I smiled again and gently volunteered an enthusiastic looking woman sitting near the window.

"Okay," she said nervously, "I am Daniela. I am commercial engineer. I have 38 years."

"Anything else?" I asked her.

"I married?" The silence that followed was interrupted only by the sound of an older gentleman taking notes. Studious. Inside the hearts of these gentle folk, I thought, there must be a Latin person struggling to be set free. Needless to say, there was no salsa dancing that night. That is not to say the students are boring; they are, however, extremely reticent. In general, I found the students to be very interested in English and in American pop culture in particular. It seemed to be a given that English was a key to unlocking something or another, and that having it was important. Students were warm to me and each other. The men offered me their hands as they entered and exited the room. Male and female students greeted one another with a kiss on the cheek and understood that, as an American, I did not.

I suppose the teaching lessons to be learned here are that (1) not all Latin American cultures are so similar and (2) Chilean students tend to be a formal, quiet group.

Issues for Reflection

1. Don't generalize students by their language. Chileans, Cubans, and Spaniards may speak Spanish, but culturally, they are different. Likewise, Mexicans that you taught in an ESL setting may behave differently in an EFL classroom in their own country.

2. In an ESL setting, it behooves you to know as much as possible about the cultural groups that you teach. Likewise, in an EFL setting, you should learn as much about the country as you can before you go there. Knowing as much as possible about your students' culture will help you gain their respect and help you be a better-prepared teacher.

CASE #2

Conversation Class in Portugal
Adults; Private Language School
Scott M. Culp

I currently teach EFL to adults in a private language school in Portugal. I would describe my current students as working adults and recent college graduates, the majority of whom have some contact with English in their professions or as part of their future career plans. After five years in Lisbon, I am now teaching in the northern city of Braga, Portugal's third largest, in a vibrant area known for its concentration of important national industries, agricultural activity, and several respected universities and polytechnic institutes.

I very much enjoy teaching in Portugal. In some ways, it is unique; in other ways, it is similar to my previous teaching settings. My experience in teaching English to international students over the past fifteen years had been in both the ESL and EFL settings, in the United States, Canada, France, Portugal, and Slovakia. I have taught all types of classes, from free conversation to grammar and composition. These previous experiences have been extremely helpful in developing a good teaching style here in Portugal.

Students in a high-intermediate or advanced conversation class in Portugal almost universally request that the teacher do nothing more than set up a salon, a delightful series of non-guided discussion classes focusing on randomly chosen subjects. The model that Portuguese students prefer runs along the lines of a slightly more organized version of the standard talk among friends that can be overheard at any local café. Here students do not expect the teacher to give hand-outs or to write anything on the blackboard; likewise, they themselves do not expect to have to write or take notes of any kind. "Let English wash over you" may be an accurate image of their expectations. Curiously—or maybe not—students choose not to discuss much about the culture of English-speaking countries; they would rather talk about local or world events, general culture or the arts, family life or their own day-to-day worries. Since the choice of topic is critical in a conversation or speaking class, this is an important caveat for newcomer teachers here to know.

Of course, this option is nice for the instructor, who could then dispense with the burden of more formal lesson-planning and become a member of the spirited coffee chat, but there is an educational limitation. As tempting as this format may be, in such a class the majority of students (even the strongest ones) invariably fall into a trap: They rehash basic vocabulary as opposed to using richer words or expressions, they repeat certain errors in grammar and pronunciation, and they lack the ability or the content to sustain longer speech.

Students may feel comfortable, but in this situation there is very limited linguistic growth. In this free-wheeling model, students receive good practice in listening comprehension, and their ability to understand global meaning naturally improves (mostly from the teacher's contributions to the conversation), but the students themselves are not making improvements in their own speaking skills, which is what they are in class to achieve.

After indicating to my students that a class with nothing but open conversation had its limits, they agreed to allow me to modify the format of class. I now include frequent short activities to enrich vocabulary based on themes—such as money, driving, or education—and I occasionally focus on higher-level grammar concepts (e.g., *to have something done* or *to be about to do something*) when a structure presents itself as naturally occurring as part of a conversation, i.e., the proverbial *teachable moment*. The grammar intervention took place after the fact on the day following its appearance in natural conversation. The introduction of *Read and Retell* activities also became popular once the students realized that they could increase the number of minutes they actually spoke if they took ownership of a story, news item, or event and had to recount all the details to the rest of the class.

The popular impression in Portugal (and in other countries in my experience) is that a student can improve his or her English conversation skills simply "by doing" in the same way that a runner can increase strength and stamina by running every day. However, *doing* is not the same as *building*, and this realization gets the students to rethink how they study English. The desire to have an open conversation still runs strong, and I did not abolish it completely since the students found the chaotic back and forth of a lively discussion both fun and satisfying. Part of their learning experience has to be the understanding that building skills is just as important as practicing them. Thus, a good recipe for successful teaching here includes a teacher with good training in and knowledge of ESL grammar and other learning needs such as vocabulary and pronunciation. (See Appendixes A, B, and C.)

Issues for Reflection

1. Choose topics that are meaningful to your students. Again, this is part of a good needs assessment.

2. It is critical to find out your students' expectations of the daily class meetings as well as the overall course. Why are your students in your class? Scott's students wanted to *do* English rather than study or learn English. He sought a comfortable middle ground through activities that allowed students to talk, which is the goal of any conversation class, while at the same time forcing them to practice newly learned grammatical structures.

3. Your job is to push your students to go beyond what they can already do. Again, with an early needs assessment, you would be able to gauge the approximate level of your students as well as what they are capable of accomplishing within your course.

CASE #3

Teaching Speaking in the United Arab Emirates
Adults; Colleges
Nancy Fahnestock

I teach college math to non-native speakers in the United Arab Emirates (UAE). In actuality, my job is a combination of math and EFL, as I will explain. Teaching a subject (i.e., academic content besides English) to UAE students is challenging, but my years of teaching math and my training in ESL enable me to do a good job with my learners.

The UAE is a federation of seven emirates (Abu Dhabi, Dubai, Sharjah, Ajman, Umm al-Qaiwain, Ras al-Khaimah, and Fujairah). It occupies an area of 83,000 square kilometers along the southeastern tip of the Arabian Peninsula. Four-fifths of the UAE is desert, yet it is a country of beautiful, contrasting landscapes. I have been here two years now, and I love my teaching job. To be sure, there are challenges—as there are with any teaching situation anywhere. The UAE has an intriguing traditional culture and a safe, very welcoming environment—and a huge component in this is the people, whom I love working with. I live in Al-Ain, a city that is traditionally more conservative than larger UAE cities such as Dubai or Abu Dhabi.

All of my students are female Arabic speakers. They range in age from 18 to 40. The students have studied English for eight years before they arrive in my class, but communication is still a real problem for them. Since all college classes here are taught in English, it is imperative that the students develop good speaking and listening skills so they can do well in their non-English classes, such as math.

Students are tested and placed according to their level. The lowest-level students go into the Diploma Foundations program, where I teach. My students usually range from scores of 0 to 50 (on a 0–200 scale). This potentially wide range of abilities can make teaching these students a challenge.

In my first semester here, I have to admit that I did not realize the importance of speaking in this math classroom. While I did have some ESL students in my math classes in the United States, non-native students were rarely more than 20 percent of my class. Here in the UAE, I teach math to a class that is composed completely of non-native speakers.

Near the end of the first semester here, I suddenly realized that I had some students who had not spoken a word of English to me. My focus, after all, is math; we spent almost all of the class working on material to help the students pass the exam at the end of the semester in order for them to go to the next level. Once I realized my students' need for more speaking practice, I immediately began a different approach. Not only did I want to see their answer, I also began to ask them to explain what they had done to get the answer. In other words, what were their steps? My focus was on developing speaking fluency, and math was at the same time the vehicle and final goal.

One challenge that I face is the fact that the women want to help each other; in an attempt to do so, they will translate without being asked to. I have to constantly remind them that we will only translate once we have attempted all other ways to communicate the concept and have not been successful.

Another challenge I face is that some of my students have a difficult time relating to authentic activities because they are so extremely sheltered that they cannot relate to activities outside the classroom. To work on this and at the same time their speaking skills in math, I give them a larger task to work on: a project. I have the women design a T-shirt that they will sell in order to make a profit for a charity. The T-shirts are all done on paper; however, some students have gone so far as to have their actual T-shirt made. Through this, my students learn about buying the shirts for one price, selling them for another, and the amount they need to sell in order to raise a certain amount of money for their charity. This also gives them an opportunity to use some artistic and creative skills.

Once the project is completed, they must make a presentation to their class. They must explain what the charity is, why they have chosen it, and who the charity benefits. They must also explain the math portion of the project, for example, how many shirts they must sell in order to reach the required target donation amount.

For the most part, the level of the students I teach is so low that I really focus on communication. I want to work on building their confidence to speak in English and making them feel comfortable. If they understand my meaning and I understand their meaning as they attempt to express themselves, I make only obvious corrections. I do not expect that my students will speak with perfect grammar. My first goal is to develop fluency; accuracy can follow.

Whether you are teaching ESL or EFL, I have found that students appreciate it when the teacher shows a genuine interest in them and their culture. I am presently studying Arabic, so either before or after class, I sometimes ask my students questions that I have about Arabic. Of course, their explanation has to be in English—so that it can be beneficial to me as I'm learning Arabic but more important so that my students have to practice explaining things in English. Just as important as this language aspect is the fact that my students know I'm making an attempt to learn their language and their culture. I have found that this is motivating for the students as we both struggle together to speak another language.

Issues for Reflection

1. In some ways, Nancy's course is an example of ESP, or English for Specific Purposes. The students' main reason for English in this class is to discuss math. Thus, a great deal of the language she needs to teach, including both vocabulary and grammatical structures, is about math.

   In an ESP course, students often want a combination of general English and specific English. For example, if you are teaching a speaking course to nurses, then you will need to introduce specialized vocabulary related to nurses in addition to the general type of English. For grammar, you might need to teach the structure *have* + OBJECT + PAST PARTICIPLE as in, *You need to have your blood checked,* in the second week of the course though this structure would be taught much later on in a regular conversation class.

2. As with many programs, Nancy's students focus heavily on the final test. Rather than ignore this, Nancy found activities that would practice speaking and at the same time help prepare the students for the final exam. Thus, the students were more motivated to attempt these activities.

3. Rather than stick to the traditional classroom set of activities, Nancy designed special projects for her students that required everyone to put their English skills into practice.

4. Finally, Nancy's transition from ESL in the United States to EFL in the UAE has been made smoother by her desire and attempts to learn as much about her students' country and culture as possible. This is important for several reasons. Knowing about the students' culture allows you to understand them better and, as a result, teach them better. Knowing about their culture is a sign of respect for your students. Knowing about their culture makes them respect you more as a teacher and as a person. The students will have a better relationship with you as their teacher, and this is a win-win scenario.

CASE #4

Teaching English in Mexico and China
Adults; University
Salvador Venegas Escobar

I'm a Mexican teacher who learned most of his English in Mexico. I began to study English 26 years ago and just a year later began teaching it. I've taught English in various kinds of settings but mostly at the university. In the spring of 2005, I had the opportunity to teach EFL at a Chinese university. I was therefore in a unique position to compare teaching EFL to Mexican learners and Chinese learners. Here are my impressions of both groups in terms of cultures, classroom behaviors, language needs, and language learning.

The first thing I faced in China was class size. In Mexico, I'm used to relatively small groups of 20 to 25 students. In China, I taught large classes, with 60 to 70 students. However, the one conversation class that I'll talk about here had only 35 students, still a large number when you are trying to get students to speak.

The second thing that I noticed was a difference in classroom manners. The Chinese learners were extremely punctual and respectful. When I entered the room to begin teaching, practically everybody was there already, which was most definitely not the case with my Mexican students. In China, once I entered the classroom, I would be met with an intimidating silence. At first, I thought this was a good thing because it would make class easier for me. However, their lack of responsiveness would throw me off at the beginning, but I soon got used to it. While my Mexican students speak up whenever they have questions, I learned that if I wanted my Chinese students to participate, I would have to elicit responses and be very patient for them to come up with a response.

In Mexico, my students and I share a common first language, but this was not the case in China. One benefit of having students and the teacher speaking the same first language is the ability to discuss difficult grammar or vocabulary differences in the shared native language. However, having a teacher that speaks the same language as the students—especially in an EFL setting where speaking is the supposed goal of the course—doesn't always help and can indeed be a liability. For example, many of my Mexican students will still use Spanish when speaking to me no matter how many times I ask them not to or how often I pretend not to understand them. In contrast, the students in China had to speak English in order to communicate with me. There was simply no other way to communicate. To me as a teacher in a speaking class, this was a plus.

As far as learning styles, I would say that Chinese students are more accuracy-oriented whereas Mexican students are more fluency-oriented, so I had to work on different goals for each group. In China, I tended to work toward discouraging their memorizing of dialogues and more toward improvising speech. My goal was to increase the amount of speaking by the Chinese learners. In Mexico, I tend to work more toward getting the grammar right. I try to make students aware of what they should be saying as opposed to what they are in fact producing.

Pair and group work seem to work very well in both cultures—as long as you make sure they're using English most of the time. With monolingual classes, you can't always avoid their using their mother tongue to speak to each other, but at least you can help by creating engaging activities (such as information gap and role play activities) that will make the learners use English more.

Issues for Reflection

1. Classroom procedures can vary greatly from country to country, as this teacher experienced firsthand in China and Mexico. If these students had been in an ESL setting, they would have had to deal with the language issues as well as a new set of classroom expectations. What you consider normal or standard classroom procedures may not be so normal or standard for all students.

2. Being able to speak the language of your students is an advantage. Many would argue that it is a disadvantage because students will expect you to speak to them in their language, but you control this: *Limit it!* If you are explaining a really difficult word or a hard grammar structure, then by all means, use your common language. However, for communication, including explaining directions, use the target language.

CASE #5

Teaching Conversation in Canada
Adults; Adult Education; College
Carmen Valero

I have been an ESL teacher in Canada for more than ten years and a TESL trainer for five years. There are a number of key things to remember when teaching conversation in a multi-cultural environment such as Canada.

The first thing to be consciously aware of when entering a Canadian ESL classroom as a teacher is that your students are generally new or fairly new to the country. They will most likely be experiencing symptoms of culture shock and having some degree of difficulty in adapting to their new Canadian way of life. For these reasons, the more relevant conversation topics and vocabulary themes would be those related to introducing Canadian culture and to settlement issues—for example, informing students of the programs and services available to newcomers as well as covering routines such as how to see a doctor and how to return defective merchandise. Let's not forget some of the very unique Canadian terminology—such as *toque, toonie,* and *eh?*—that needs to be introduced. As for pronunciation, we need to point out our North American way of devoicing our 't''s as when we drink *wader* instead of *water*. Language meets the real world when we have to explain what we really mean when we tell students to "dress warm" in the winter.

Second, Canadian ESL teachers need to be prepared to deal with the diversity of a multi-cultural classroom. This is a powerful caveat: You must always keep in mind that the students are as foreign to each other as you are to them. There may be issues of racism, gestures, or behaviors that are taboo in some cultures while not in others, and occurrences of cultural misunderstandings. I can recall instances of playing music in the classroom, pairing students of the opposite sex together, showing the bottom of my shoe, giving the class a "thumbs up," and pointing at the board with my index finger—all of which were highly offensive to some students. For this reason, Canadian ESL teachers needs to be aware of cultural differences and have as wide a range of cultural knowledge as possible while at the same time allowing for the students in the class to develop a new understanding of Canada's multicultural society and of each other. This can be achieved by discussing topics related to culture, such as customs and traditions, and by implementing cultural teaching strategies in the lesson plan. From my experience, these do in fact make for very interesting conversation topics and equally bring students and teachers closer.

The greatest advantage and disadvantage to being a Canadian ESL teacher is that in addition to being an expert in the language, you must have a background in sociological and sociopolitical issues in order to effectively teach newcomers, particularly in the conversation class. You spend a lot of time researching cultures, dealing with emotional settlement issues, contemplating the appropriateness of conversation topics, and walking on eggshells for fear of being offensive until you reach an adequate comfort level. At the same time, it is a highly rewarding and excellent learning experience that will most definitely be life-changing and play a significant role in your own cultural identity.

Issues for Reflection

1. It is important to know which actions are considered taboo by your students' culture. For example, you should not make the okay sign to Brazilians, show the sole of your shoes to Arabs, or point with any finger but your thumb in Malaysia. By the same token, you should know which actions from certain cultures are considered rude here, including asking people about their salary or arriving two hours after dinner has started.

2. This teacher mentioned sociopolitical knowledge. Teaching requires you to know more than the subject matter, but with ESL students, this is even more true. You need to know something of politics, geography, history, and culture to be an effective teacher of international students.

CASE #6

Teaching Conversation in Qatar
Adults; Bridge Program
Bob Campbell

I taught conversation in Qatar, which is a small country located on the Persian Gulf. The goal of the program was to prepare the country's top high school graduates for success in universities. Our focus was on Academic English, and the program was intensive.

Qatar is a conservative Muslim country, and teaching there can provide many challenges for Western teachers. You must be extremely sensitive to the cultural norms and religious beliefs of the students. In conversation classes, many topics were viewed as unacceptable. Sex, dating, drugs, alcohol, religion, politics, and the ruling family were not discussed. For many Western teachers, controversial topics provide the basis for a stimulating lesson. In order to make "safe" topics, such as animal rights, more interesting, I would build the students' interest by giving extreme or humorous examples. I also brought a lot of enthusiasm to each topic, and I believe this carried over to the students.

Another challenge in our program was that it was coeducational. This is almost unheard of in Qatar. Before coming to our program, the students had never studied in a classroom with members of the opposite sex. While they were confident of their speaking ability in general, speaking in front of the opposite sex was another story. It was necessary to provide an environment in which the students felt comfortable expressing themselves. We spent a lot of time just getting to know each other through a variety of activities. I provided encouragement, humor, and patience, which helped the students to feel safe enough to contribute to the discussions.

One of the main areas that I focused on in conversation classes was accuracy in speaking. Qatar is unusual in that the vast majority of the population is made up of foreign workers, and English is widely used for communication. Therefore, my Arabic-speaking students had grown up using English and felt very comfortable with their speaking ability. However, they were rarely corrected when they made errors. The general feeling among the students was that as long as they could make themselves understood, they would be fine. To focus on accuracy, I used Simulated Oral Proficiency Interviews, which are based on the ACTFL (American Council for the Teaching of Foreign Languages) guidelines. Depending on the level, questions involved tasks such as giving directions, complaining, and supporting an opinion. I believe this helped the students focus on their errors and make adjustments leading toward accuracy in speaking.

Finally, maintaining the students' interest was always a challenge. To accomplish this objective, teachers must be able to go beyond mundane tasks such as the basic open discussion of "What did you do this weekend?" Through my years of teaching, I learned a good repertoire of solid communication activities. Besides those listed above, we gave presentations, held debates, and negotiated problem-solving activities—all of these with specific directions and goals. This variety was useful in holding the students' attention and providing motivation.

While the circumstances and suggestions I mentioned are specific to my experience in Qatar, I believe they have practical applications in other situations as well. Stimulating interest, providing a safe environment, valuing accuracy, and using a variety of activities can help to make a conversation class successful in many situations.

Issues for Reflection

1. Some countries are more conservative than others. Teaching a conversation class there can be challenging because you need topics that will provoke discussion yet are not considered unacceptable in that culture. This teacher noted that topics such as sex, dating, drugs, alcohol, religion, politics, and the ruling family were definitely not discussed in this particular country.

2. Coeducational classes can be an issue in certain countries. If you are the foreigner teaching in such a situation, follow the lead of your national colleagues.

3. Accuracy in speaking was a problem, so this teacher brainstormed a solution using standardized tests that the students would respond to. Instead of viewing final tests as something evil, use them as another tool in your teaching.

4. A conversation class needs conversation tasks. You can't just tell students to turn to their partners and talk about whatever they want to for 20 minutes a day. To be the best conversation teacher possible, you need to develop a solid repertoire of teaching ideas. Almost all teachers know how to play hangman, but how many *other* activities can you name off the top of your head?

   There are several easy ways to increase your grab-bag of ideas. Talk to colleagues and see what their favorite ideas are. Consult books on speaking, including Chapter 4 in this book. Check out Internet sites for ESL/EFL teachers. Attend conferences where teachers are presenting "how to" ideas for the classroom.

CASE #7

Teaching Conversation in Japan
Adults; University
Brent Wolter

I taught English in Japan for about thirteen years, with almost ten of these years spent in various Japanese universities. The one thing you'll find about Japanese university classes is that there is no typical setting. I had everything from discussion classes of about 8 students to conversation classes of 70.

The size of your class obviously impacts how you teach the class, even more so when it is a conversation or speaking class where student participation is desired. In general, I would say that most classes were usually somewhere around 35 students. In addition to differences in class size, student motivation and willingness to participate vary considerably as well. This is due largely to the fact that most Japanese universities now classify English (often taught by a native speaker) as part of their students' general education requirements. In addition to class size, this requirement affects students with a wide range of feelings about English, from those who love it to those who deplore it and everything in between.

Although it can be misleading to generalize, clear patterns tend to emerge from students within particular faculties. This means that one class period can be spent with a group highly motivated students who are genuinely willing to learn, followed by a group of students intent on just doing the minimum of whatever is necessary to pass (and in the worst-case scenarios, little more). Still, it is my overall impression that *most* students see English as important, even if their willingness to work to improve their English is sometimes lacking.

As for what does or doesn't work in the Japanese university setting, in my experience, students were willing to follow instructions as long as the instructions were clear and unambiguous. This is very important. This often meant that sudden shifts in classroom activities could be bogged down in complex explanation, so I usually stuck with a few activities that I repeated on a weekly basis. (I should also add here that classes usually only meet once a week for 90 minutes, meaning you only see students fifteen times during the semester.) Of course, there is always the option of explaining things in Japanese, but it seemed that universities typically frowned on anything in Japanese, as it seemed (in their eyes) to defeat the rationale for employing native speakers in the first place.

Getting students up and out of their seats to take part in activities was never that problematic for me in most of the places I worked. However, I often found myself stuck in lecture halls with immovable rows of benches with fixed chairs. The most recent place I worked could be likened to the seating configuration on a 727; two rows of two seats on either side with a row of three or four seats down the middle. This was hardly designed for conversation lessons.

If there is one specific thing that I learned in my time there teaching conversation it is that any type of speaking activity needed to be extremely well structured if it was to have a reasonable chance of success. This should probably go without saying, but you would be surprised how many books had discussion prompts that read, "Now discuss the good points and bad points of college life with your partner." This type of unstructured discussion prompt will usually not work in the Japanese university classroom (despite the seating arrangements) unless there has been some sort of scaffolded build-up that gives the students the language and (as important) the confidence to do so. In the end, I began using an extremely structured approach that focused on topics that would never require knowledge from the world at large. In other words, I tended to focus on personal experiences as a start, and then I would work up to ideas and opinions if I felt the students had the ability and the rapport with one another to discuss such things.

No matter what the topic was, however, I gravitated toward an approach that first invited students to compose questions they could ask to get model answers from other students (yes, that's right, questions rather than answers). After this I would offer some gently corrected versions of their formulations, plus my own more natural types of spoken expressions (e.g. *What is/was* ____ *like?* rather than *How about* ____?). Armed with this arsenal of correct expressions, I then allowed students to ask their partners, while their partners responded with genuine answers. This was topped off by a final free discussion on the topic in randomly determined groups of three or four.

This practice seemed to work fairly well—as long as the students had the ability and willingness to participate in some basic conversation with partners. I never tried it on really low-level learners though, so I am not sure how it would have fared with such groups. I suspect if they had sufficient motivation, there would have been a way to make it work. Lacking this, however, I would have probably used techniques that required less on-the-spot pressure and a lower risk of what Japanese students might interpret as public failure to perform a task that puts them in an uncomfortable position in the public eye.

I enjoyed teaching university classes in Japan. With knowledge of the students' culture as well as learning expectations, I was able to teach English speaking and conversation despite the large class sizes and obstructive seating arrangements.

Issues for Reflection

1. It's important to remember that not every person in your classroom is motivated to learn English. Some university students may be there because it's a required course. (This phenomenon is true in other types of classes as well. For example, some company classes have students who may be there only because their boss told them to attend.)

2. Routine may seem boring to you, but it is comforting to many students, especially to those with weak listening skills or weak overall proficiency.

3. Keep activities simple. Remember that what may seem quite simple to you can be extremely complicated to someone who has never done that activity before—even more so if the directions are being delivered in an unknown language.

    Consider a simple game such as tic-tac-toe if you've never played it or seen it demonstrated. Without using pencil and paper or any visual demonstration, use only words to explain how to play this game to someone and you'll see how difficult an explanation for a simple game can be.

4. Notice how Brent had his students do tasks, not topics. Too many conversation books have prompts such as, "Now discuss the pros and cons of having only one child." You need to have smaller tasks that work on appropriate vocabulary and structures to help scaffold this discussion activity.

5. Some form of conversation can be done with students even in large classes. For novice teachers or teachers accustomed to classes with 12–15 students, suddenly facing 40–60 students can be daunting. Seek advice from other teachers who have taught these large classes in that country or university.

CASE #8

Teaching Conversation in Vietnam
Adults; University
Le Pham Hoai Huong

Though there are surely differences in certain groups of college-aged students, I am writing about students in the B.A. in English program at Hue College of Foreign Languages in Vietnam. Since these students are in an English program, their motivation tends to be quite high.

Students in this college program have three hours per week to practice oral English. Because this amount of time is relatively low, it is up to the teacher to maximize student speaking and listening whenever possible. In class, students work in pairs and small groups to discuss topics given in the textbook or given by the classroom teacher. In my experience, students also enjoy role plays to practice functional language. They usually have a textbook written by Western authors to follow.

Classroom interaction usually falls into two kinds: teacher-whole class or student-student. In class, students wait for the teacher to assign tasks to them; they rarely if ever initiate topics for discussion. In a Vietnamese classroom, the teacher clearly has all the power and respect. Students almost never interrupt the teacher.

The students have a good relationship with each other. They usually sit in the same place, close to the same classmate, for the whole semester. Sometimes the classroom discourse is collective. Every student likes to contribute to the chain of discussion if interested.

Under the umbrella of speaking skills, we cover many things in our classes. Vietnamese students at this level and in this kind of program are actually quite good at grammar rules and at using English expressions—which they have memorized—communicatively. One definite weakness, however, is pronunciation. Our students need to work a lot on pronunciation. Students often experience negative transfer from their first language; they transfer their pronunciation habits from Vietnamese to English. For example, final consonant clusters such as /ts/ in *cats* or /zd/ in *realized* are extremely difficult for the students. Their accuracy in pronouncing these ending sound combinations is a problem since Vietnamese does not have such final consonant clusters.

Motivating students is not a problem. The students are highly motivated to learn oral English for their future work prospects. However, they are timid about acting out plays or dialogues in front of the class. When unsure of what to do, Vietnamese students do what many non-native students do: They tend to use the mother tongue, especially when working in groups.

Choosing the topic for discussions is an important step in planning a good class. As most of our textbooks were written by Western authors primarily for an ESL audience, topics in the books can sometimes produce no talk. This is logical since students may not have any idea about a given topic, such as laws in Britain and children's rights. I have found that my university-age students in Vietnam really enjoy discussing topics that are more familiar and more meaningful to them, such as love, travel, and education.

You will enjoy teaching speaking skills to Vietnamese students. They are respectful, have a positive attitude toward learning English, and can be a joy to work with.

Issues for Reflection

1. All teachers would like their students to have more class time, but this is simply not a possibility in many cases. One of your most challenging objectives is to make the best use of limited class time. In an EFL setting especially, but also in many ESL settings, students have little to no contact with the target language outside of class. The teacher has to remember that any practice must take place inside the class. Pair work and group work can multiply the amount of practice.

2. Role plays can work well, but this activity depends on the personality of the teacher and the students. If you present this activity with the right attitude, your students will get into it. Even some of the most quiet students may end up surprising you. (See Activity 15, Chapter 4.)

3. Don't confuse teaching conversation with teaching grammar. Students may have had extensive experience with grammar rules but very little practice in actually speaking. Your job then will be to maximize student speaking. (This is not to say that grammar is unimportant. Every ESL teacher should know ESL grammar well.)

4. Students expect the teacher to deal with pronunciation at some point. Students clearly recognize that their pronunciation may hinder their ability to converse fluently in English. You should know enough about ESL pronunciation, including where sounds are made (e.g., labio-dental, velar), how sounds are made (e.g., stops, sibilants), whether they are voiced (e.g., /s/ is voiceless, /z/ is voiced), and ESL minimal pair problems that are specific to your students' first language (e.g., /b/ and /v/ for Spanish speakers, /i/ and /ɪ/ for almost all non-English languages). Knowing all of this information does not mean that you should teach it but rather that you can teach it—when it is pertinent. (See Appendix B.)

5. Once again, we see the importance of the topic in a conversation activity. This teacher wisely opted for topics appropriate for Vietnamese university-age students in Vietnam (i.e., EFL versus ESL).

CASE #9

Teaching Conversation in Brazil
Adults; Language Schools
Catherine Flores

During part of my 25 years of teaching ESL and EFL, I had the opportunity to work in Brazil, where I taught all levels of English from beginners to advanced. In this experience in the Brazilian EFL classroom, I learned that Brazilian students are very inquisitive, and they like to talk and share stories. Unlike some groups of students, Brazilians do not usually have a problem expressing their feelings or opinions quite openly.

My experience teaching conversation classes in Brazil has led me to understand Brazilian culture better. As a result, I have a better feel for Brazilian students' expectations regarding their English classes and their English teacher. One of the most important expectations of Brazilian students is that you as the teacher know enough about Brazil to know that Brazil is not a Hispanic country. Brazilians do not like to be perceived as Hispanics. They speak Portuguese—not Spanish—and often make a point of their cultural differences.

For the most part, getting Brazilian students to speak up in class is not a problem. They feel very comfortable expressing their opinions and sharing information about their culture. Students are eager to speak and express their thoughts. Since Brazil is a country of youth, classes must be dynamic and provide an arena for open discussions. In fact, in these open discussions, conversation classes can become very heated when students debate an issue. If they are passionate about a subject or topic of discussion, Brazilians will go out of their way to express those feelings. At times, this can be perceived as arrogant by other cultures, but I found this par for the course in my classes in Brazil.

The concept of time and punctuality varies from culture to culture. Brazilians are relaxed about meetings and deadlines. You will often find students arriving after class has started and then jumping right into the discussions being held in the classroom without any concern about their tardiness.

Classroom interactions are a little different from what I was accustomed to in my North American ESL classes. In Brazil, students may at times seemingly interrupt a classmate in an attempt to answer more rapidly. It is important for the instructor to be aware of this classroom dynamic to better guide the class activities and permit equal opportunity of participation. Brazilian students work well together on a task. However, there is a common interest among themselves in establishing relationships first before working on a class project, instead of immediately focusing on the task and letting relationships develop as they work on the task.

All cultures have different notions of social space and physical contact. Brazilians are very warm and friendly, and they consider touching a sign of acceptance. In fact, upon meeting someone, you may receive an *abraco,* or embrace, which involves a squeeze of the arm and a kiss on the cheek.

In my experience, Brazilians tend to have good fluency; however, they expect the instructor to correct their pronunciation and mistakes when speaking at all times. Topics I found that worked well were questions about societal customs and practices, environmental issues, food and cuisine, and sport activities. I would recommend that you stay away from topics regarding politics, religion, and alternative lifestyles. All in all, conversation classes in Brazil tend to be energetic and active, with many students jumping in to give their opinion.

It is very important for an instructor to have an understanding of different cultures and customs, which will help the teacher to comprehend students' expectations and be better prepared to teach any English class. Brazil has its unique customs and classroom situations, and being aware of these will make your teaching job much easier.

Issues for Reflection

1. Know your students. Brazil may be in South America, but it has a different culture, history, and language than its neighboring Spanish-speaking countries.

2. Some groups can become quite passionate when discussing topics. As a teacher, you need to be able to rein in these emotions to maintain the flow of a discussion. This is not an easy skill for novice teachers.

3. This teacher found that Brazilians seemed to interrupt each other in class discussions. In an EFL setting, this is not a problem since it appeared to this teacher to be normal and not upsetting to any of the students. In an ESL setting, however, a conversation teacher should know from the beginning that different cultures will bring different conversation patterns (not related to their first language but rather to their first culture) to the classroom. This can be problematic, and teachers may need to explain the new norms.

CASE #10

**Teaching Speaking and Listening to Teachers in China
Adults; Teacher Training for Public and Private School Teachers
Jan Pilcher**

I was recently invited to teach a multi-week seminar on teaching English to Chinese teachers of English. I was one of four American teachers who participated. We worked with approximately 80 attendees from the surrounding school district—which has more than 800 high schools!

Before arriving, we did not have a complete picture of the specialties of the seminar teachers, how the classes would be structured, or even what the capabilities of the teachers (our students) would be. We were given a class schedule the night before the first classes were to begin. We met the students in the afternoon and quickly determined that there was a significant range of English comprehension levels among the students. Good teachers can learn to cope with multi-level classes, but such classes are not the ideal. Because we were trying to impart content (here, ways to teach English) and because time was such a critical issue (we had only a handful of weeks), the 80 teachers needed to be grouped by proficiency level.

We responded to this assessment need. On the first morning of class, the four of us took twenty students each and administered a basic oral comprehension test using a variety of picture scenarios. During lunch, the four of us organized the students into four groups. By the time lunch hour was finished, we were ready to teach leveled classes.

There are many teaching opportunities in China today, and some training settings will allow more flexibility than others. Our site was very good in this aspect. The four of us took time to negotiate, by way of suggestion, a four-class day instead of a five-class day. Logistically, this was much better: This fit better with having four teachers and four groups of students. We would see each student one time each day, and we could adjust our lesson plans according to the level of the class. The compromise was that we still had a four-and-a-half-hour teaching day with two-and-a-half hours in the morning and two hours in the afternoon. It worked great!

Our students were wonderful. All of them were employed as English teachers in public and private schools. Ages ranged from 21 to nearly 55. Most were women, but there were a number of men, too. Levels of proficiency ranged the whole gamut: A few were hardly able to put together three words at a time, while others could carry on a lively conversation.

Our curriculum for the week consisted of three areas: reading skills, pronunciation skills, and teaching methods for teaching listening. In my class on teaching listening, I managed to incorporate a different listening skill exercise in each class, which usually ended with a game. We tried to practice each game at least two times during the two weeks so students could remember how to play. At first, the students were somewhat shy, but after a few attempts at different games, I felt like I almost needed to wear a helmet to referee! They said that they never played games in class because their classes were so large. This was a valid caveat, so I had to modify the games so they could be played by large groups.

In my language learning and teaching experience, songs seem to be universally popular. They loved to sing so we taught them some popular old rock songs. You could not go wrong with a Beatles standard, but we got several requests for the Carpenters song *Yesterday Once More*. I spent two nights looking around the city music stores for a copy. I found one with the English words already printed in a booklet! I made a copy in a cloze format for each student. They had to fill in the blanks as they learned the song. We all sang together doing karaoke on the weekend!

You never know how a certain technique or teaching idea will go over. What is successful with one group can often flop with another—and vice-versa. To my surprise, one of the most interesting classes involved U.S. coins. In class, I passed out handfuls of pennies, nickels, dimes, and quarters. There is history on each coin, and many of the coins today are different. The quarters were cool because we could look for each state on a map and then try to describe the designs. They each got to choose a few coins to take home to their own classes for show and tell. I think one of the most important points here is that the students perceived this use of realia as something clearly related to the language, culture, or country being studied. Never underestimate the use of good realia to spice up a conversation class—whether it's an actual restaurant menu, a magazine advertisement, or even coins!

From what the teachers told me, language teaching in China tends to focus heavily on learning the pieces of the language—grammar, idioms, and patterns. In this short special workshop, I really believe that teachers were able to learn some new ideas for teaching listening (and speaking). I hope they will try to have more fun in class after working with me for a few weeks. I know that I certainly enjoyed working with these Chinese teachers. Teaching is always easier when you have such enthusiastic and motivated learners!

Issues for Reflection

1. One of the most common and effective ways to use a song for listening is to create a cloze activity for the song. In a cloze activity, you write out the song lyrics and then delete certain key words or phrases. Students then listen to the song to fill in the blanks. By the second or third time you play the song, many students will start singing along whether you have asked them to or not. (For those who consider this more of a listening rather than speaking activity, I would like to note that at any point in a conversation, one person is listening, and without good listening skills, that person would not be able to respond to the other person's words. Listening is conversation, too.)

   Choose slow songs. Delete words that students can catch when they listen to the song. Delete some easy words and some hard words. By hard words, I do not mean difficult semantically. I mean that the words are hard to catch in the song because of the combination of words around them. Remember that you are practicing *listening*, not spelling of previously unlearned vocabulary.

2. Consider Jan's comment that, "You never know how a certain technique or teaching idea will go over. What is successful with one group can often flop with another—and vice-versa." As you plan your speaking class, you will of course choose activities that you think will be successful with your group, but just because an activity does not work well in that class does not mean that it won't work well with another group. As you reflect on the activity after the class, think about how the activity could have been modified to be more successful.

3. Realia gets students interested. If you are practicing ordering food in a restaurant, bring in actual menus from a restaurant. If you are discussing clothing, use the clothing store flyers or advertisements in newspapers. Be creative. Realia can also be attained easily on the Internet.

4. Short-term assignments in China, especially during June, July, and August, are abundant. Numerous postings are on the Internet. Teaching in one of these short-term assignments in China is an excellent way to get some EFL teaching experience in a short time. However, it is critical to do your homework before you choose your program. How organized is the program where you'll be teaching? Will you have materials? Who are the students? What about references? Can you talk to some teachers who taught there last summer?

CASE #11

Teaching Conversation to High-Intermediate Learners in the United States
Adults; Intensive English Program
Tim Wilson

I currently teach high-intermediate conversation skills at a large university in Florida. The Intensive English Program involves approximately 150 students whose cultural backgrounds vary from Korean to Hispanic, from Middle Eastern to French. The largest population of students in my communication skills class come from South Korea, Japan, and Venezuela, while the remaining students come from other countries such as France, Saudi Arabia, Colombia, and Kuwait.

Although the students were of various backgrounds, their desires to pursue an American university education were very similar. Many of my communication skills class consisted of ages ranging from 18 to 28 with the average being centrally focused around 22. In addition, the class consisted mostly of males rather than females, and in this particular class, the majority of students planned to pursue a degree in business. Therefore, I took into account in the lesson planning their pursuit of passing the TOEFL® for college admittance, their need for everyday communication and expression, as well as the need and interest for business communication skills.

We focused on communication styles in various situations such as at work, at a party, in the classroom, on a date, and even in arguments. I found that the students liked to discuss situations that related to them and understand vocabulary words that mattered in these situations. For example, I remember discussing the different dating styles in the various cultures and trying to understand such words and phrases as *flirting, hitting on,* and *he's got the hots for someone.* When these topics were raised, I saw how the majority of my relatively quiet Korean students began to speak up, ask questions, and even provide advice (and at times, even some good advice!) on how to date.

Overall, what worked well with my students in communication was not only looking at topics of interest and relevance but also for them to see these situations illustrated. I understood very quickly that many of these students were visual learners because they would easily grab concepts and vocabulary that they either saw written on the board or acted out in a movie clip. Therefore, I would repeatedly go to the simple yet reliable blackboard to allow the vocabulary words to be visualized. In addition, we would group words together on a topic and then create a situation where they needed to be used—for example, using such terms as *flustered, experience, working up the ladder,* and *kissing up* in a situation where Student A is being interviewed for a job and Student B is the angry interviewer.

As time went on, I saw these students gain more confidence in trying these activities because they became more comfortable with each other, especially within their language skills. I learned several important things from my teachers (that is, the students of my communication skills class). First, never force the speaking: Allow students little by little to trust you, to trust the process, to trust each other, and eventually to trust themselves. Second, by understanding my students' interests and learning styles, I was able to teach not the way **I** learn but rather the way **they** listen and engage.

The difficult task of the communication teacher is to lay yourself and your agenda aside and then just go with the students' flow!

Issues for Reflection

1. One of Tim's most important points is the effect of writing new vocabulary on the board. Vocabulary growth is critical in improving oral proficiency. As new words and phrases come up in class, write them on the board. Students will greatly appreciate your use of the board. Train students to jot down these new phrases.

2. Grouping vocabulary by theme can help learners assimilate the new vocabulary better. It helps establish a mental network for the words. At the same time, it motivates students because they can see a real situation where these words would be useful.

CASE #12

Teaching Speaking to Low-Proficiency Learners in the United States
Adult Education; College
Anh Ly

I currently teach a high-beginning level class at a large college in California. Our school serves more than 25,000 adult students at more than 60 sites. Our classes are open entry and open exit. A majority of our students are immigrants from Mexico, South America, and Southeast Asia. The remaining students are from Africa, Ukraine, Japan, China, and other countries.

There are 45 students in my beginning-high ESL class; 98 percent of my students are Hispanic and 2 percent are categorized as Asian or other. Their ages range from 18 to 65. Some of them are newcomers, and some of them have been living in the United States for more than twenty years. Their academic background varies greatly, with some illiterate in their mother tongue to others with a university degree in their native language; this vast difference in their learning abilities makes keeping them focused on learning the language a great challenge.

Even though reading, writing, and grammar are being introduced to prepare the students for subsequent higher levels, we place more emphasis on survival skills, which are largely listening and speaking. My students—as with a great many adult learners—are more interested in learning the rules of grammar, however.

Teaching conversation to our different ethnic groups of students can be difficult. I have noticed that new Asian students are less likely to participate in conversational activities compared to my naturally outspoken Hispanic students. However, it is a greater task for me to retain some of my Hispanic students' attentiveness to completing their assigned homework and obeying classroom rules. Given this combination of learner characteristics, a successful teacher must be able to take control and direct students regarding what to do. In fact, I would say that these particular classroom management skills are essential and help me to be a stronger and better teacher.

Since there are various cultures and customs in this class, cultural differences are often emphasized so that students can be easily merged into the mainstream of American society. In our conversations, we often mention and compare the differences of the American cultures versus students' native cultures.

In class, the ultimate goal is for my students to practice conversations in pairs. I have found that it is important to give students the vocabulary they need to perform the pair task and to provide them with an example, either in the form of a written example or a live demonstration, before the actual activity. Therefore, before my students practice conversation in pairs, I go over vocabulary relating to the topic of the lesson, practice conversation models, role play with a couple of students, and have some students volunteer role play in front of the class.

I am always impressed by my student's persistence in learning the English language; most of them come to class after long workday hours with only a few hours of sleep. Some students even come to class without having eaten dinner. My students are driven. They know that by mastering the English language, many doors of opportunity will open for them to have a better future.

After eight years of teaching, I have learned a great deal from working with my students. I have learned that a good teacher has seemingly infinite patience, knows a great deal about the subject matter, is able to motivate students, and respects learners' differences. To be certain, many of them do need the repetition, repetition, and repetition that I heard about in education classes and teacher workshops, but the picture of good teaching and good learning is actually much more complex.

Issues for Reflection

1. Anh's adult students in the United States need survival skills, so the topics that she will use in her class would be different from those used in an EFL setting.

2. Many adult learners who have some previous training in languages expect classes to focus on (or at least mention) grammar. It is important for the teacher to be aware of what ESL grammar issues are. In other words, once again we see a need for speaking teachers to know ESL grammar well. (See Appendix C.)

3. Before having students do their conversation practice in pairs, Anh reviews vocabulary that the students will need. Again, it is important for students to have the necessary vocabulary and grammar for conversation activities. If they don't have this, then the speaking activity quickly becomes nothing but a vocabulary or grammar lesson, which was not the point of the conversation activity.

CASE #13

Teaching English Conversation in Japan
Adults; Language School
Kevin Novenario

English conversation is a huge business in Japan. Currently, there are hundreds of English conversation schools all over Japan, employing thousands of teachers. I work for one of the largest of these language schools. My school also offers courses in Spanish, Italian, French, Chinese, and German. While there are courses geared toward standardized English tests such as the TOEFL® and TOEIC® exams, mainstream conversational English is the primary focus of this school. Specialty classes for business English and travel English are also available.

In the mainstream classes, the students are from all walks of life, from junior high school students to senior citizens. Their reasons for studying English are similarly varied, but the majority study for the following reasons: as a hobby, for traveling, for business, and to communicate with foreigners.

Another type of class is a language lounge, where the students come in and talk to each other using the target language. Because students view this type of class as an opportunity to practice and interact with a real native speaker, the language lounge is very popular. In these classes, the instructor is present only as a moderator. Teachers have no planning to prepare, and students have no homework to complete. Some schools sell package deals in which students buy a set number of tickets that they can redeem for a lounge slot that is convenient for their schedule.

English conversation training starts early here. We have classes available for elementary school-age children, divided into three age groups. There is even a special class for very young children in which the mothers also participate in the class activities.

There are very few true beginners at my school, since English is a required subject from the first year of middle school until graduation from high school, six years total. Still, as English education in the public schools is primarily grammar-translation based, Japanese students can be quite inexperienced as far as English conversation ability is concerned. Students may be able to analyze the grammar of a rather complicated sentence, but they often lack the ability to carry on the simplest of conversations.

The method of instruction in conversation classes is quite different from that used in a traditional Japanese classroom. In our regular classes, there are a maximum of four students per class. Use of Japanese in class is strictly against school policy. While there are a few grammatical structures and vocabulary words introduced in each lesson, the lessons focus primarily on English conversation and communicative ability. The lessons are 40 minutes long and are structured to provide as much student talking time as possible.

A sample lesson may go as follows: First, the teacher and students greet one another and make some small talk. Then an assessment activity is given. The students are presented a situation and try to say what they can on the topic. Some sample topics include free-time activities, making a hotel reservation, and the pros and cons of a factory. The purpose of the assessment is to see which students are talkative/quiet, as well as to check what language the students may already have going into the lesson. New vocabulary and grammar are then introduced—usually a model conversation with interchangeable vocabulary words.

A listening activity is also part of the lesson. First, the teacher presents some questions to the students, models the language in a story or conversation (which gives the teacher an opportunity to do some voice acting), and then checks students' answers for comprehension. At the heart of the lessons are language activities and an application. The activities give the students a chance to reinforce the target language through various tasks such as sentence completion, matching, or paraphrasing. In the application, the students try to apply as much of the target language as possible, away from the textbook, usually in a role play or discussion. Finally, the teacher points out what the students did well, what could be improved, and offers some activities for review.

Forty minutes is not a lot of class time, so it is important to prepare and then maintain a good flow of good activities in the class to maximize this limited time. Japanese students tend to be reserved, but activities with clear directions can certainly help them come out of their shell in class.

Issues for Reflection

1. Having taught in Japan, I concur with Kevin's statement that English conversation is big business in Japan. This has two repercussions for you as a teacher. First, there are many conversation teaching positions available in Japan, and you should really do your homework to find out as much as possible about the school. In addition to all of the pertinent job details such as salary, housing, and visa requirements, you will want to know about the school's students, curriculum, schedule, and materials available. Second, many people of all ages attend English conversation classes. Find out if you will be teaching adults, children, or both. All of these points have an impact on the conversation class that you teach.

2. You may teach in a school that has a conversation lounge. In this setting, you are not teaching as much as you are simply managing a conversation for a small group. The advantage is that it is less work for you in many ways, but the disadvantage is that you have to maintain a conversation with small but reticent groups for several hours during the day. This can be more demanding than you might imagine.

3. Kevin describes the many Japanese learners who have studied English but still cannot function much in English, a group that we usually call *false beginners*. Teaching false beginners can be a challenge because novice teachers may incorrectly assume that the students need to be taught English from zero since their proficiency level is so low and would seem to indicate no knowledge. Perhaps a better way to think about false beginners is not that they have no knowledge but rather they have no *active* knowledge. As Kevin points out, the teacher has to provide activities that focus on speaking practice.

4. In an EFL setting (and sometimes in an ESL setting), all of the students share a common native language. In this case, the teacher's judicious use of the students' language can be helpful at times. However, Kevin's school had an official policy against using Japanese in class. It is important to work within any existing rules regarding the use of the students' native language and plan accordingly.

CASE #14

Teaching Conversation in Korea
Children; Language School
Bobby Wheeler

I currently teach conversational English to elementary and middle school students at a language academy in Seoul, South Korea. My school is a franchise of small academies with original curriculum and study materials for children to develop strong English speaking and listening skills.

For Koreans to enter into a university, they must take many difficult exams, including one testing English fluency. Since education is a top priority for parents in Korea, they send their children to academies, or *hogwons*, to receive additional education beyond what they receive at the public schools. Many parents believe that their child's education is not sufficient in the public schools, so they are willing to pay large sums of money to send their child to an English *hogwon*.

My job as an English teacher is not to teach students difficult language or give tests that are impossible to pass. Instead, I am a conversation teacher and my job is to be an English speaker and give the students exposure to English immersion taught by a native speaker.

I usually teach six classes a day, all lasting 50 minutes. My largest class will have only nine students, so this small number definitely helps with classroom management. In addition, students receive more personal attention. My favorite conversation class is one composed of four boys and four girls. Their English is limited, but I can tell that that they are extremely bright. These particular students are only eleven years old, but they have been studying in this *hogwon* for a few years already.

I begin the conversation class with several warm-up questions such as, *What day is it today?* or *What's the weather like today?* Beginning with simple warm-up questions allows the children to make a transition from thinking in Korean to English. To reinforce speaking in English only, the students have sticker cards, and when they speak Korean they receive a yellow sticker. As simple as this sounds, this penalty card system works wonders for classroom management with this group of students.

After the warm-up questions, we watch a conversation situation on the computer. The students listen to the conversation several times and then repeat it. After they finish the repetition, I assign roles from the conversation to different students. When the students act out these conversation roles, they better understand the context of the words and will be able to use them in a practical situation in the future. We then practice using different vocabulary so the students will understand that the vocabulary has many applications. In essence, these are simple drills, but I always try to make sure the contexts are not sterile. The utterances should be meaningful to the students. For example, *Mom, can I watch TV? No, you must do your homework first!* can be changed to *Mom, can I play on the computer? No, you must clean your room first!*)

The students in the class are similar in many ways. Korean is their mother tongue. They all are from middle-class Korean families. Furthermore, their parents push them hard to be as successful as possible in the future. In this regard, teaching these learners is a simple task since they have similar backgrounds and goals. On the other hand, the lack of classroom diversity can be a bit of a drawback since all of the students share the same customs, beliefs, and culture. It is often easier to talk when people have differences, not similarities.

The goal of each class meeting is to get the students to speak English whether or not they speak correctly. I do not directly teach grammar rules; instead, the students learn from trial and error and repetition. I never directly present or explain a grammar rule because children do not know how to analyze grammar in the same way that adult ESL students can. The more that I can get the children to speak, the more chances they have to learn English from their mistakes; the more they talk, the less shy they become.

Teaching conversational English in Korean *hogwons* is a rewarding experience. I enjoy working with Korean students because Koreans push themselves hard to become fluent in English. They are a very motivated group. Knowing English gives Korean children an educational advantage, so there is certainly a huge sense of personal satisfaction in helping a child gain access to a brighter future.

Issues for Reflection

1. Children learn differently. You can't overtly teach grammar patterns to children. In an EFL setting, students are not exposed to much if any English outside of class. Using activities that have repetition of vocabulary and grammar patterns built into them is an effective technique for teaching children. It's one reason that songs work so well with children. They will sing the same song over and over.

2. In an EFL setting, there will be less diversity than in a typical ESL class. Therefore, common ESL textbook activities in which students ask each other where they are from or what the name of their school is (when they are in fact all in the same school) will not be effective. *Remember:* People have lengthy discussions about differences, but they have very short discussions about similarities—until they find a difference.

CASE #15

Teaching ESL in Canada
Adults; Community College
Mark Limacher

I've been teaching ESL at a community college on the west coast of Canada for more than ten years. Conversation is one part of an integrated class in which all four skills are taught. The average class size is twenty students ranging in age from 18 to 80 (really!). About half are international students who plan to enter university in Canada; the other half are immigrants who are studying English to enhance their employment opportunities. It is not uncommon for a single class to have students from ten or fifteen different countries.

The curriculum at our college is based on an outcomes approach: students are tested on what they can do with what they know. For example, students are taught how to make small talk, including various common expressions and small-talk skills such as holding the floor, avoiding a question, and turn taking. For their assessment, they will need to make small talk in an unrehearsed situation and demonstrate their abilities. After each assessment, they receive feedback on their performance and are given multiple assessment opportunities to improve on their initial performance. This approach to teaching is quite challenging because it requires the development of a lot of materials, giving feedback is laborious, and the students are unfamiliar with the approach. On the plus side, students often make quite remarkable progress over the term.

One interesting aspect of teaching students from such a wide range of countries is the opportunity to observe the value that different cultural groups place on speaking and listening skills. For example, my classroom experience suggests that students from some cultures such as Iran or Somalia are often very good at learning conversation skills. They are often both accurate and fluent and have excellent pronunciation and strong nonverbal skills. They appear to be very sensitive to the techniques Canadians use to convey multi-layered messages orally and are good at imitating these communication patterns. In contrast, students from some other cultures, such as China, may struggle with listening and speaking activities. Of course, this isn't because of any inherent lack of ability, but rather, it appears that grammar, reading, and writing are more valued in some cultures, while oral self-expression isn't as important. An intriguing aspect of this for me as the conversation or communication teacher is helping students who apparently place less value on speaking skills develop sensitivity to the ways that stress, intonation, and non-verbal communication are used.

The students who come to the college have a wide range of needs, goals, and educational backgrounds. Combined with the age and cultural differences, the class is a place of high diversity. The teaching generally is challenging, but it is very rewarding, especially watching the students as they form a strong, supportive learning community.

Issues for Reflection

1. Once again, we see a teacher comment on the correlation between how talkative students are and their different nationalities. When planning a class, take this into account as you choose activities that encourage all students to participate equally. (In other words, you want tasks that require all students to speak.)

2. Mark mentions the specific way that assessment is done at his school. Good teachers consider assessment from the very beginning of their planning and build in appropriate activities. Again, assessment is not a negative. Assessment tells the students (and the teacher) how much progress they have made and which areas still need improvement. Tying assessment more closely into the class activities is a wise and motivating move on Mark's part.

CASE #16

Teaching Conversation in Japan
Young Adults; University
Darren P. Bologna

For three years, I taught freshman English at a medium-sized private university in Chiba, Japan. Our school had about 3,500 students specializing in learning languages and/or cultures. I usually taught eight 90-minute classes per week, of no more than 30 students. The level of the students' conversation skills was minimal upon entrance.

The students were all eighteen-year-old freshmen. They came from high schools where they had learned English by rote memorization in order to pass a university entrance exam. Therefore, they had had little, if any, experience speaking English besides some stock phrases and questions such as *Can you use chopsticks?* I found that if you vary your answers from the expected answer list that the students have in mind, don't worry—they won't miss a beat but rather will continue by asking other stock questions.

In accordance with the teaching philosophy of the university, I tried to emphasize functional English. I did not worry the students too much about little things like grammar. When a grammar point had to be made, students would get a distant look in their eye that teachers called "the 100-yard stare." I found the students to be very knowledgeable about U.S. culture, music, movies, and fashion. I also found that the students who had a tangible goal in which they would use English were much more motivated than students studying English because they want to understand *Legally Blonde* or another movie better.

Ironically, my best classes were weekly 90-minute English classes designed for non-English majors. Initially, I was hesitant to teach these courses because I thought the students would have little motivation to learn English since it wasn't their major. However, they were a joy to work with for an interesting and quite surprising reason: These students had experienced none of the Western teachers' interactive methods. Most of their instructors were Korean, Indonesian, or Thai who employed the same teaching style the students had just left behind in high school, that is, a teacher-centered, learn-this-material kind of class. Therefore, when I set up interactive and communicative activities for them, these students would absolutely have the greatest time sitting in groups, completing conversation puzzles, and playing games that the English major students took for granted because they were exposed to it on a daily basis.

Classroom management in Japan is really the teacher's responsibility. I say this because the students come to the table with awe-inspiring respect for the *sensei* (teacher). The students expect you to lead the class, to give clear, unambiguous directions, and to act in the full role of *sensei*. You need to emphasize group skills rather than individual skills. There will not be a student who raises their hand or yells out an answer. This goes against the grain of Japanese culture; you must allow the group time to come to consensus and give their answer. This Japanese expression "The nail that stands up gets hammered down" says it all.

To succeed as a university teacher in the Japanese university classroom is quite easy provided that you're patient. Consequently, you have only yourself to blame if you destroy that. Anger is very destructive, instantly ruining classroom harmony. The Japanese view anger as a character flaw of weak self-discipline rather than as a sign of strength. If you become angry and lose your cool, the class will never forget. The students will begin to take you down a destructive road of passive-aggression in which they demurely resist anything you do to move the class forward thereafter.

In conclusion, Japanese university students genuinely appreciate the time you spend creating innovative lessons. They are quite sensitive and know when you have spent your time and energy to improve the class. Also, be patient in bringing your interactive teaching methods to a new class; it takes time to acculturate them. However, the absolutely hardest part of teaching will be your last class with the tearful good-byes and the disposable cameras lined up to take a picture with *sensei*.

Issues for Reflection

1. Patience is an enviable virtue. It is important to have a plan but at the same time be able to go with the flow when diversions happen in class.

2. Some cultures exalt the role of the teacher so much that students can be quite comfortable with the teacher doing the bulk of the talking, which is by definition a teacher-centered classroom. In speaking classes, the focus should be on the students, not the teacher, and all activities should aim for maximum student speaking.

   I've heard novice teachers say things such as, *These students don't have anything to say* or *These students won't talk because they don't know anything.* Sometimes it is not that students aren't able to talk but rather that they aren't accustomed to talking in front of the whole class or even the teacher.

   Let's reverse cultural roles for a moment. Imagine that during one of *your* professor's lectures in one of *your* history classes, you stood up during one of your professor's sentences. After a brief moment of incredulity, the professor stopped for a second. Exactly at that precise moment, you said, "I don't agree with that. I think the war was caused by. . . ." Can you imagine how uncomfortable everyone would be? Well, maybe it's just as uncomfortable for students of certain nationalities (e.g., Japanese, Taiwanese, Malaysian) to speak up in class—even when you have asked them a direct question.

   As several teachers have mentioned in this chapter already, you may need to spend a great deal of time waiting for your students to get accustomed to you and your teaching style before they play volleyball instead of bowling. (See Chapter 5, p. 187, for reference.)

3. Many recent TESOL graduates leave with their new degree and many ideas for communicative, student-centered teaching. However—and this is a critical caveat—this does not mean you should start implementing new techniques that your students are not familiar with. It is important to work within students' expectations, too, while you gradually make any changes you wish.

CASE #17

Teaching Conversation in Germany
Adults; Business English in a Private School
Karina Clemmons

The old fallback conversation starter question "How's the weather today?" just didn't cut it in the private school where I taught in northern Germany. It was always cold and rainy, and no one wanted to be reminded of it! Instead, I prepared myself for conversation classes by poring through international newspapers and news magazines on the train on the way to the school or the business where the class would take place.

The German adults that I taught at a school specializing in business English were serious about their conversational ability. Because most German students, regardless of their track in the vocational, mid-level, or university-bound public high schools, have had English classes in secondary school, my conversation classes were mainly intermediate and advanced English proficiency levels.

My school offered teacher resources that included a collection of conversation role plays related to business ethics, but I prepared for my conversation classes by keeping up with current events. Politics was the most popular topic among my students, and I had to be on my toes to disprove the popular German belief that Americans know little about or are simply uninterested in international affairs. My students loved to discuss regional and national politics, debate international relations, and theorize on the latest business trends. The school where I worked provided copies of national and international newspapers as well as weekly news magazines for its teachers to peruse. I always skimmed these resources and kept my ear tuned to the news for current events that might interest my students as conversation topics.

In addition to politics and business, another favorite topic of my students was talking about their jobs. Since many mid- to large-sized German companies do business within the European Union, English has become the lingua franca for many of their employees. Employees were expected to be proficient in English, particularly in conversational transactions when dealing with vendors and customers. My students were keenly aware of the perception that speaking English well would improve their employment prospects and make them appear educated, competent, and knowledgeable among their professional and social peers.

While some ESL teachers hold the philosophy that natural conversational flow should not be interrupted with corrections, my German students wanted corrections. In the middle of a heated discussion about the effects of the current multi-party coalition in the German legislature, my students would pay rapt attention to my correction of their use of the future perfect progressive tense. In fact, at times it seemed their evaluation of me as their English teacher was directly correlated to my ability to explain obscure grammar points without hesitation.

Many veteran ESL teachers can relate stories of painful conversation classes when students were so reluctant to speak that the teacher's mind raced to think of ways to fill the awkward silence when a planned activity failed miserably. My students in Germany, however, were uninhibited about talking in conversation class. Our classes were lively, interesting, and intellectually challenging for student and teacher alike.

Issues for Reflection

1. Karina points out the importance of the topic that you choose for your conversation class. Becoming familiar with your students' needs as quickly as possible can mean the difference between a successful class and an unsuccessful one.

2. Because these students were interested in current events, the teacher had to spend some time outside of class trying to get information about current news, politics, and business. Likewise, if your students are interested in the stock market or art, then you should try to inform yourself about these subjects so you can take advantage of their interests in your conversation class.

3. Adult learners often want to be corrected. If you are not familiar with ESL grammar, you cannot offer good explanations to explain students' errors. In addition, students rightfully expect you to know ESL grammar rules because you are the teacher. (See Appendix C.)

I agree wholeheartedly with this student expectation. Any native speaker can have a conversation with a student, but only a knowledgeable teacher can effectively deal with ESL students' errors. This means recognizing the error as well as knowing whether the error is from first language interference (e.g., Spanish students' use of *have* in *I have hungry*) or from ESL universal errors (e.g., all students' use of *be* in *Every day I am wake up early* or confusion of participles in *The movie was very interested*). It also means knowing whether the error is serious enough to warrant a correction or is merely a blip that is part of the second language acquisition process. If correction is warranted, then teaching experience and training will tell the teacher the best way or ways to practice the error.

CASE #18

Teaching Conversation in China
College; University
Jennifer Miller

I taught EFL in China for several years at a university in Wuhu, China. (Yes, it really is pronounced "woo-hoo.") The conversation classes I taught consisted of English majors. For two years, I had these same 30 students for two hours a week of conversation class. Anyone who has taught Chinese students can relate to the fairly nonexistent concept of class participation in a Chinese classroom—at least in any sense of the Western idea.

I was the first foreign teacher these students had, and in most cases, I was the first foreigner they had spoken to. Many of my students came to the university from the surrounding countryside and were petrified to converse with a native speaker. You can imagine then how that would complicate a conversation class. Furthermore, the general experience of their high school English classes had been structured around grammar translation and rote memorization. Developing conversational English had not been high on the list of priorities.

However, little by little, bit by bit, I built a relationship with these students, and they began to become more comfortable in oral production. Initially, we stuck very close to the fairly uninspired textbook assigned by the university. I would introduce cultural segments to keep things interesting, but the oral production was based on reading sample dialogues from the text and then making minor modifications to practice other vocabulary.

Over time, the relationship between student and teacher was strengthened, and their ability to verbally express themselves, as well as their comfort in doing that, grew. We were able to venture into more and more conversational areas. However, throughout this time, it remained important to incorporate both model dialogues for them to follow, or later in the developmental process, an appropriate amount of time for them to prepare themselves for the conversation.

One of the last units we covered before they finished conversation class at the end of their sophomore year was a unit based on the movie *Dead Poets Society*. This movie had great appeal to the Chinese students on many levels. They loved the romance and the tragedy, and the issues themselves were very real to the students. Like the characters in the movie, my students were confronted with pressure from parents and school authorities to achieve, the threat of suicide from confused and overburdened classmates, and confusion over the clash between traditional teaching methods and seemingly unorthodox new teachers (their foreign teachers!). After viewing the movie, we spent several class periods discussing it as a class, going over characters and themes, answering comprehension questions, and engaging in informal debates.

At the end of the unit, we arranged the class in a circle (which really meant sitting at odd angles all over the furniture which was nailed to the floor) for a final discussion of the movie. One of my favorite teaching memories is when the students actually took over the conversation and engaged in a discussion regarding the movie and its application to their lives that didn't require me for prompting or commenting. It had taken two years, a lot of preparation, as well as a fair amount of relationship (building) to see my students participate in a full-scale class discussion, but the wait was worth it. My patience and persistence had paid off.

Issues for Reflection

1. It may take a long time for students to feel comfortable enough with a teacher and their classmates to actively engage in speaking in class. Teachers may have to work patiently but hard at gaining students' confidence. Only then can speaking happen. Jennifer mentions this regarding teaching in China, and I experienced the same thing in Japan.

2. In some EFL settings, you may be the first and only contact that your students have had with a native speaker of English. In addition to not knowing you individually yet, they may have never met an English speaker, so students need time to adjust.

3. If your students' proficiency level is sufficient, then challenge them with activities such as movies. Never attempt to show a movie and discuss it in one class period. If you do this, students are most likely responding to what they saw, not what they heard, which means you have wasted an opportunity to practice listening, which is a vital skill in conversation. Jennifer wisely spread the movie out over several classes.

CASE #19

Teaching University English Classes in Korea
Adults; University
Bryan T. Stoakley

For five years, I taught English in Korea at a university that put much focus on learning English. I led conversation classes, where writing and grammar instruction was nearly non-existent, in two different formats.

In the first format, we had regular university classes, required for all undergraduates, composed of 30 students. They met once a week for two hours and were almost always filled with students of the same major and year. The other format was one that students, staff, faculty, and adults in the community paid extra to attend and took place four days a week for four hours. Also, students were not grouped by major but by level with no more than fifteen students per class. In both formats, I had to continually confront the teacher-centered mantra that the Korean education system promotes.

A general obstacle—and arguably the most important—that an English teacher must overcome in Korea is students' reticence. This obstacle is not because the students can't speak English, but because they prefer not to—until they become comfortable making mistakes and/or are comfortable with the teacher and their peers. This situation occurs because nobody wants to make mistakes and be labeled stupid, so they choose not to speak and thus not make any errors.

To make the students feel comfortable, we played many conversation games that helped them bond with their new classmates. Some games were prefabricated board games, and other activities were just fact-finding missions for the students to learn about each other.

It is also imperative for students to realize that mistakes are natural and not to be looked down upon. In order to lighten the mood regarding mistakes, I would sometimes speak Korean where I would inevitably make a mistake and then we would discuss, in English of course, what I did wrong and how I could improve my communication method. I could almost always transfer my mistake to theirs, so they realized the importance of analyzing mistakes. Similarly, when teaching pronunciation I made it a point to make the lesson humorous and goofy. For example, when forced to act like a bumble bee when attempting to make the /z/ sound, everybody relaxed and had a good time.

Another technique that I successfully used to get students to communicate in English was to give them advance notice of the topics/questions we would discuss/answer for the next class meeting. Frequently, I let them choose the topic to be discussed, and I created vocabulary, phrases, and questions to be addressed. Through advance notice, the lower-level students were allowed to prepare their answers beforehand, which enabled them to participate in class instead of having the higher-level students control their group's rhythm.

Group work is a necessity. In group work, there is less stress about making mistakes for two reasons. First, there are fewer people who will hear your mistakes. Second, working in groups means more individual time to practice talking. When the students were doing group work, I could then walk around the class and help them out with communication strategies (that they had already learned) one on one.

Through these techniques, I was able to implement just about any lesson and it would be successful, which means that students participated (spoke), learned new vocabulary and phrases, and used it all in a meaningful (and less stressful) way.

1. Korean students are accustomed to a teacher-centered classroom, so in your planning, you will have to think about activities that get students to do almost all of the talking. At the same time, you should realize this change will not happen overnight and initially you are likely to have many nearly silent classes. Be patient. Build rapport. Explain the activities well. Demonstrate the activities before letting students practice. Teach vocabulary and structures necessary to successfully complete the tasks.

2. Bryan let his students choose the class topics. In addition to owning the lesson, another advantage is that students know in advance what the next topic will be and can plan accordingly. If they want to participate, they can consult their bilingual dictionaries to look up key words or phrases that they might need for the next day's speaking activity.

3. In cultures where classrooms are viewed as a medium to reduce errors, teachers may find it difficult to convince students that making mistakes is a natural, not a negative, part of the language acquisition process. This is especially important for learners who have been conditioned to remain quiet in class instead of participating more actively.

CASE #20

A Year in the Life of an ESL Teacher on the Canadian Prairies
Adults; Various Settings
Frieda Lepp Kaethler

Teaching speaking is a complex intertwining of fluency and accuracy tasks along with a host of socio-cultural/linguistic knowledge and understanding of discourse patterns. For learners, knowing what to say, when and how to say it, in what register, and with appropriate intonation and rhythm can be like trying to play all instruments of an orchestra at once by oneself. Speaking is often the most desired skill and yet the one learners are most reluctant to engage in because it involves the risk of real-time language action. However, when these myriad factors actually do come together, the result is a kind of small epiphany.

Short-term contracts, the bread and butter of most rural Manitoba ESL teachers, have allowed me the privilege of tasting ESL in various settings in this region. My fall semester begins with juggling two locations. From Monday to Thursday, I teach in the small city of Steinbach, a farming community founded more than a century ago by European immigrants. Recently we have been inundated with a new wave of Russian and German immigrants, some with families as large as a baker's dozen. My solitary learner from Turkey only came the first few days. After that her children got sick, and she left for a month-long visit to her family in Turkey. This leaves me with a group of mainly women from the same language backgrounds, a setting more common to EFL. I'm currently trying new experiments in eliminating L1 in the classroom.

This is settlement language, and my initial needs assessment confirms my hunches that they want mainly speaking. We spend many pleasurable classes role playing making doctor's appointments and parent-teacher interviews, all propelled by imminent real-life needs. My routine warm-up is an opening question (to make taking attendance more interesting). After a "buddy buzz," each learner answers the question as his or her name is called. One morning my question is, "If you could study anything you wanted, what would you study?" My eyes widen as people who are primarily trades workers speak of studying engineering, medicine, and architecture, if given the chance. I am suddenly aware of how the circumstances of their lives have prevented them from pursuing these dreams. All their energy for now and for the foreseeable future goes into subsistence for themselves and their children.

On Fridays, I drive 25 minutes west to Providence College, a rural campus out in the middle of the wheat and sunflower fields of the flat Red River Valley basin. Here I teach English for Academic Purposes to international students who are preparing to enter college or seminary. These students tend to be predominantly Korean, though this year I am thrilled to have a class in which there is no common language background. In this speaking/reading class I often begin with a conversation board with questions. Later we move into topics such as "asking questions on campus" or "language for being a group participant." Vocabulary and pronunciation lessons flow out of these topics and the readings. An illuminating moment came last week with the question, "Where do you hope to be in ten years?" Juan Pablo from Peru said he hoped to have an import-export business in his home city of Lima. The income from his business would be used to finance a liberal arts college that he would like to found. What a vision!

Spring finds me back in Steinbach at my local college teaching a TESOL certificate course to young college students, who frequently do their practicum overseas. Grading their assignments is like a free trip to a university in the Ukraine, a public school in Korea, and a rural school in Cameroon. Just yesterday, I "looked in" on my TESOL student, Aubri, teaching a group of Swahili-speaking women in Tanzania. Her biggest struggle was to get the women, unaccustomed to communicative language teaching, off the page and into real-life conversation.

This past summer, my temping schedule allowed me to do a short stint at the University of Manitoba. My students were from China, Brazil, Chile, and Mexico. The speaking highlight here was a request by my Mexican architect student to meet with her and her architect husband after class to discuss his projects. In the university coffee shop, I was treated to a personalized virtual tour of this young architect's work on his laptop, where I learned about environmental architecture. The Spanish architect Gaudi was his primary influence, and I was thrilled to have a front-row seat.

I firmly believe in teaching speaking/pronunciation (along with grammar, vocabulary, and a host of other considerations) in the context of themes meaningful to the learners. However, it is difficult to measure the magic that happens when all of these come together in real-life conversations between people.

> **Issues for Reflection**
>
> 1. Frieda begins her story by mentioning fluency and accuracy. Teaching speaking involves a delicate balance of the two. Some groups will want to focus more on accuracy, and your job will be to work on their fluency. Conversely, some groups gravitate toward fluency and have to be convinced of the need for better accuracy. The teaching point here is reflected in Frieda's opening words: "Teaching speaking is a complex intertwining of fluency and accuracy tasks. . . ."
>
> 2. A short but productive warm-up activity is a good technique for opening the class. Some teachers do this while they call the roll; others do this as their first classroom activity of the day. A simple direct question such as the one Frieda used can generate a great deal of interest even when students are just starting class. In addition, this kind of high-interest fluency activity at the beginning of class motivates students to come on time so they can take part in it.

Conclusion

As you have seen, these stories are from all over the globe. The students are learning English for a multitude of different reasons. In spite of all the differences—and there are many—these teachers also report a good number of similarities. The learners want to speak English. The learners' goal in learning English needs to be taken into account. Teachers should view their class at the same time as one group of learners and as individual learners. Teachers need to know about English—something about grammar, pronunciation, and vocabulary. Teachers need to have good classroom management techniques. Learners learn conversation best by *doing* activities, so teachers need to have good activities prepared.

In the next chapters, we will learn about some of these effective speaking activities, including how to construct them and how to use them in class, as well as some unsuccessful activities and how to avoid them.

4 Twenty Successful Activities

This chapter includes twenty useful, practical, and fun speaking activities. There are literally hundreds of speaking activities described in numerous books, articles, guides, and websites for teachers—and you should certainly use these resources as you attempt to find activities that match your students' needs. However, because there is so much information available and you have limited time resources, you might feel overwhelmed.

In this chapter, I have limited the material to information on twenty activities that *I know firsthand are successful with both ESL and EFL groups. I have used them successfully in both ESL and EFL settings.* However, because no one knows your students, their needs, their personalities, and their proficiency better than you, it is up to you to decide the suitability of using these twenty activities for your classes.

As previously discussed, what happens in a conversation classroom can vary tremendously. The activities can range from simple activities such as language games or repetition drills for pronunciation to more complex group discussions of controversial topics with differing levels of original student talk in between. The activities explained in this chapter represent this full gamut and are listed here in no special order. Some of these activities will work well with your groups as they are; others may need to be tweaked to fit the dynamics of your classroom situation.

The information for each activity is organized as follows:

Title: sometimes includes information on the ideal number of participants

Description: brief explanation of what the activity is and what it accomplishes

110

<u>Needed</u>: lists materials needed to complete the activity

<u>Preparation Steps</u>: explains what the teacher must do to prepare for this activity

<u>In Class</u>: details the steps for successfully completing this activity

<u>Caveats and Further Suggestions</u>: lists potential problems and suggestions for follow up

<u>Example</u>: gives an actual example of the activity that you may use in your classes

<u>Source</u>: indicates the source—a publication, a website, me, you (the teacher), your students

In this chapter, we will look at twenty activities that work well in speaking classes. *Heads up:* In Chapter 5, we will look at ten activities that failed, so try to think about what exactly makes the activities in this chapter successful.

Activity 1
Find Someone Who

DESCRIPTION

Students use a checklist as they walk around the room trying to find a person who has a certain characteristic. When students find "someone who drives a truck" or "someone who was born at home," they write that person's name on their checklist of paper and move on to the next person with the hope that that person meets one of the other characteristics on the master list. *The goal is to meet and talk to as many people as possible within the time limit in order to put one name by each of the characteristics.*

NEEDED

1. A piece of paper listing 15 to 20 characteristics.
2. A copy of the paper for each student.

PREPARATION STEPS

1. Prepare 15 to 20 characteristics using vocabulary that your students are familiar with. Since this is a fluency activity, the purpose can be to review or recycle vocabulary and perhaps even learn one or two new words, but the main purpose of this activity is to get students talking for a purpose and, thus, limit the difficulty of the language used. As with all fluency activities, aim for a level below your students' actual proficiency level.

2. Try to vary the questions so that it will be easy to find a person for some characteristics but not so easy for others. Easy questions that most people can answer *yes* to include "find someone who has more than one brother," "find someone who watches TV at night," or "find someone who likes to eat fish." It is usually harder to find the one or two people who can answer *yes* to "find someone who is an only child," "find someone who was born in December," or "find someone who usually reads the newspaper every morning." Mix up the easy and difficult characteristics on your sheet.

IN CLASS

1. Announce that the class is going to do a brief interview activity in which each student will ask people a question to find out if they do a certain activity. The goal is to ask everyone in class until students find someone who does that activity or has that characteristic.

2. On the board, write two examples of characteristics from your sheet. Tell students not to give the answer right now. Ask them to think how they would answer if someone asked them right now, "Excuse me. Do you read the newspaper every morning?" What would their answer options be? (*Yes, I do* OR *No, I don't.*)

3. Hold up a copy of the checklist of characteristics. When students find someone who says yes to one of their questions, they should write that person's name on their checklist sheet and go on to the next question with another person.

4. Important: A student can write a person's name only once. Thus, if Maria reads the paper every day and she is an only child, no student can write Maria's name twice on the checklist.

5. Pass out the papers. Ask everyone to stand up. Begin the activity. You, as the teacher, should participate as well.

CAVEATS AND FURTHER SUGGESTIONS

1. This is a great icebreaker for the beginning of the course. It's also a good way for you to learn your students' names and something personal about each of them.

2. You might decide to give a prize to the student who completes the activity first or within the time limit. There is a caveat to offering a prize. When the activity is timed, sometimes students get so focused on winning the prize that they just start writing in people's names.

3. As a follow up, when everyone is seated again, ask students to introduce someone and say something about that person. For example, Maria could say, "Everyone, I'd like to introduce Joseph to you. [Joseph raises his hand so everyone knows who he is.] I found out today that Joseph has two dogs."

Example of Find Someone Who

1. _____   Find someone who has a pet.

2. _____   Find someone who has at least one grandparent still alive.

3. _____   Find someone who takes showers instead of baths.

4. _____   Find someone who ate at McDonalds® in the last week.

5. _____   Find someone who drives to school every day.

6. _____   Find someone who owns more than two watches.

7. _____   Find someone who was born south of the equator.

8. _____   Find someone who drank coffee at breakfast today.

9. _____   Find someone who has visited more than five countries.

10. _____   Find someone who speaks more than two languages.

11. _____   Find someone who was born in January.

12. _____   Find someone who has visited Canada.

13. _____   Find someone who is good at math.

14. _____   Find someone who does not like broccoli.

15. _____   Find someone who is an only child.

16. _____   Find someone who likes rice better than potatoes.

17. _____   Find someone who likes pizza.

18. _____   Find someone who likes blue better than red or orange.

19. _____   Find someone who was born in August.

20. _____   Find someone who can swim well.

Source: Keith S. Folse.

Activity 2
Find the Differences

‖‖DESCRIPTION

Two students each have a version of a picture or drawing, but the two versions have some differences. Without showing their papers to each other, they have to talk about their pictures to identify all the differences.

‖‖NEEDED

1. Two similar yet different versions of a picture, one labeled as A and the other as B (see p. 117).

‖‖PREPARATION STEPS

1. You may find two versions of the same picture in a teacher resource book or teacher website.

2. If you can't find suitable material, you can also create two versions of the same picture. The picture does not have to be elaborate to work well. Some things need to be exactly the same, some things should be a little different (e.g., the cat in A is gray, the cat in B is black), and some things should be completely different (e.g., the cat in A is a dog in B; they are the same size and are in the same location in the picture).

3. You will need to make enough copies of A for one-half of your class and of B for one-half of your class.

4. Some teachers prefer to organize the copies in pairs (i.e., one A and one B) and put a paper clip on each pair. This speeds up getting the papers out to everyone correctly so that partners do not end up with two copies of the same version.

‖‖IN CLASS

1. Announce that you are going to do a **Find the Differences** activity. If you've never done this before with your students, draw two large versions of a simple picture on the board. It should NOT be similar to the actual pictures (unless you have weak students and want to review vocabulary). Explain what students are to do, and then demonstrate with the pictures on the board. Ask if anyone can find a difference. Repeat it, and then write it on the board. Continue until everyone can find three or four differences.

2. Pre-teach or review key phrases such as "Is there a _____ in your picture?" or "Does your picture have a _____?" Other questions might include "What color is the _____?" or "Is the _____ on the left or the right of the _____?" Write these phrases on the board or on a wall chart.

3. Put students into pairs.

4. If you are worried about students looking at each other's pictures, you could have them sit back to back instead of face to face. If they are sitting face to face, you might bring in file folders to stand up on the table as a sort of dividing screen. (This might seem silly, but students seem to like the prop.)

5. Pass out a paper-clipped set of pictures to each pair of students.

6. Tell students to start talking and finding differences. Allow students 5 to 10 minutes to work on this task.

7. At the end of time, you have two options:

   a. Have students (without looking at their partner's papers) tell you the differences so you can write them on the board. If a student uses incorrect language, repeat the sentence correctly and write it correctly on the board.

   b. To practice fluency, repeat the process once more before checking the answers. Do this by having all the A students stand up. (The B students remain seated.) Then have the A students move to a different part of the room to find a new partner. Now repeat Step 6. When time is up, then do Step 7a.

▌▌CAVEATS AND FURTHER SUGGESTIONS

1. Students must not see their partner's paper. If students can see each other's paper, then this is no longer a two-way activity but rather a one-way activity. It can then be solved by one student without using any speaking. (In other words, it becomes a one-person activity, much as when you work by yourself to do this activity in a newspaper without talking to anyone.) (See pp. 48–49 regarding two-way activities.)

2. Make sure that students have a good grasp of some of the general questions that they'll need to complete this task. (See In-Class Step 2.)

3. If you have never done one of these activities before, I recommend that you try it with another native speaker (or better yet, get two friends to try this out; in this way, you can actually observe and record the phrases objectively) to see which phrases and questions native speakers would ask when doing this task.

Example of Find the Differences

Picture A

%<----------%<----------%<----------%<----------%<----------%<----------%<-----

Picture B

Source: Folse, K. (1993). *Talk a Lot: Communication Activities for Speaking Fluency.* Ann Arbor: University of Michigan Press.

Activity 3
Drawing a Picture

▌▌DESCRIPTION

Two students each have a different picture or drawing. Student 1 can see the picture. Student 1 explains to Student 2 how to draw the picture while Student 2 draws. Student 2 can and should ask clarification questions throughout the process. Afterward, the process is reversed as Student 2 explains his or her picture to Student 1.

▌▌NEEDED

1. Two pictures, one labeled A and one labeled B. You will need pictures that are easy to explain how to draw and are easy to draw. However, if the drawing is too easy, then there is little need for useful communication. Remember that you actually <u>want</u> communication to break down. You want some confusion. Confusion must be repaired, and this repair will be done by speaking and listening, also known as *negotiation of meaning*. (See pp. 40–42 regarding *negotiation of meaning.*)

2. One large but simple drawing to use in the pre-activity class demonstration. (See In-Class Step 1.)

▌▌PREPARATION STEPS

1. Look in a teacher resource book or access a teacher website to find two pictures. They will be completely different, but they should be similar in complexity to allow drawers to succeed in getting the gist of the picture for their renditions.

2. You will need to make enough copies of A for one-half of your class and of B for one-half of your class.

3. Some teachers prefer to organize the copies in pairs (i.e., one A and one B) and put a paper clip on each pair. This speeds up getting the papers out to everyone correctly so that partners do not end up with two copies of the same picture.

▌▌▌IN CLASS

1. Announce that you are going to do a **Drawing a Picture** activity. If you've never done this before with your students, then have a student (preferably one of your more vocal students) go to the board. Have the student face the board and not look back at the class. On a large sheet of paper, draw a simple drawing, such as a mountain with the sun on top to the left and two houses to the bottom right. Now have the class members take turns telling the student at the board how to draw this picture. Encourage the student at the board to ask questions if needed.

2. Pre-teach or review key phrases such as "Can you repeat that?" or "Tell me again. Where does the _____ go?" Write them on the board.

3. When you are certain that everyone understands the activity, put students into pairs.

4. Allow students 10–12 minutes to work on this task. It is usually more difficult than it appears at first.

5. At the end of the time limit, you have two options:

   a. Have students (without looking at their partner's papers) tell you the differences so you can write them on the board. If a student uses incorrect language, repeat the sentence correctly and write it correctly on the board.

   b. To practice fluency, repeat the process once more before checking the answers. Do this by having all the A students stand up. (The B students remain seated.) Then have the A students move over to a different part of the room to find a new partner. Now repeat Step 4. When time is up, then do Step 5a. I really prefer this second option for this activity because students are rarely able to give correct or complete information for the picture. This allows for much more real fluency practice. In fact, before checking, you could even repeat this step again, so that each drawer works with three different informants.

▌▌▌CAVEATS AND FURTHER SUGGESTIONS

1. The temptation to peek is high. Do your best to make sure that students cannot see their partner's paper.

2. Make sure that students have a good grasp of some of the general questions that they'll need to complete this task. Think about the necessary vocabulary as you select the two pictures for this activity. (*Suggestion:* If you have studied a certain set of vocabulary, such as *living room furniture* or *eating out at a restaurant,* then try to find such a picture.)

3. If you have never done one of these activities before, I recommend that you try it with another native speaker (or better yet, get two friends to try this out; in this way, you can actually observe and record the phrases objectively) to see what phrases and questions native speakers would ask when doing this task.

For example, for the two pictures used in this activity, students' vocabulary needs may include these words and phrases.

Words: picture   roof   sun   tree

stripes/striped   gray   black   cloud

window   door   number   floor (story)

man (person)   big   little (small)

Phrases: next to   between   to the right   to the left

There is ___.   Is there ___?   There are ___.   Are there ___?

There isn't ___. There aren't ___. Where is ___?   What color is ___?

above   below   first   How big is ___?

Do you have ____ in your picture?

Does your picture have ___?

My picture has ___.   My picture doesn't have ___.

How about ___?   What about ___?

Is the ___ to the left/right of the ___?

How many ___ are there?

Example of Drawing a Picture

You can use any picture in this activity. Keep them as simple as possible. Here are two possibilities that are simple yet complex enough to be drawable after some (required) interaction.

✂-----------✂-----------✂-----------✂----------✂----------✂-----------✂----------✂-----

Picture A

✂----------✂-----------✂-----------✂----------✂---------✂-----------✂----------✂-----

Picture B

Source: Folse, K. (1993). *Talk a Lot: Communication Activities for Speaking Fluency.* Ann Arbor: University of Michigan Press.

Activity 4
Information Gap: Simple Completion

▌▌DESCRIPTION

Students work in pairs to trade or verify missing pieces of information to complete a task such as a train schedule, a simple map of an area, or a family tree.

▌▌NEEDED

1. An A form (for half the students in your class) and a B form (for the remaining half of your class) of an information gap activity.

▌▌PREPARATION STEPS

1. On your word processor, create one master form of the information gap activity. Ideally, this is a collection of information. (It is words, not a picture.) This could be a simple train schedule with columns—such as destination, platform, and departure time—or even a grocery list.

2. Save your master copy from Step 1. Now create two more copies. Label one as A and the other as B.

3. Delete four or five pieces of information from Version A.

4. Delete four or five different pieces of information from Version B. Be sure not to delete the same piece of information from both A and B. If you are using the train example, then do not delete the platform number for the train to Boston. One of the students must be able to find this information on one of the versions.

5. You will need to make enough copies of A for one-half of your class and of B for one-half of your class.

6. Some teachers prefer to organize the copies in pairs (i.e., one A and one B) and put a paper clip on each pair. This speeds up getting the papers out to everyone correctly so that partners do not end up with two copies of the same version.

7. An important preparation step is for you to think about two things: the language in the sheet (e.g., for our train schedule example: *platform, destination*) and the language students need to complete this information gap activity (e.g., "What platform is the train to Boston leaving from? Can you tell me what time the train to Los Angeles is leaving?"). Some teachers prepare a list of these questions on a large sheet of paper to post on the wall; others prefer to write these on the board or on a overhead transparency.

▍▍▍IN CLASS

1. Explain that you are going to do a pair work activity. Put the students into pairs.

2. Hold up an example of the two sheets (which have a large A and B written on them) and explain that in a minute, you'll give each pair an A sheet and a B sheet. Each sheet has information about _____ (the topic: a train schedule, a family tree, etc.), but explain that each sheet has only part of the information. Pairs need to work together to find out their missing information so that they end up with two complete and identical sheets.

3. Distribute the papers. Tell them not to look at each other's papers. Let them begin.

4. If you think your students may be confused by this kind of activity, then the first time you do this, you should write a simple example on the board and have students run through it with you.

▍▍▍CAVEATS AND FURTHER SUGGESTIONS

1. It is important that the language on the sheets is already known to the students. The purpose of this activity is the language that ensues in trying to complete the missing pieces—not the words on the page.

    If you choose a topic that is too difficult, then that becomes the lesson instead of the speaking fluency. (Remember that this is a conversation or speaking class!) For example, if you design a school schedule that lists classes such as Civics, Algebra, and Home Economics, then students will spend a lot of time on those words—and that is a very poor activity for speaking fluency. A better choice for a school schedule would be simple, easily understood classes such as English, Math, and History. In this way, students will not even think about the names of the classes (which is the goal) but instead focus their time on the relevant missing pieces of information (e.g., the room number for the Math class or the teacher's name for the English class).

Example of Information Gap: Simple Completion

Student A

Who Is Who? At the United Nations

Four people are eating lunch at a cafeteria at the United Nations in New York City. These four people are from four different countries. They have four different jobs and four different hobbies.

Directions: Work with a partner to find out who is who. Ask questions such as "What is Pablo's job?" "Where is _____ from?" or "How old is the man from Senegal?"

Name	Age	Country	Work	Hobby
Jason	33			
Pablo		Mexico	interpreter	
	31		operator	chess
	35	Kuwait		

Source: Folse, K. (1993). *Talk a Lot: Communication Activities for Speaking Fluency.* Ann Arbor: University of Michigan Press.

Example of Information Gap: Simple Completion

Student B
Who Is Who? At the United Nations

Four people are eating lunch at a cafeteria at the United Nations in New York City. These four people are from four different countries. They have four different jobs and four different hobbies.

Directions: Work with a partner to find out who is who. Ask questions such as "What is Pablo's job?" "Where is _____ from?" or "How old is the man from Senegal?"

Name	Age	Country	Work	Hobby
		Canada	English teacher	traveling
	37			reading
Pierre		Senegal		
Saleh			translator	tennis

Source: Folse, K. (1993). *Talk a Lot: Communication Activities for Speaking Fluency.* Ann Arbor: University of Michigan Press.

Activity 5
Information Gap: Group Problem Solving

▌▌DESCRIPTION

Students work in groups (of three in this example) to trade or verify missing pieces of information to complete a task such as a family tree, train schedule, or a simple map of an area.

▌▌NEEDED

1. One copy for each student of the main sheet for the information gap activity; some of the information is filled in on the page with the rest to come from student-student interaction.

2. A set of clues or pieces of information for each person in the group; if students are working in threes, then you need three sets of different information for Student A, Student B, and Student C.

▌▌PREPARATION STEPS

1. On your word processor, create one master form of the information gap activity. Ideally, this is a collection of information. (It is words, not a picture.) This could be any number of things, including a simple train schedule, a grocery list, or a family tree.

2. Save your master copy from Step 1 to serve as your own answer key. You WILL need this for yourself!

3. You will delete most (but not all!) of the information from the master, one piece at a time. As you do, you will assign that information to either A, B, or C. For example, if you delete "Susan" from the family tree, you should write a clue such as "Susan is the grandmother" or "Susan is married to Jake."

4. Difficulty of the clues: The clues are important. You can actually make the interaction easier or harder—depending on the level and brainpower of your students. To make an easy clue, just put the information directly as it is. For example, in a family tree, say, "Susan is the grandmother." To make it more difficult, say, "Susan has two granddaughters." On the tree, there is space for only one grandmother, so Susan must be the grandmother, but the clue did not say this directly. (The clues in the example on page 130 are good models for clues that make you listen, think, and then have to negotiate meaning.)

5. Interaction from the clues: To increase interaction among the three students, you can make a clue for Student A that says, "Jake is married to Susan." Since the family tree has many blanks with neither Jake nor Susan filled in, Student A will read the clue but not know what to do with it. This will create some confusion, and Students B and C will talk about it. However, you have cleverly given a clue to Student B that says, "Susan is the grandmother," and the family tree might contain only one pair of blanks for grandparents at the top. Thus, Student B will say, "But wait. I know that Susan is the grandmother." Then Student C will say, "Okay, then Jake is her husband because my clue says 'Jake is married to Susan.'" Remember to include some obvious clues and some not-so-obvious clues.

6. You will need to make enough copies of the A clues for one-third of your class. Do the same for the B and C clues.

7. Some teachers prefer to organize the clues in sets (i.e., one A, one B, one C) and put a paper clip on each set. This speeds up getting the papers out to everyone correctly so that partners do not end up with copies of the same clues.

8. The language preparation suggestions from the previous information gap activity still apply. Think about the language that students actually need to complete this task.

▌▌IN CLASS

1. Explain that you are going to complete an information gap activity in groups of three.

2. Put students into groups of three. Explain the activity.

3. Distribute the master sheet to all students. (If the puzzle is simple enough as in the forthcoming family tree example, you could draw it on the board and have students copy it on their own paper.)

4. Distribute the packets of A-B-C clue sheets to each group of three. Tell them not to look at each other's papers. Each student should take one clue sheet and fill in as many pieces on the master sheet as possible. Allow 5 minutes for this.

5. Have students work in groups of three now to exchange information. Again, make sure that they cannot see each other's paper. This is a speaking activity, not a reading activity. *Suggested time limit:* 10 minutes

▌▌CAVEATS AND FURTHER SUGGESTIONS

1. It is important that the language on the sheets is already known to the students. The purpose of this activity is the language that ensues in trying to complete the missing pieces—not the words on the page.

2. You control the level of difficulty and interaction of the clues. No one knows your students' proficiency better than you, so control accordingly.

3. Students may seem to get a little frustrated, but this is okay. They will feel a real sense of accomplishment when they complete this puzzle—which they can and will do.

This activity has clues that are important but inadequate to solve the puzzle. The clues are intentionally not direct to force students to ask their partners to repeat clues several times until things start to make sense.

Example of Information Gap: Group Problem Solving

Information Gap: Who Is Who?

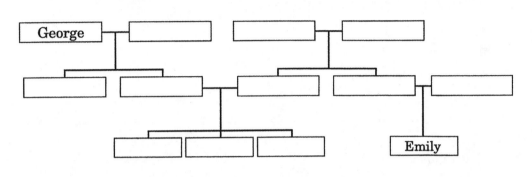

Source: Folse, K. (1993). *Talk a Lot: Communication Activities for Speaking Fluency.* Ann Arbor: University of Michigan Press.

Student A Clues

- Emily is Dennis's daughter.
- Doris is Emily's grandmother.
- Karen is Maria's aunt.
- Rosa is Cathy's mother-in-law.
- Jimmy is Luke's nephew.

✂----------✂----------✂----------✂----------✂----------✂----------✂----------✂----------✂-----

Student B Clues

- Cathy is Dennis's sister.
- Maria is Luke's niece.
- Hal is George's grandson.
- Ben is Doris's husband.
- George is Cathy's father-in-law.

✂----------✂----------✂----------✂----------✂----------✂----------✂----------✂----------✂-----

Student C Clues

- Karen is Emily's mother.
- George is Luke's father.
- Luke is Hal's uncle.
- Steve is Doris's son-in-law.
- Emily is Jimmy's cousin.

Activity 6
Ranking

DESCRIPTION

Working in small groups (perhaps five to seven students), students will rank a series of real-world items (usually six to ten items) in order and then discuss their rankings to reach a group consensus. The goal is for the group to come up with answers that match the actual correct ranking.

NEEDED

1. A master list of ranked items (e.g., countries by population, items by price, or football teams by wins). These should be real-world items that are relevant to the students. Include the actual figures to explain the ranking (e.g., population, prices, number of titles).

2. A list of these items in the incorrect order. (If you write this list on the board, you need nothing else; some teachers prefer to write this incorrect list on an overhead transparency so that it may be used for other classes.)

3. Overhead projector (if you use the overhead transparency option).

PREPARATION STEPS

1. Prepare a list of ranked items; usually six to ten items is good. Fewer than six is too easy to solve, and more than ten is too complicated.

2. Prepare a list of these items but in the incorrect order. You can write the list of items on the board, in which case you need only a list for yourself, or you can prepare the list on an overhead transparency.

IN CLASS

1. Explain that you are going to do a ranking activity. Explain what the verb *rank* means.

2. If your students need an example, write an easily solved scrambled list on the board. For example, you might write the list "orange blue black red chocolate" and ask the students to rank the words by length, with 1 being the shortest and 5 being the longest.

3. Write your list of items on the board. Have the students copy your list. Write the directions on the board. Be sure to identify which number is the lowest and which number is the highest. (In other words, you don't want some students to think that 1 means the most while others think that 1 means the least.)

4. Give students 5 minutes to work individually to rank the items.

5. Have students work in groups. Their goal is to come up with one group list that ranks the items.

6. Give the answers (say and write them) to find out which group came the closest to getting the correct answer.

CAVEATS AND FURTHER SUGGESTIONS

1. Use a topic that is relevant to your audience. For a group of teachers in Chile, I demonstrated this activity with a listing of the population of six South American countries. For your students, you could have them rank the prices of six common items that they themselves might buy. Use a supermarket advertisement as your expert source of prices. (Bring the advertisement to class as proof of the authenticity of the prices.)

2. Choose a ranking that is actually guessable. In other words, it should be difficult but not incredible to come up with the answer. If the answer is too obvious, then there is no discussion. The example about the length of the words is a good example of ranking but a horrible example of a speaking activity because no one has anything to discuss. The length of the words is clearly visible.

3. The number of items should be between six and ten. If you have only three, four, or five items, most people can get the answer correct with some knowledge— and maybe some luck—through a process of elimination. If you have more than ten, then the differences between the items is not so large or discernible, so the activity will fail because no one can get the correct answer (except by luck) and because there is no real distinction between the items. In other words, you are asking students to do a task that is practically impossible.

4. Research supports the importance of repetition of newly learned vocabulary to help move it from short-term to long-term memory. To accomplish that here, make sure that two or three key vocabulary words that you want to emphasize are present and are underlined. (In the example on p. 133, the key word might be *population*.)

5. This activity could be used in a content course, for example in a K–12 setting, where you want to practice an important ranked list in your subject (e.g., the planets in order from the sun or the ten largest U.S. states by size) and at the same time provide some speaking practice for your ESL students. Of course, it is important to make sure that no student has access to the correct ranking order until after the activity is over. In other words, don't let anyone open a book!

Example of Ranking

Directions: Rank these from biggest (1) to smallest (6) in terms of population.

____   The *population* of Argentina

____   The *population* of Bolivia

____   The *population* of Chile

____   The *population* of Colombia

____   The *population* of Ecuador

____   The *population* of Peru

Answer:
1. Colombia   2. Argentina   3. Peru   4. Chile   5. Ecuador   6. Bolivia

Activity 7
True or False?

▌▌DESCRIPTION

Students work in small groups of three to four to correctly identify which one statement of four about the speaker's family is false. The goal is to trick the other students into choosing the wrong sentence.

▌▌NEEDED

1. A good example for this activity: four believable sentences about yourself, three of which are true and one of which is false.

2. A bad example for this activity: four sentences, three of which are obviously true and one of which is obviously false.

▌▌PREPARATION STEPS

1. Prepare a good example and a bad example to use as a demonstration of this activity.

▌▌IN CLASS

1. Announce that you are going to do a speaking activity in which students have to guess whether their partners are telling the truth or lying. You could preface this by writing the phrases *to tell the truth* and *to tell a lie* on the board. As an opener, you might ask who is good at lying.

2. Demonstrate this activity using the good example. Tell students to listen carefully. Say your good example of four sentences. (If students cannot understand something, repeat it several times, but let them ask you for clarification of language or pronunciation; in other words, encourage negotiation of meaning here.) Give students a moment only to think about your statements. Read them again. Then have students take turns to guess which one statement they think is false. To increase the drama a bit, have them vote for the one they think is a lie by having them raise their hands as you say, for example, "Okay, who thinks number 1 is a lie?" "Ok, who thinks number 2 is a lie?" After everyone has voted, then reveal your lie.

3. Now do the bad example. If you have come up with a really bad example, then everyone should be able to guess the lie very easily. (Use something like "I am from Denmark"—provided that you are indeed not from Denmark!) Point out and maybe discuss why this is a bad example for this activity.

4. Now have the students write out four statements about themselves. They should write three true statements and one lie, but all should be believable. Allow approximately 5 minutes.

5. Now have the students get into groups of three to four students. Tell them to take turns going around their groups reading or saying their statements aloud. Other students can ask for repetition or explanation of words, but they cannot ask for more information about the fact. At the end of each person's turn, the other group members should guess which statement they think was false. The speaker reveals the answer, and then the next group member reads his or her statements, etc.

6. After everyone has had a turn, bring the class back together as a group and ask which person in each group was able to lie the best. Who was able to trick the group members? For fun, have those people—that is, the good liars—try out their four statements on the whole class now.

CAVEATS AND FURTHER SUGGESTIONS

1. This activity has very few potential problems as long as students understand what kind of statements are good and which are bad for this particular activity.

2. Students could write out their four statements for homework to allow class time to be spent on speaking instead of silent writing.

3. For review and reinforcement, you could add a specific language component here by telling the students that each statement must contain certain recently studied vocabulary (e.g., school subject names, family relationships) or grammar (e.g., comparatives, past tense).

4. A variation of this can be done as a pre-reading activity. Write four statements (three true, one false) about the content of a reading passage. Have students try to identify the false statement. Instead of telling them the answer, have them read the passage. This often gives students additional motivation or purpose in reading a passage and adds some speaking to a paper (reading) activity.

Example of True or False

(These sentences are about my family. These sentences will vary according to the individual, of course.)

1. My middle name is Scott.
2. I was born in New Orleans.
3. My parents met on a blind date.
4. I have three sisters.

Activity 8
Auction

▋▋DESCRIPTION

In this speaking game, teams (two or three) of students (three to six members; no more than six ever) work together as they compete to "buy" correct sentences.

▋▋NEEDED

1. A sheet with fifteen to twenty sentences on it; about 35 percent of the sentences should have an ESL error, most of which are related to something you have covered in class.
2. Play money (from a game like Monopoly®).

▋▋PREPARATION STEPS

1. Prepare a list of fifteen to twenty sentences that contain either a grammar point (e.g., comparative, gerunds and infinitives, present perfect tense) or a vocabulary item (e.g., words such as *perturb, absurd, relative*; or idioms such as *out of the blue, the bottom line, come up with*).
2. Create an error in about one-third of the sentences.
3. Make sure that the errors are ones that your students might make. Grammar errors might include omission of articles for some Asian languages, Russian, and Arabic (e.g., "The main reason that I am attending this English school is to get much better job") or word order for many languages (e.g., "No one really understands why did that man rob the bank").
4. Prepare enough copies of this handout so that each student receives a set of sentences.

▋▋IN CLASS

1. Announce that you are going to do a language game called **Auction**. Write the word *auction* on the board. Ask if anyone can explain what an auction is. If no one volunteers, then demonstrate an auction.

2. This auction is similar to other auctions. Your goal is to buy good items, but the items here are sentences. This auction has 15 (or the number you chose) sentences for sale. Your goal is to buy only good sentences.

3. Pass out the sentence sheets to each individual. Let the individuals work on this alone for about 10 minutes. Explain that their goal is to identify which sentences are correct and which are wrong. Do not allow them to talk to each other or to consult dictionaries or textbooks.

4. Put the students in teams of three to six students. Try to avoid having more than three teams. Ask each team to select a captain. The individuals in each team should number themselves 1, 2, 3 (4, 5, 6). The captain will be number 1.

5. Allow the teams about 10 minutes to consult to determine which sentences they think are correct (and which are wrong—though that is not needed in this game).

6. Distribute money to each team. For ease, avoid giving out more than two kinds of bills. For example, give each team a set number of 100s and 50s. Do not give out 5s, 10s, 50s, 100s, 500s, and 1,000s. Choose only two denominations. (This will make bidding easier to follow.)

7. Explain that you are going to start the bidding in a minute. The goal of each team is to buy as many correct sentences as possible. Buying an incorrect sentence does not count against a team, but, of course, it costs them money. Thus, a good strategy sometimes is to buy a sentence that no one wants with the hope that it might be correct.

8. The bidding cannot be done by all students at the same time. This would produce chaos, but—worse in a speaking activity—not everyone would have an opportunity to speak. The bidding for Sentence 1 will be done by only the team captains, who are number 1. The bidding for Sentence 2 will be done by only the number 2 people. Before the bidding starts for each sentence, the teacher must say the student number that can bid for that particular sentence.

9. Start the game. Say, "This is number 1. It is open for only Student Number 1 on your team. Only that person can speak for your team. I will ignore anyone who is not a number 1." Read sentence number 1 aloud. If it has an error, do not emphasize the error. After reading the sentence, say, "Does anyone bid $50 (or whatever the smaller bill is that you distributed)?"

10. When the bidding appears to be nearing an end, announce, "Okay, this group [point to group or say Student A's name] has bid [$300 or whatever the amount is]. Are there any other bids?" If any team makes a new bid, then you accept that bid and say, "Now I have a bid of $400. Any other bids?" followed by "$400. . . . Going. . . .Going. . . .Gone!"

11. Make a record sheet on the blackboard. If there are three teams, make four columns or boxes—one for each team and one for the sentences that no one wanted. If Team B bought Sentence 1, then write a 1 in the box for Team B. If no one wants the sentence, then write number 1 in the "unsold" box. At this time, do not indicate whether the sentence is correct.

12. Continue until you have gone through all the sentences.

13. When the game is over, go over the sentences one by one. If a sentence is correct, circle that sentence number on the board. The winner is the team that has the most circles.

14. Leftover money is useless. Thus, teams should spend their money. After all, that is goal of going shopping.

▌▌▌CAVEATS AND FURTHER SUGGESTIONS

1. Make sure the sentences are not too easy or too difficult. Ideally, there will be two or three correct sentences that are very easy to identify as correct. Teams will energetically bid for these.

2. Be sure that the last two or three sentences are correct. At the very least, make sure that there are some correct sentences near the end of the list. If not, the game will die out quickly. Students need to have a reason to keep up their momentum till the very end.

Example of Auction
(Two or Three Teams of up to Six; Smaller Groups Are Better)

Note: You need to create sentences for your students based on what they have studied. Here are some grammar and vocabulary examples. Note that an X indicates an incorrect sentence, but this should not be included on the student sheet.

Grammar:

1. Did you take the books that was on the table? (X)

2. I am interested in buying a new car.

3. Why he went is a mystery to me.

4. You saw the accident by the lake, don't you? (X)

5. Alaska is larger than Texas, but Texas has many more people.

6. In Britain, winter storms they can bring winds gusting to 50 mph or higher. (X)

7. Saturn is the sixth planet from the sun and has over twenty-one satellites. (X)

8. Omaha, Nebraska, is the place where the Platte River joins the Missouri River.

Vocabulary:

1. CLUMSY has a negative meaning.

2. ITEM = thing

3. He drank two BEETS before dinner. (X)

4. REFUSE means to connect something again. (X)

5. HOWEVER = sin embargo (Translations are only possible if all of your students speak the same native language, if you speak the language well, if your school or program approves of the use of translation, and if you think translating certain words will be beneficial.)

Activity 9
If You Were the Judge (Real Court Cases)

▌▌DESCRIPTION

Students read and consider the facts of a real court case to come up with their own verdicts as if they were the judge.

▌▌NEEDED

1. A court case that is written at the students' proficiency level on a legal question that they can understand.

▌▌PREPARATION STEPS

1. Find a court case on a topic that is of possible interest to your students.
2. Summarize it in two or three short paragraphs. It is important that students not have to read very much for this speaking activity.
3. Modify the language so that almost all of the words and expressions are already known by your students; keep new vocabulary to a minimum.
4. Make a copy of your modified version of the court case for each student.

▌▌IN CLASS

1. Write a word or phrase that is important to the court case. Ask students to tell you anything they can about this topic. For example, if the topic is a theft, then let students come up with words and phrases. Write all of these on the board as a sort of brainstorming session.
2. Pass out the court case. Let students read the case individually. This should not take more than 5 minutes.
3. Read the court case out loud. Emphasize certain facts. Ask if anyone has any language questions. Ask students to tell you the court case in their own words.
4. Just as students are about to start discussing what they think should happen, transition to the homework assignment, which is to write in approximately 50 words what they would do if they were the judge.

5. In class the next day, put students into groups (of three to five) to discuss their decisions. Can they reach a consensus? Allow 10–15 minutes for this discussion.

6. When you call time, you have four options:

   a. Allow students to form different groups to discuss the matter further. If they are in groups of three, have them count off 1-2-3. Have the number 1 students stay, the number 2 students move to the left (if the groups are in some semblance of a circle arrangement), and the number 3 students go to the right. Allow no more than 10 minutes for this second discussion. You can repeat once more.

   b. Have a whole class discussion of what the judge should do and why. Try to elicit specific reasons for each group.

   c. End the discussion by giving the judge's decision (see page 146). Ask if the students are surprised by this decision. How many of the students came up with a decision that was the same as that of the judge?

   d. Do 6a, 6b, and 6c.

▮▮CAVEATS AND FURTHER SUGGESTIONS

1. The choice of the court case is critical. A search on www.google.com of "court cases" as well as keeping up with current events can help locate interesting cases.

2. The language in the court case summary that you write must be simple. In addition, the summary must be brief. It is important to make sure that students in a speaking class do not get bogged down in a reading activity, which is what happens often when teachers try to use newspaper or magazine articles as a springboard for discussion. Remember that you are teaching a *speaking* class.

Example of a Real Court Case—with Supporting Exercises

Exercise 9.1

Read this court case about a divorce.

Herman and Viola Alston separated in 1985. Two years later, in 1987, Viola Alston filed for divorce. In her divorce petition (request), Mrs. Alston did not seek alimony or a share of the marital property. At that time, Mrs. Alston was a clerk with the federal government and Mr. Alston was a prison guard with the District of Columbia.

A few days after Mrs. Alston filed the papers for a divorce, Mr. Alston had the winning ticket for the Lotto. In fact, the jackpot that he won was over a million dollars: $1.1 million. Under the terms of the lottery prize, he receives $44,000 a year after taxes in lottery payments. Mrs. Alston thought that part of this money should go to her, so she re-filed her divorce papers and demanded alimony. (In other words, when Mr. Alston won the lottery, the couple was still married. Mrs. Alston had filed the divorce papers, but Mr. Alston won the lottery before the divorce was final.)

Mrs. Alston said that she did not ask Mr. Alston for anything at the divorce because she knew that he did not have any money or savings.

Exercise 9.2

If you were the judge, what would you do? Does Mr. Alston have to pay half of his prize money (or any part of his prize money) to Mrs. Alston? _____

_____

Write two or three reasons for your answer.

1. _____

_____

2. _____

_____

3. _____

_____

Exercise 9.3

Work in small groups. Discuss your decision and your reasons. When you finish, your teacher will tell you the result of the case.

Exercise 9.4

If you won $1,100,000, what would you do with the money? Remember that you have $44,000 each year. You do not get the total amount of money in one payment.

_____

_____

_____

_____

_____

_____

Can you think of any problems that might result because you have won so much money?

_____

_____

_____

_____

Exercise 9.5

Work in groups. Compare your answers to those in Exercise 9.4. Which answers are the most interesting or unusual?

Source: Folse, K. S., & Ivone, J. (2002). *First Discussion Starters: Speaking Fluency Activities for Lower-Level ESL/ EFL Students.* Ann Arbor: University of Michigan Press.

ANSWER to Exercise 9.2

When the case went to court, the decision was in favor of Mrs. Alston. The court said that Mrs. Alston had a right to some of the lotto money. Mr. Alston was not happy with this decision, and he used his legal right to appeal (protest) this decision to a higher court. The circuit court (the regional court) listened to both sides of this case. In the end, the seven judges voted 6–1 in favor of Mr. Alston.

The judges gave two reasons for their decision. First, Mr. Alston used his own money to buy the Lotto ticket. The second reason is related to the first reason. The judges said that in this case, one person did not help the other person get the Lotto ticket in any way. Therefore, the money was Mr. Alston's. The decision of the judges was not unanimous (6–1), but almost all of the judges agreed with Mr. Alston's side of the situation.

Activity 10
Liar (Groups of 4)

DESCRIPTION

Working in groups of four, one of three students acts out a given situation without letting the fourth person see who did the action. Then all three students repeatedly deny and accuse the others of doing the activity. Only one is lying. The fourth student must listen, continue asking, and correctly guess who the liar is.

NEEDED

1. A list of actions that you want your students to perform.

2. Any props or realia necessary for the actions on your list. For example, if you want students to open a dictionary, then each group of four students will need a dictionary.

3. A student with a watch with a second hand.

PREPARATION STEPS

1. Make a list of actions that can be demonstrated or performed easily by a member of all the groups of four students.

2. The actions can practice specific language points.

   a. *Vocabulary*—If animal vocabulary is being reviewed, then you can have students draw a snake, make the sound of a horse, or draw a picture of a cat.

   b. *Grammar*—If you have covered irregular past tense, then have students *draw/drew* a giraffe, *take/took* a (stuffed) cat, or *write/wrote* the word *snake* on the board.

3. You will need approximately six to ten actions to do this activity once. Depending on the class, this could take between 20–40 minutes.

IN CLASS

1. Explain the liar game. Explain that students will work in fours. One person is the guesser, and the other three are the possible actors. Explain that the guesser will turn his or her head so that he or she can't see and that only one person will actually do the action. Then the guesser will have 30 seconds to accuse someone. That person (and all three people) will deny doing the action—even if they are the one who did this. At the end of 30 seconds, the guesser must guess who he or she thinks actually did the action.

2. Demonstrate this activity one time. Ask three volunteers to come to the front of the room. You will be the guesser. Make sure there is a marker by the whiteboard or large sheet of paper. Turn your head so that you can't see. Now tell them that one of them should take the pen and draw a cat. Ask one student in the audience to tell you when they have finished. When they have finished, turn to face the cat drawing and the three students. Now have someone time you for 30 seconds by saying "Ready? Set? Go." The guesser will begin by accusing someone, "I think Susan drew the cat." And then Susan (and each of the three) will DENY this by saying, "No, I didn't draw the cat. Mark drew the cat." And then Mark will respond by saying, "No, I didn't draw the cat. Ann drew the cat." And then Ann will deny this and accuse either Susan or Mark again. The guesser must jump in if there is silence and accuse someone. The goal is to generate statements to help the accuser guess who the liar is. The game continues this way for 30 seconds.

3. Explain some strategy for the guesser. The guesser needs verbal and nonverbal feedback to help guess who the liars are. Therefore, it is important for the guesser to have a steady stream of input, so he or she must keep asking questions. If there is silence, the guesser needs to jump in with, "So B, did you draw this? Come on, you drew this, didn't you?"

4. When time is called, then the guesser should say, "I think [A, B, or C] drew the cat."

CAVEATS AND FURTHER SUGGESTIONS

1. The purpose of this activity is to get learners to produce a target form numerous times in a very short time span. For example, here the target is the three forms of *draw* in past: affirmative *drew*, negative *didn't draw*, and interrogative *Did you draw…?*

2. Plan your list carefully. I thought that I could put a list of past tense verbs together quickly. While I can put together a list of irregular past tense verbs quickly, it would not be a list of irregular past tense forms that anyone can illustrate in class. For example, *draw/drew a picture, take/took a coin,* and *write/wrote a word* are all good because they can easily be acted out by many groups in the classroom. However, *go, eat,* and *see* are irregular, but they are difficult to act out.

   Consider *see/saw.* What can you come up with? "I saw the cat." Well, this is not as good as a phrase that produces a result. If I say, "I drew the cat," then there is a new cat on the board. If I say, "I took the dime," then the dime is gone. You need language that lends itself well to this activity. If you choose well, this is a wonderful activity that really gets students talking.

3. We mentioned briefly the notion of getting students to say the target language point as many times as possible in the short time span. In a normal drill in class, I might get students to repeat "I drew it, I didn't draw it. Did you draw it?" perhaps five or six times in 30 seconds. However, in this liar activity, all four people usually say at least eight to twelve examples of the target language points in 30 seconds, which is an amazing feat.

Example of Liar (Groups of Four)

Activities with irregular past tense verbs that can be demonstrated in most classrooms:

- draw a _____
- write _____ on the board
- take _____
- cut a piece of paper (Note: you'll need paper and scissors.)
- tear a card (Note: you'll need cards.)
- put _____ (in a place) (e.g., put the pencil on the floor)
- bend a _____ (Note: you'll need a card, a coat hanger, or an aluminum can.)
- drink _____ (Note: you'll need small cups and some beverage.)
- throw _____ (perhaps a paper across the room?)
- eat _____ (Note: you'll need small candies for this.)

Source: With apologies to whoever designed **Liar.** I saw this activity at a TESOL conference so long ago that I don't recall the presenter or the conference.

Activity 11
Pair Talking (Minimal Pairs and Difficult Sounds)

▌▌DESCRIPTION

In this activity, students work in pairs from a sheet with four pictures. Student A must describe one picture to Student B, and B must be able to identify the exact picture. Student B does this by asking Student A questions. The activity is difficult because the pictures practice difficult sound pairs for ESL students such as /b/ and /v/ for Spanish speakers and *-teen* versus *-ty* (for most ESL students).

▌▌NEEDED

1. Sheets with a series of four illustrations that are very similar and that feature difficult sounds for ESL learners; an ideal sheet might have six sets of four illustrations.

2. Indicate with a check mark or dot the exact picture that the student must describe; on the A sheet, mark one picture for number 1, 3, and 5; on the B sheet, do the same for 2, 4, and 6.

3. You will need one sheet per student.

▌▌PREPARATION STEPS

1. You can find examples of this in *Targeting Listening & Speaking: Strategies and Activities for ESL/EFL Students* (Folse & Bologna, 2003).

2. Alternatively, you could draw or find your own illustrations. In this way, you could target the activity for the language needs of your own students.

3. You will need an A copy for half the class and a B copy for the other half.

▌▌IN CLASS

1. Explain that you will do a **Pair Talking** activity. Demonstrate this the first time by drawing four boxes on the board. In each box, draw an illustration that is similar in some way to the other illustrations. Instead of drawing, you could also write these four items that are similar sounding to ESL learners: 50   15   fifteen   fifty

2. Have a student serve as a volunteer. Ask that student to give her answer once. Then you can ask questions if you want. "Is it a number or a word?" or "Is it greater than 20?" The goal is for the student to ask you questions.

3. Student A asks Student B about number 1. Then Student B asks Student A about number 2. Student A continues with 3 and 5, while Student B continues with 4 and 6.

CAVEATS AND FURTHER SUGGESTIONS

1. Choose the illustrations carefully. <u>Remember</u>: The goal is confusion. When there is confusion, communication breaks down. When this breakdown occurs, it must be repaired, and our goal is negotiation of meaning, which will happen during the repair.

2. This activity should be repeated several times. As long as students do not mark up their papers too much, they can still use them several times. Repeating this activity with different partners on different days is a good recipe for building better fluency.

Example of Pair Talking (Minimal Pairs and Difficult Sounds)

Directions: Work in pairs. You (Student A) work from this page, and Student B works from a different page. Take turns describing the pictures marked with a dot; your partner can listen and ask questions to identify the correct picture and place a dot by the correct picture. You (Student A) describe questions 1, 3, and 5, which are on this page. Student B describes questions 2, 4, and 6, which are on a different page. You (Student A) go first.

Student A

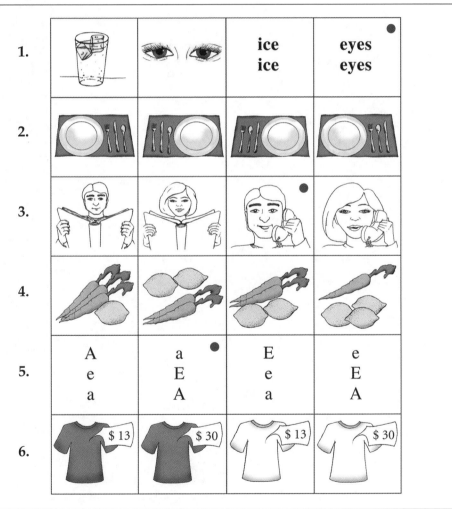

Source: Folse, K. S., & Bologna, D. (2003). *Targeting Listening & Speaking: Strategies and Activities for ESL/EFL Students.* Ann Arbor: University of Michigan Press.

Example of a Pair Talking (Minimal Pairs and Difficult Sounds)

Directions: Work in pairs. You (Student B) work from this page, and Student A works from a different page. Take turns describing the pictures with a dot; your partner can listen and ask questions to identify the correct picture and place a dot by the correct picture. You (Student B) describe questions 2, 4, and 6, which are on this page. Student A describes questions 1, 3, and 5, which are on a different page. Student A goes first.

Student B

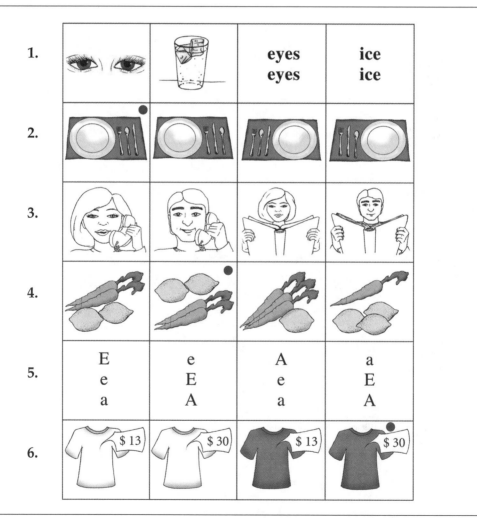

Source: Folse, K. S., & Bologna, D. (2003). *Targeting Listening & Speaking: Strategies and Activities for ESL/EFL Students.* Ann Arbor: University of Michigan Press.

Activity 12
Communication Crossword Puzzles

▐▌DESCRIPTION

Students work in pairs or threes to solve a crossword puzzle cooperatively. Some of the clues are on the page with the puzzle, but about half of the clues are divided among the two or three students.

▐▌NEEDED

1. A simple crossword puzzle, no more than ten letters by ten letters in size.

2. Clues for the puzzle words, half of which are on the same page.

3. A set of clues for each person in the group; if students are working in threes, then you need three sets of clues for Student A, Student B, and Student C.

▐▌PREPARATION STEPS

1. Prepare two copies of the crossword puzzle, one with all the words filled in and the other blank.

2. Make a list of the clues for each word.

3. Write about half of the clues on the puzzle sheet.

4. Divide the remaining clues into three groups labeled A, B, and C.

5. In general, only one student will have each clue. However, to create a little confusion and therefore the need for negotiation of meaning by the speakers, give clues for one word to two or more of the students—but not the same exact clue. For example, if 6 Across is *aunt,* then Student A's clue might be "your uncle's wife," but Student B's clue might be "sounds like *ant,*" while student C's clue might be "your cousin's mother."

6. Some teachers prefer to organize the clues in sets (i.e., one A, one B, one C) and put a paper clip on each set. This speeds up getting the papers out to everyone correctly so that partners do not end up with copies of the same clues.

▐▌IN CLASS

1. Announce that you are going to do a crossword puzzle. Ask how many students know what this is. Ask who in class does crossword puzzles in English or in their native language.

2. Explain the meanings of the words *down* and *across* in crossword puzzles. (This may seem easy to us, but why do we call it down instead of vertical or across instead of side or horizontal?)

3. Distribute the puzzle sheets to the students. Give them 5–10 minutes to fill in as many of the clues as they can.

4. Put students into pairs or groups of three. Explain that you will distribute clues for each student in the group, A, B, C. Students should use the clues to continue solving as many of the remaining words as possible. Allow 5 minutes for this. No peeking at other students' puzzles.

5. Now let the students discuss their answers. At this point, students will still have missing words in their puzzles. They can talk about the missing words by giving clues or explaining the words. They cannot say the words or spell the words; they cannot show their papers to each other. This is a speaking activity.

CAVEATS AND FURTHER SUGGESTIONS

1. Students must know the words in the puzzles. The language should be at their level or below to be a true fluency activity.

2. Do not use a computer program to generate your puzzle. I don't care how "easy" this is. I've never seen one produce a good puzzle. In a good crossword puzzle, the words cross. Most computer programs and novice designers make crossword puzzles that are more than half empty space. This is not a crossword puzzle. (Notice how the sample crossword puzzle of 100 squares on page 157 has only 36 that are black. The majority of the squares have letters, which means that the words are crossing.)

3. When you have inserted the main words in your puzzle (the example uses family words), then add small words that are the glue of the puzzle. These are words such as *the, from,* and *eight.*

4. Remember that your students are non-native speakers, so try to give clues that are meaningful to them as English learners. For example, if the answer is *the,* then don't give a technical clue such as "article," and don't give a useless clue such as "a short word." Think ESL! How about "____ United States" or "____ middle" (i.e., words that in English require *the*)? Likewise, for *eight,* you could say "between seven and nine" or "sounds like *ate.*"

5. See page 285 for answers to the puzzle on page 157.

Example of Communication Crossword Puzzles (Pairs)

Use the clues to solve the puzzle. Some clues are missing.

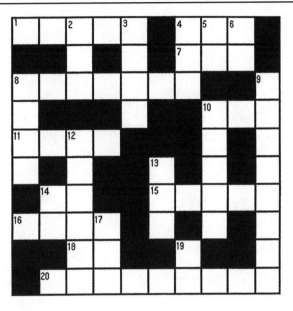

ACROSS

1. a month of the year
7. half of a pair
11. abbreviation for abbreviation
14. What's the name _____ the book?
16. Do you _____ today's date?
18. the same as 6 down

DOWN

2. walk very, very fast
4. abbreviation for a day of the week
5. _____ apple, _____ orange
10. My birthday is June _____.
14. I played tennis _____ Tuesday.
19. What time _____ it?

Source: Folse, K. (1993). *Talk a Lot: Communication Activities for Speaking Fluency.* Ann Arbor: University of Michigan Press.

Crossword Puzzle Clues for Student A

3 down: a strong, dangerous animal

17 down: abbreviation for 20 across

The second letter of 8 across is *I.* The sixth letter is *L.*

15 across: Saturday comes _____ Friday.

4 across: abbreviation for March

6 down: letters that mean "again"

8 across: the 16ᵗʰ U.S. President

✂----------✂----------✂----------✂---------✂---------✂----------✂---------✂-----

Crossword Puzzle Clues for Student B

12 down: July comes _____ August.

The second letter of 7 across is *N.*

9 down: a day of the week

20 across: the middle day of the week

10 across: a beverage

13 down: abbreviation for January

8 down: 366 days is a _____ year.

Activity 13
Twenty Questions
(Pairs, Small Groups, or Whole Class)

▌DESCRIPTION

In this commonly used activity, students take turns asking *yes-no* questions in an attempt to guess what the teacher (or a designated student) is thinking of. The game is called **Twenty Questions** because the maximum number of questions allowed is 20.

▌NEEDED

1. A list of items that your students know the names of.

▌PREPARATION STEPS

1. Prepare a list of items that your students know the names of.

2. If you have lower-proficiency students or want to make the game more finite, then either prepare copies of the same list of items for everyone or prepare an overhead projector transparency of the list so that students can only use items from this list for the game. (Alternatively, you could also write the list on the board.)

▌IN CLASS

1. Announce that you are going to play **Twenty Questions.** In case students have not seen this game before, do a quick demonstration. It is important to reiterate that only *yes-no* questions are acceptable.

2. This game can be done as a whole-class activity, which is what I suggest initially until students are familiar with the rules and have the proficiency to operate in perhaps three or four groups in your class.

3. If a person gets a *yes* answer, which is at least partially luck, then that person gets to ask the question again. This is advantageous because you can only make a specific guess such as "Is it a cat?" or "Is it a doorknob?" if you have the floor—that is, it is your turn to ask a question. If a person gets a *no* answer, that information is certainly useful, but the turn passes to the next person. This element of luck is crucial in speaking activities. It allows the weaker students to gain an upper hand at times, something that often annoys the higher-proficiency learners and at the same time motivates them more.

4. The person who guesses the speaker's word receives one point, and then the turn to be the speaker passes to someone else (who thinks of an item and answers the *yes-no* questions).

CAVEATS AND FURTHER SUGGESTIONS

1. This game can be done in pairs, but it is more fun in small groups of three to five people.

2. Some students may initially work better from a list of specific items. If you choose this option, then make sure the list has items that are similar. For example, don't put "cat dog giraffe rock snake snail" because rock is the only non-living object; when someone asks, "Is it alive?" and gets a *no* reply, then the next speaker automatically knows to ask, "Is it a rock?" and the speaking stops. The caveat then is that a specific list often aids people, but that list needs to have many similar objects in it, such as five famous people, five animals, five colors, five pieces of furniture, five countries, etc.

3. Think about the language needed to play this game well and teach that language. Beginning students can ask, "Is it an animal?" or "Can you eat it?" but you also need to teach "Does it have anything to do with school?" or "Is it bigger than a _____ ?"

4. This speaking activity can be used to practice (1) *yes-no* questions, (2) *can* ("Can you eat this thing?"), and (3) recent vocabulary, as well as other language points. For example, if you make the students identify the question number (e.g., the second question), students can then practice ordinal numbers, which is meaningful practice for saying the date (March 20th) since the numbers in **Twenty Questions** will never go over 31, the number of days in a month. (See example on page 161.)

Example of Twenty Questions (Pairs, Small Groups, or Whole Class)

Teacher:	(thinks of one object but does NOT say it: *diamond*)
Student 1:	Here is the first question: Can you eat it?
Teacher:	No, you cannot eat this. Next student.
Student 2:	Here is the second question: Is it alive?
Teacher:	No, it is not alive. Next student.
Student 3:	Here is the third question: Is it expensive?
Teacher:	Yes, it is expensive. It is still your turn. Ask another question.
Student 3:	Here is the fourth question: Is it bigger than a shoebox?
Teacher:	No, it is not. Next student.
Student 4:	Fifth question. Is it smaller than my hand?
Teacher:	Yes, it is smaller than your hand. It's still your turn.
Student 5:	Is it more for men or is it more for women?
Teacher:	That is not a *yes-no* question. One more try.
Student 5:	Ok, is it more for men?
Teacher:	No, it is for both men and women, but more women have this than men.
Student 6:	It's my turn. This is the sixth question. Does Maria (another student in the class) have this? (The teacher glances at Maria.)
Teacher:	No, I don't see it today, but she might have one. Next student.
Student 7:	Seventh question. Do you have this?
Teacher:	Good question, but no, I don't have this.
Student 8:	Eighth question. Is it jewelry?
Teacher:	No, not exactly, but it's connected with jewelry. (The teacher gives a hint to motivate the students and maintain the activity.) Next student.
Student 9:	Is it similar to a rock?
Teacher:	Yes, it is similar to a rock.
Student 9:	Is it a diamond?
Teacher:	Yes, that is my word! Now it's your turn to think of a word for the group.

Source: Keith S. Folse. This is a transcript of a Twenty Questions activity from my class.

Activity 14
Solve the Mystery: Finish the Story

▮▮DESCRIPTION

Students work in small groups or as a whole class to try to figure out the ending of a real story.

▮▮NEEDED

1. A real story that has an interesting or surprising but realistic ending. In other words, the ending should be surprising but plausible, given all the facts.

▮▮PREPARATION STEPS

1. Find a story that has a surprising but plausible ending. It should be on a topic that your students can relate to or are interested in.
2. Rewrite the story to make it short and easy to comprehend. Reduce the new vocabulary load as much as possible.
3. You can make a copy of the revised version for everyone, put it on a transparency, or read it to the class. Of these three, the last one is the least recommended because most students want to study the case somewhat.

▮▮IN CLASS

1. Introduce the topic of the story as a pre-activity. For the example story for this activity, which is about a passenger dilemma on a train, ask questions such as, "How many of you have ridden on a train?" and "Can you compare trains in _____ [the student's country] and the United States?" This last question will generate some interesting comparisons; in Japan, for example, people ride the train perhaps five or six times a week at a minimum. In the United States, only a small percentage of people ride trains regularly.
2. Transition from your general pre-activity talk to the story on the paper. Read the story slowly (as students follow along with you if they have the paper, too). When you get to the ending, do NOT reveal it. For homework, have students write in 50 words or less what they think the ending is and why.

3. In class the next day, put students into groups of three to five to discuss their answers for how they think the story actually ended.

4. After they have finished discussing their possible solutions to the mystery, then play the *yes-no* game. They can ask you any question they want about the topic, but all questions must be *yes-no* questions only. You can listen to a question, but all your answers must be either *yes* or *no* (and a little help if you wish to give that). You may need to teach key phrases such as, "Does the reason have anything to do with _____?" or "Was the person alive?"

5. At the end of the discussion, you can reveal the answer.

▌▌CAVEATS AND FURTHER SUGGESTIONS

1. Make sure the story is real and that the ending is plausible.

2. Keep the story brief.

3. Since this is a fluency activity, limit new vocabulary. Again, for a fluency activity, you don't want $i + 1$; instead, you want $i - 1$.

   In a fluency activity, you want students to get the maximum amount of speaking practice. If there are too many new words or phrases, then the students will focus on the new vocabulary instead of the speaking task. The languages in the task, that is, the language on the paper or in the book as well as the language that students need to complete the task, should be at the students' level *(i)* or just below their level *(i − 1)*.

Example of Solve the Mystery: Finish the Story

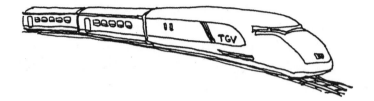

Read the following true story.

> The TGV is the fastest train in Europe. It can reach a speed of 185 miles per hour
> (300 kilometers per hour). A unique incident occurred recently aboard one of the
> bullet trains. A passenger was riding the TGV. When the train arrived at Tours, the
> police and several specialists met the train. They were there to help the passenger,
> who was not able to leave the train on his own.

Think about the situation described above, and then come up with three possible
answers for this question: Why was the passenger unable to leave the train? Write
your answers here.

_____

_____

_____

_____

_____

_____

Source: Folse, K. S. (1996). *Discussion Starters: Speaking Fluency Activities for Advanced ESL/EFL Students.* Ann Arbor: University of Michigan Press.

Activity 15
Role Play (Pairs)

▌▌DESCRIPTION

In this activity, students use their creativity and personality to play the role of a specific person while interacting with another person in the role play.

▌▌NEEDED

1. A story, incident, or court case with several parts to it.
2. Perhaps a list of the characters.

▌▌PREPARATION STEPS

1. Find a story that is of interest to your class. It could be one you have already discussed in this class. It could be a story that everyone knows, but you must change one part. For example, you could do Cinderella, but make Cinderella naughty instead of nice.

2. Figure out a list of the possible characters that your students with their level of proficiency could play the role of.

3. You can prepare small slips of paper with a role on each one, or you can just list the characters on the board. For each character, be sure to put a phrase or sentence that tells something about the character of the person; in essence, this is telling the student how to act. For example, you might write "a very difficult restaurant customer—when you order your food, be sure to ask for many details about the food."

▌▌IN CLASS

1. Announce that you are going to do a role play. The first time you do this activity, some students will need much more information and clear directions.

2. Put students into groups of whatever number that you have planned for. If you have eight roles in the story, then break the students into groups of eight before you distribute the roles (i.e., one role for each student).

3. Distribute the roles. Students should not know each other's roles; they will reveal it through speaking. In a role play, you should spend some time telling people who you are and why.

4. Give students some class time (no more than 10 minutes) to write down some of the things their character would need to say. In addition, this time is for students to consult each other in their first language or their dictionaries so that they can have the words they need. This is a real opportunity for students to push themselves to help their language grow as they actually attempt to stretch their current limited English (i.e., their interlanguage).

5. Begin the activity. Students introduce themselves and discuss their views about the topic.

CAVEATS AND FURTHER SUGGESTIONS

1. Choose a good story. Choose good roles.

2. I have often thought that this activity was a bit on the hokey side and that a role play is risky in class. My experience has been the opposite. I'm always surprised to see who ends up doing the talking in these events.

Example of Role Play (Pairs)

Directions: Put students in pairs. Student A will role play number 1, 2, or 3. Student B will role play number 4.

Student A

1. You are a client of Mann, Inc. You bought a DVD player that is not working well. Your DVD player is under warranty. A friend of yours tried to fix the DVD player, but was not able to. Your friend used to work as a technician at Mann, Inc. You must call the Customer Service Center and ask them to repair it.

✂----------✂----------✂----------✂---------✂---------✂----------✂---------✂-----

Student A

2. Your DVD player doesn't work because your six-year-old child put a piece of gum in it. Your DVD player is under warranty. Now you want Mann, Inc., to exchange the DVD player for a new one. Call Mann, Inc., and speak to a Customer Service Representative and demand for the product to be exchanged for a new one.

✂----------✂----------✂----------✂---------✂---------✂----------✂---------✂-----

Student A

3. Your teenaged son lost your DVD player. He took it to a friend's house, and it disappeared. Your warranty will expire in two days. You want Mann, Inc., to give you a new DVD player. You paid a lot of money for the DVD player, and you believe that because it is under warranty, Mann, Inc., must give you a new one. Call a Customer Service Representative at Mann, Inc., and demand a new DVD player.

✂----------✂----------✂----------✂---------✂---------✂----------✂---------✂-----

Student B

4. You are a Customer Service Representative for Mann, Inc. You have been given orders from your supervisor to make every effort to <u>not accept</u> merchandise back for an exchange or for repair. You must do your best to refuse to exchange a product or have a product sent to Mann, Inc. Service Center, even if it is under warranty.

Source: Monica Allison and Valerie Mann-Grosso, two experienced ESL/K–12 teachers.

Activity 16
Flexible Odd-Person Out (Groups of Three)

DESCRIPTION

Students work in groups of three to identify who has an object that is different; in other words, who is the odd-person out?

NEEDED

1. Sets of four cards.
2. Paper clips for each set of cards.

PREPARATION STEPS

1. On every set of four cards, write four words of two similar pairs. For example, you can write two animals and two colors: *cat, dog, red, white.* The pattern is always A-A-B-B.

2. On the other side of the card, write a number on all four to identify them as a set: 1-1-1-1 and then 2-2-2-2, etc.

3. This activity generates a good amount of speaking and goes rather quickly, so the number of card sets you will need to prepare depends on the number of groups of three in your class. Each group of three will need about five sets of cards. If you have around twenty students, that would mean up to seven groups of three students, so you'll need seven times five or 35 sets of cards. This may sound like a lot, but it should take you less than 15 minutes to prepare these cards, and you can reuse them many times.

IN CLASS

1. Put students in groups of three.

2. Explain odd-person out. Students will work in groups of three. They will receive a set of four cards clipped together. All cards must be kept number side up. Each person takes one card without showing it to anyone. (There will be one left over; that card should stay face down.) Students take turns saying what is on their cards. The person with the different card must indicate that he or she has the different item and explain why it's different by saying, "My card is different because _____."

3. Make sure students understand that they cannot show their card to anyone, but they can repeat the word and can ask questions about other students' words to understand what is written on the card. Also, the extra card must stay number side up.

4. Give each group about five sets of cards, number side up.

5. Tell them to begin by removing the clip from one set of cards. Each student should take one card and leave the extra card number side up.

6. They should take turns saying what is on their cards. The odd-person out should identify him- or herself and explain why the card is different.

7. After they are finished with one set of cards, they should put all four cards back together, put the clip back on them, and then go to the next set of cards to repeat the process.

8. When students are finished with their five sets, give them more cards so they can continue.

9. It is okay if students get the same set of cards more than once because it is unlikely that they will take the same combination of three cards from the four.

IIICAVEATS AND FURTHER SUGGESTIONS

1. The difficulty of this activity can be increased or decreased quite easily. Simply choose different vocabulary. Choose common words such as animals, colors, and numbers, or choose more difficult words such as positive adjectives (*excellent, outstanding*) and negative adjectives (*distraught, ashamed*).

2. This activity can also be adapted to content area classes easily. It can be used in biology (*organ, organ, system, system*), in geography (*sea, sea, ocean, ocean*), or even in math (7 x 3, 25 – 4, 44 ÷ 2, 14 + 8) [the answers are 21, 21, 22, 22—but all four are different math operations].

3. The genius of this activity is that you can (and should!) repeat it many times to develop students' speaking fluency. Even though the cards are the same, it is unlikely that students will have the same combination of cards. Each set of four cards actually has four different three-card combinations. Consider these combinations for cat dog red blue: (1) cat, dog, red; (2) cat, dog, blue; (3) dog, red, blue; (4) cat, red, blue. There is only a 25 percent chance then that the students will get the same combination of cards; even if they do, they don't know this until they have taken the cards, and there is even less chance that the same person who had the odd-man out card will have that same card again.

Example of Flexible Odd-Person Out (Groups of Three)

Make these eight sets of four cards:

Set 1:	a banana	a strawberry	a lemon	a cherry
Set 2:	rice	Coke®	Pepsi®	popcorn
Set 3:	ears	eyes	toes	fingers
Set 4:	an apple	a cat	a dog	a lemon
Set 5:	basketball	chicken	turkey	skiing
Set 6:	a sister	grandmother	a son	an uncle
Set 7:	a cake	car	a cookie	a bus
Set 8:	the sun	a cloud	blue	yellow

Source: Folse, K. (1993). *Talk a Lot: Communication Activities for Speaking Fluency.* Ann Arbor: University of Michigan Press.

Activity 17
English Language Question Task Cards

▌▌DESCRIPTION

Students work in pairs or small groups (three to four) to figure out the answer to a grammar (or vocabulary) question task. These questions can be of several types, but they are designed to raise learners' consciousness of the grammar point (or vocabulary word). The goal is for students to discuss answer options and reach a consensus.

▌▌NEEDED

1. For the entire class, you'll need a set of about 30 grammar question task cards. These cards should not be the small note cards but rather the 5" × 7" (U.S. size). Alternatively, you could print these out on half sheets of paper.

▌▌PREPARATION STEPS

1. Write the question tasks. These question tasks can be of several types—from traditional multiple-choice to inductive learning. In any case, the content should be appropriate and meaningful to the age, proficiency level, and goals of your students.

   These grammar examples are all aimed at intermediate-proficiency learners:

   1a: multiple-choice:

   The customer was frustrated because the clerk _____ English at all.

   (A) had not speak   (C) has not spoken

   (B) did not speak   (D) was not spoken

   1b: error identification:

   The customer was frustrating because the clerk did not speak English at all.

   1c: Task: Explain the difference in these sentences.

   (A) I was eating when he knocked on the door.

   (B) I ate when he knocked on the door.

   (C) I had eaten when he knocked on the door.

1d: Task: What is the rule from these examples?

    (A) I was talking on the phone when someone knocked on the door. OK

    (B) I talked on the phone when someone was knocking on the door. POSSIBLE BUT UNUSUAL

    (C) I was eating dinner when the phone rang. OK

    (D) I ate dinner when the phone rang. POSSIBLE BUT UNUSUAL

2. Number the cards from 1 to 50 (or the total number you create).

3. The answers can be written on the back of the card or on a separate card. If you use a separate card, make sure to number both the question task card and the answer card with the same number.

IN CLASS

1. Announce that you are going to do a communication activity in pairs (or small groups of up to four—as you like). The purpose is to figure out some problems about English. (You can announce that the questions are mostly about grammar or vocabulary, or you can just leave it at English.)

2. If this is your first time to use this activity in this class, you might demonstrate one of the cards with some students in front of the room.

3. Put the students in pairs or groups.

4. Pass out some cards to each group. Then have the students begin discussing one card at a time.

5. Students should check the answers on the back of the card only after they have discussed the answers. Most groups are good about doing this. However, if your group is the type that will look at the answer almost immediately, then you will need to make two cards—one for the question task and one for the answer.

6. Time permitting, have students take five new cards to begin again.

CAVEATS AND FURTHER SUGGESTIONS

1. This activity works well if you choose material that is at the students' level or maybe just beyond (or even several steps beyond). This is supposed to push learners, not just get them to recall previously learned information.

2. This activity can be repeated numerous times. You can literally have hundreds of cards prepared. This activity works well with classes that don't begin on time because many students come late (for whatever reason). This is a good opening activity because it really is an activity that is confined to one small group; thus, if a certain person is absent or comes in late, that student has missed what was on the card, but not a whole class activity.

3. The idea behind these tasks is to get students to think about these structures, i.e., to raise their consciousness or awareness of these structures. Such activities are referred to as "consciousness raising" tasks and are discussed in several articles (see Sharwood Smith, 1981; Ellis, 1991; Fotos & Ellis, 1991; Fotos, 1993).

Examples of English Language Question Task Cards

Four examples for upper beginning–level proficiency.

1. *multiple-choice:*

    It is now 2:30, and my classmates and I _____ in the speaking class.

    (A) am sitting   (C) sit

    (B) are sitting   (D) were sitting

2. *error identification:*

    <u>Washington is</u> the capital <u>of U.S.</u> now, <u>but</u> for a short time New York City <u>was</u>.

3. *Task: Explain the difference in these sentences.*

    (A) I take a shower.

    (B) I am taking a shower.

    (C) I took a shower.

4. *Task: What is the rule from these examples?*

    (A) I make eggs for breakfast every day. OK

    (B) I make eggs for breakfast now. NO

    (C) I am making eggs for breakfast now. OK

    (D) I am making eggs for breakfast every day. NO

Source: Keith S. Folse

Activity 18
Battle: Find It First

▌▌▌DESCRIPTION

In this activity, students (in pairs or groups of three) take turns asking *yes-no* questions to identify a certain picture that one student has marked.

▌▌▌NEEDED

1. A series of drawings that differ in only a few characteristics. (For this example, we will use drawings of fifteen houses.)

▌▌▌PREPARATION STEPS

1. You can find this activity in different professional publications. Otherwise, you'll have to draw the illustrations yourself.

2. If you opt to draw these yourself, then pick a theme for the illustrations. It should be something that can have multiple versions by adjusting only three or four characteristics.

3. After you get your theme, draw a simple illustration of it. Then make a list of possible adjustments before you draw. For example, the houses in this activity are all the same size. The variations come from the roof color (black, gray, white), the number on the door (13 or 30—a common pronunciation problem for ESL learners), the location of one tree (to the left, to the right), and the location of the door (on the front left, on the front right).

4. You will need a copy of the sheet for each student.

▌▌▌IN CLASS

1. Announce that you are going to do a speaking and listening activity about some houses. Hold up one of the sheets and show everyone that the sheet contains fifteen houses that are similar yet different.

2. Explain that this activity requires students to listen, think, and then ask questions so that they can guess the person's picture as quickly as possible.

3. Put students in groups of three. They should label themselves A, B, and C. Student A will go first.

4. Explain that A will pick a house to live in. Then B and C will take turns asking *yes-no* questions to try to identify A's house. B begins with a *yes-no* question. If A answers *yes,* then B continues. If A answers *no,* then C asks a question. The goal is to be the person who gets a *yes* answer to an exact question such as, "Do you live in house K?"

5. After B or C has guessed A's house, then A and C try to guess B's house. Finally, A and B try to guess C's house.

6. Keep track of the number of questions asked before the house is identified. The winner is the group member who guessed the house with the fewest questions. If B and C are guessing A's house, and B asks a question, C asks a question, and then B solves the house identity by asking, "Do you live in house G?" (and A says *yes*), then the score is 3 for B. (Student B asked only two questions, but C's question counts also.)

▌▌CAVEATS AND FURTHER SUGGESTIONS

1. Students love this simple activity. It doesn't get much simpler than this.

2. This game is based on a children's game called Battleship®. The basic premise here is a binary system of *yes* or *no* possible answers for a finite set of questions (here, approximately four: the roof color, the door number, the tree location, and the door location). However, this is information for you as you design similar activities, but you don't have to share this strategy with the students yet! Let them figure it out.

Example of Battle: Find It First

Directions: Work in groups of three. One student will choose one house but will not reveal which one. The other two students will take turns asking *yes-no* questions to try to guess which house was chosen. If the answer is *yes*, then that student continues asking. If the answer is *no*, then the other student asks a question. The goal is to guess the picture first and in the fewest number of turns.

Source: Folse, K. (1993). *Talk a Lot: Communication Activities for Speaking Fluency.* Ann Arbor: University of Michigan Press, p. 72

Activity 19
Tell It Three Times: 3-2-1

DESCRIPTION

This is a fluency-building activity in which students work in groups of three. Each student tells a story in relation to a prompt given by the teacher. Each student has 3 minutes to tell the story. After getting into new groups, students then have 2 minutes to tell the same story. Finally, in yet another group, they have 1 minute to tell their stories. This activity is usually called 3-2-1 because of the decreasing time allocation.

NEEDED

1. A list of no more than five questions.

PREPARATION STEPS

1. Prepare a list of five questions that can serve as prompts. The prompts need to be general enough so that a native speaker could talk about it for 3 whole minutes but specific enough so that it could be answered in 1 minute if necessary.

2. Use only known language in the prompt.

IN CLASS

1. Announce that you are going to do a communication activity called 3-2-1. Tell the students that the numbers refer to the time limit of 3 minutes, 2 minutes, and 1 minute.

2. Put students in groups of three. Have them decide who is A, who is B, and who is C. This is important.

3. If possible, try to have your groups set up in a loose circle or square or rectangle. In other words, you should be able to see a sort of line connecting the centers of all the groups. This is important when students change groups in a few steps.

4. Once the students are seated in groups as you want and they have identified themselves as A, B, and C, tell them that you are going to give them a topic. Student A will have three minutes to talk about this topic. Students B and C can ask questions, but Student A should be doing almost all of the talking. After 3 minutes, you will say "new speaker," and then Student B must talk about the topic. After 3 minutes, you will say "last speaker," and then Student C must talk.

5. Begin Round 1 by saying, "Ready? Set? Go. Okay, the prompt is *What are some things that you like to do on the weekend?"* Repeat the prompt if necessary or write it on the board, but if you have chosen the right language, it should almost never be necessary to write the prompt on the board.

6. After all three students have spoken, ask Students A and C in each group to stand up. Only the A students should move to a group to the right. Only the C students should move to a group to the left. (B does not move.) In theory, this will efficiently produce new groups for Round 2.

7. Begin Round 2 by saying that you're going to do the same thing but the new time limit is only 2 minutes. You should manage the time and make sure that each person gets only 2 minutes. The listening students should ask questions to help the speaker if necessary.

8. After all three students have spoken for 2 minutes in Round 2, then ask A and C to stand up. Once again, only A moves to the right and only C moves to the left. This will produce new groups for Round 3.

9. In Round 3, announce that each student has only 1 minute to tell everything that he or she has been saying in 3 minutes and then in 2 minutes.

10. Start Round 3.

IIICAVEATS

1. The first time students do this activity is always a little difficult because they are not sure of the parameters of the task.

2. This is a fun, amazing, fluency-building activity. I'm always impressed by how much language happens when students do this activity. There is just enough structure to this so that even the most quiet, reticent students produce tons of language.

3. For many reasons, students often change the content of their responses in the 3-2-1 activity. You need to tell students that this is not only okay but natural. As you get input from other people, you realize that your answer should be changed. This is a good sign because it means that you are able to understand what others are saying in English. Students are negotiating meaning.

Example of Tell It Three Times: 3-2-1

1. Tell us about your pets (present or past). If you don't have any pets, explain why and then tell about other people's pets.

2. Who were the best and the worst teachers that you have ever had? Explain.

3. If you could choose three jobs that you would like to have, what would they be and why? Can you think of any jobs that you would definitely not want to have? Why?

4. What are the two happiest events in your life? Give details.

5. If you won a million dollars in the lottery, what would you do with the money? Think of three specific things. Can you think of any possible negative things that might happen as a result of winning this prize?

Activity 20
Strip Story

▌DESCRIPTION

Students say and listen to their part of a short narrative (as many times as necessary) in order to put themselves in the correct sequence.

The teacher selects a short narrative, usually a joke with a surprise ending, and cuts it up into six to ten strips. Each student gets one strip of the story. The students must then stand up and say (or read) their strip of paper as many times as needed until they can put themselves (and their strips) in order.

▌NEEDED

1. One short narrative, usually a joke.

2. Strips of paper (usually six to ten), with a different piece of the story printed on each one.

▌PREPARATION STEPS

1. Find a short narrative that is of interest to your students. The narrative should have a surprising twist at the end. A good choice is a joke.

2. Most narratives are too long. Eventually, you will need to divide the story into six to ten pieces (depending on the size of your class/groups), so don't choose a really long story at all.

3. Edit the story down to the bare essentials or facts.

4. Remove all unclear or unfamiliar vocabulary or grammatical structures. This is a fluency activity, so if you include (too much) new language, students will not be able to complete the task. They will focus on the language, not the story.

5. After you've simplified the language and reduced the content, you should have enough material to create the strips.

6. Your learners will work in groups of six to ten. An ideal number is somewhere in the middle, usually seven or eight. You most likely have more than ten students in your class, so you can (and should) have several groups doing this activity simultaneously. For example, if you have 24 students, then design the story for three groups of eight students. If you have 28, then design your story for four

groups of seven students. The smaller the number in your groups, the easier (and shorter) this task will be. (You don't want this task so easy that students can complete it quickly!)

7. Once you have determined the number of strips (i.e., people in groups in your class), then divide your narrative into that number of parts. If your number is eight, then divide your narrative into eight relatively equal pieces.

8. Write the story on one sheet of paper. Leave spaces between the parts of the story. Then with scissors or a paper cutter, break the story into strips (with one piece of the story on each strip). Be careful that the first part and last part aren't given away by their placement on the page.

9. Clip the strips together. If you have 24 students and your story has eight pieces, then you will have three groups of eight strips. Each group will have a clip on it. Alternatively, put the strips in an envelope or plastic sandwich bag.

IN CLASS

1. Announce that you are going to do a strip story. Put students into groups of whatever number you have planned for. If you have 24 students with eight pieces in the story, then break the students into three groups of eight.

2. If your room is big enough, have the three groups get into different areas of the room so that they won't overhear the other two groups. The students should be standing up.

3. Only after the groups are established and after they have gotten into their respective corners of the room should you give each group one set of strips. Tell each student to take one strip.

4. Each student should read the strip. Students can memorize the content verbatim or just the gist. They should then put the paper away and not look at it during the activity.

5. At this point, the teacher should announce that students in each group should take turns going around the group telling what their papers say.

6. Students should put themselves in what they believe is the correct sequence of the story.

7. Students can and should say their line as many times as necessary. Some will have to say theirs four or five times, others only once or twice.

8. Students cannot show their strips to anyone else. This is a speaking-listening activity only.

9. When the group believes that it has the correct sequence, the teacher should go over to listen to the solution. The teacher only says *yes* or *no.* If the teacher's response is *no*, then the group should continue working.

▌▌CAVEATS AND FURTHER SUGGESTIONS

1. Don't collect the strips until the activity is finished. The first time I did this, I made the mistake of collecting the papers so that students could not read or show their papers to anyone else. Unfortunately, some students forgot their lines and then had no way to check their papers one more time. They turned to me, and I could do nothing.

2. Make at least one piece intentionally short or easy. If you have a noticeably weaker student, then try (as inconspicuously as possible) to give that shorter or easier paper to a weaker student.

3. On the master sheet, do not list the steps in the correct order. Mix them up on the sheet (before you cut them up). I didn't do this the first time I created a strip story. When I cut up the pieces, the cuts were slightly irregular, and students were able to match up the edges of the strips to solve the correct order instead of using language.

4. Model a strip story once for your class. The first time that you do a strip story, students may be confused. This is not unique to strip stories; it is usual for all first-time activities. *Remember:* Even fill in the blank and matching were new at one time.

5. Do not use new vocabulary. This is designed to be a fluency activity, one in which students' goal is to speak as much as possible. If the strips have new vocabulary, then students will focus on the new vocabulary. *Remember: i − 1!* Keep the level of the language at your students' level or below.

6. The level of difficulty can be decreased or increased through the vocabulary in the story.

7. To check for the correct solution, don't tell your students the answer. Instead, when it's time to give the answer, make everyone remain standing and let one group read their version of the story. Not only is this a good way to check a speaking activity, you are now adding another listening component to this task.

8. Avoid the temptation to intervene. The good news is that your job is to do nothing. Let your students "hit tennis balls." Your job is to make sure that everyone is on task. *Remember:* Be a coach sitting on the sidelines. Limit your input to answering *yes* or *no* about sequences.

Example of a Strip Story (Groups of Eight)

■ The doctor listened and then gave the man a bottle of pills.

✂----------✂----------✂----------✂----------✂----------✂----------✂----------✂-----

■ The patient asked, "So how many of these do I take every day?"

✂----------✂----------✂----------✂----------✂----------✂----------✂----------✂-----

■ A man went to see his doctor because he was overweight.

✂----------✂----------✂----------✂----------✂----------✂----------✂----------✂-----

■ The doctor then added, "Drop them on the floor and then pick them up."

✂----------✂----------✂----------✂----------✂----------✂----------✂----------✂-----

■ "Do this three times a day."

✂----------✂----------✂----------✂----------✂----------✂----------✂----------✂-----

■ He said, "I'm worried about my weight."

✂----------✂----------✂----------✂----------✂----------✂----------✂----------✂-----

■ The doctor answered, "None."

✂----------✂----------✂----------✂----------✂----------✂----------✂----------✂-----

■ "I guarantee that you will lose weight."

✂----------✂----------✂----------✂----------✂----------✂----------✂----------✂-----

---

Source: Folse, K. S., & Ivone, J. (2002). *More Discussion Starters: Activities for Building Speaking Fluency.* Ann Arbor: University of Michigan Press.

5 Ten Unsuccessful Activities

At some point in our teaching careers, all of us have taught a bad lesson. After a bad class (and a good class, too), a teacher should reflect to try to figure out what went wrong. Just why is it that one activity can go over so well, yet another falls completely flat?

In my years of ESL/EFL work, I have been both a teacher and an administrator. I was assistant director of an Intensive English Program in the United States, level coordinator of a U.S.-based program in Malaysia and Saudi Arabia, educational director of a language school in Japan, and coordinator of a MATESOL program in the United States. In all of these positions, one of my duties was to observe teachers in their classrooms. I have seen many good speaking activities, and I have also seen some weak ones.

After observing both kinds of speaking activities—good and weak—I would sit with teachers to talk about some of the specific activities in their classes as well as the teachers' intents and activity outcomes. Too often teachers, especially novice teachers, reflect too much on the weak activities. Effective reflecting on a class is not just about the problems; reflecting is also thinking about the things that worked as well and why they worked.

In my EFL positions, I heard certain teachers complain quite often about how difficult it was to get the students to talk in class. I heard all the reasons, from laziness to stupidity to stubbornness. Certain teachers made complaints such as:

"These students just have nothing to say."
"These students are not interested in anything."

"These students don't have critical-thinking skills."
"These students won't talk. They choose not to talk."

I heard these incorrect comments from Western teachers in Saudi Arabia, in Malaysia, and in Japan. The students that we taught in the programs in these three countries were intelligent, had hobbies and interests outside of class, and spoke a great deal in their native language (evidence: classes were noisy with native language until the English teacher walked in). Thus, all of the above complaints are untrue. If the students were so quiet in class, other issues may have been involved, but the silence was not due to the students' laziness, stupidity, or stubbornness.

What was happening to cause the silence in the speaking class? Many times the problem was the activity that the teacher had chosen. In this chapter, we will look at some ineffective and even detrimental activities that teachers used in their classes. After describing the activity, I will offer some insight into why it failed.

Unsuccessful Activity 1
Presenting a Discussion Topic without Any Tasks

Situation

The teacher started the class by sitting on the top of his desk. He then asked the class, "What do you think about capital punishment?" The fifteen students stared at the teacher, who quickly added, "I mean, do you think it's a good thing?" [pause of 2 seconds] "Or is it bad? I mean, here in Japan, you don't have capital punishment, do you?" [pause of 2 seconds] "In the U.S., this is a really hot topic. Well, it used to be really controversial, and lots of. . .well, my dad, I remember, used to talk about this all the time. He thought that the best way to get rid of criminals was to 'fry' them." [pause of 2 seconds] "Does anyone else have a different opinion? What about the death sentence?"

Comments

1. You are teaching in Japan. Conversations or discussions, especially in classrooms, function quite differently in Japan. Since you are in Japan, it behooves you to learn what your students' norms are and work with those.

   The analogy that I've often heard is that a conversation in the West is sort of like a volleyball game. Anyone can start the point by hitting the ball to someone else. The other team can then return the ball or hit it to a nearby teammate and then to another teammate or even back to the original hitter before sending the ball to the other team. The other team then has various options, including the fact that anyone can hit the ball to anyone else. The only rule is that the same person can't hit the ball twice in a row. In stark contrast, a conversation in Japan is perhaps more similar to bowling. Only one person bowls at one time. Everyone else shuts up. They watch and consider the person as one person approaches the lane and finally releases the ball. They watch the ball roll toward the pins, and only after the pins have been hit can anyone else bowl.

   While this analogy is extreme, it does illustrate the fact that Japanese students in a formal setting such as a classroom are not used to many people hitting the ball randomly. The teacher was wrong to toss out a question and expect the Japanese students to play volleyball. They might have been ready to bowl.

2. In the Japanese educational system, English classes consist of learning grammar and vocabulary. I remember visiting a high school class once where the teacher checked the grammar homework by having students stand up one after another, row by row, and read a statement in which the students had filled in the correct verb form (e.g., *go, goes, going: Every day my father _____ to work by train.*). It was one of the most mechanical educational processes that I have ever seen. To be sure, this exists everywhere, but my Japanese students told me this was the norm in Japan, not the exception.

   This teacher should have known that Japanese students are not accustomed to the teacher simply tossing out an open-ended question for everyone to answer. A better way would be to plan one or two short, specific tasks about this topic before the more general discussion. For example, since this issue is about crime, the teacher could have asked the students to rank a series of six crimes (e.g., murder, personal theft, rape, burglary, arson, kidnapping) from bad to worst. The next activity could be reading about a real court case involving a heinous crime that involved a death sentence to see if the students agreed with the judge's decision or not. *Remember:* Having a topic is not the same as having a lesson plan; a plan includes specific tasks with finite goals. (See Lesson Plan #3, "White Lies," on pp. 263–265.)

3. The topic is a difficult one to use in Japan. Japan does not have capital punishment. (In fact, the vast majority of the world's countries do not have capital punishment.) There might be no spark to discuss something that the society does not have because it might not be an issue in that country. In fact, one could argue that the reason that capital punishment is an issue in the United States is that we in the United States are the odd-person out, so to speak.

   People discuss differences, not similarities. The Japanese might not have had much difference of opinions among themselves on this topic, so, of course, a spontaneous "volleyball" game did not erupt.

4. Listening skills are often weak in Japanese students because they have had so little practice in actual speaking of and listening to English. Notice how the teacher rambled on and on about his own opinions. It was an avalanche of foreign words. The teacher should have posed the question as he wrote it on the board. He should have repeated the question, and then he should have been quiet. Allowing sufficient wait time is a difficult

thing for Western teachers to do, especially if they are new and/or nervous.

Don't paraphrase your second or third attempts to communicate. Use the same words so you can help your learners. Notice how the teacher changed *capital punishment* to *death penalty*.

5. Use the board. Why didn't the teacher write *capital punishment, crime, murder, justice,* etc., on the board? People remember what they see and hear better than what they just hear (assuming that they have understood the words in the first place, which is a weakness of many Japanese students).

6. Never sit on the desk. The top of the desk and your buttocks should never meet. I'm not sure how rude this is considered in Japan, but even in the United States, I find this offensive. In addition, as a teacher, I almost never sit down unless we are all seated in a circle for group work or if the students are taking an exam (and even then I may walk around to monitor).

Unsuccessful Activity 2
Using a Task Inappropriate for Students' Age

Situation

The teacher introduced the game "Simon Says" to practice commands and review vocabulary of body parts. In this game, the teacher gives commands to the entire class. If the command is preceded by the phrase "Simon says," then you should do the action. If the teacher does not say "Simon says," then you should not do the action. For example, if you hear, "Simon says to touch your left ear," you should touch your left ear, but if the teacher then quickly adds, "Okay, now touch your other ear," you should do nothing because Simon didn't say to do it.

After moving all the desks to the sides of the room to clear the middle area, the teacher had all the students stand up against the back wall. He explained that they would play "Simon Says" and then asked them to close their eyes for the whole game. He then gave commands such as, "Simon says take two steps forward," "Simon says to touch your right foot with your left hand," "Simon says to shake your butt," and "Simon says to stick out your tongue."

Comments

1. These students were adults. The rationale for having students close their eyes was that they would not be able to copy what their classmates were or were not doing but would really have to listen. This is a good rationale, but adults do not like to close their eyes in public. It tends to make us feel very uncomfortable.

2. The requested actions were inappropriate for adults. It is rude (and embarrassing) to stick out your tongue. It is embarrassing to wiggle your behind. It is embarrassing to be contorted so that your left hand is on your right foot.

3. This was a free adult conversation class. How much conversation is happening in "Simon Says"? None.

    If students had their eyes open, they could see what others were or were not doing and then ask the teacher to repeat so that they could try to catch the meaning one more time. In this way, at least there would be some negotiation of meaning. However, with students' eyes closed, this was more like a test with embarrassing questions.

4. With any activity, ask yourself how you would feel having to do this activity. If you wouldn't like to do it, then many of your students won't either.

<u>Follow-up Note</u>: After this particular class, about half the students stopped attending. They did not return to the free conversation class.

Unsuccessful Activity 3
Using a Task Unsuitable for Students' Proficiency

Situation

A novice teacher received one of those e-mails extolling the cute but difficult aspects of the English language. She found this interesting and chose this for the basis of an entire class. In this e-mail, most of the "funny" parts were actually plays on words, but her non-native speakers didn't understand these plays on words. Examples from her sheet included:

- A chicken crossing the road is poultry in motion.
- In democracy your vote counts. In feudalism your count votes.
- Once you've seen one shopping center, you've seen a mall.
- Time flies like an arrow. Fruit flies like a banana.
- Those who jump off a bridge in Paris are in Seine.

The teacher passed out a sheet of twenty of these statements. She had the students take turns reading them aloud as a prelude to discussion. However, there was very little discussion. Students grabbed dictionaries as she spent the class explaining not the play on words, which was the point of the lesson, but rather the meanings of the words and then the play on words, and then the cultural references.

Comments

1. Think back to the last time someone told you a joke (in your native language) that you just didn't get so that person ended up explaining the joke to you. How did you react then? Did you fall on the floor laughing? No. If you have to explain a joke to someone, it's not funny. Likewise, if you have to explain not only the joke but also the meaning of each of the individual words, then there is no joke. These sentences are far beyond the English ability of most non-native speakers.
2. One reason that the content of this lesson is a very poor choice as a springboard for anything is that the language is too difficult at two levels—literal and metaphorical. The second reason that this content is

poor is that the statements contain many cultural references that only a native speaker would recognize. For each of the five statements, I offer these comments:

- A chicken crossing the road is poultry in motion.

    Students will not know *poultry*, so you have explain that word. *Poultry* is probably worth teaching. (*Vocabulary:* Avoid teaching words that have no "pay off" for the students. You want to teach and practice high-frequency vocabulary and structures.)

    Students do not know the expression *poetry in motion*. If you teach this expression, they will get it as a separate expression; they will most likely think they can now say mathematics in motion, literature in motion, etc. After teaching this expression, how useful is it to your learners?

    Finally, we have a series of jokes asking, "Why did the chicken cross the road?" You may not have realized this, but this is a part of your culture. Think about it: We don't talk about dogs or cats or snakes crossing the road; our line is always about chickens crossing the road.

    After all of this explanation, would you laugh? Would you chuckle even? Now imagine the comprehension problems faced by an ESL learner. If the students are EFL learners, they are even less likely to understand any of the cultural references if they somehow manage to understand the language issues.

- In democracy, your vote counts. In feudalism, your count votes.

    What is *feudalism*? What is a *count*? If you were in an intensive Chinese class, are these concepts for which you would like to learn the Chinese words?

- Once you've seen one shopping center, you've seen a mall.

    Many students will know that the terms *shopping center* and *mall* are very similar. However, to smile at this statement, your English has to be good enough that you know we often reduce *them* to *'em*. In addition, you have to know the idiomatic structure, "Once you've seen one ____, you've seen them all." While some ESL/EFL learners may understand the gist of this structure, they probably won't know it as an idiomatic structure that we use to mean that the current example of a "____" is not special.

■ Time flies like an arrow. Fruit flies like a banana.

What is a *fruit fly?* To laugh, you have to know that there is a pest that we call a fruit fly. In addition, you have to know that "time flies like an arrow" is a special saying in English.

■ Those who jump off a bridge in Paris are in Seine.

This is a play on the word *insane,* which is not here, but you have to recognize this play on words, which depends on your knowing the word *insane* in the first place. In addition, river names in English should take the definite article (e.g., the Nile, the Mississippi), so this example is difficult to grasp, and after it's been grasped, it is comprehensible but incorrect input.

3. The paper had twenty of these statements. Multiply all the explanation time for each statement by twenty items. That equals a lot of teacher explanation. What were the students doing? They were not talking. They were not discussing. They spent the class listening to the teacher, who was (unfortunately) so enthusiastic about these sentences. The confused students were wondering why people were seeing malls, why fruit was flying, and why insane was funny. How valuable was this conversation class to them?

Unsuccessful Activity 4
Using Discussion Prompts that Can't Generate Discussion

Situation

The teacher put the upper-intermediate students in small groups of four. She gave each group a handful of cards with questions on the cards. She told them to take turns reading the cards aloud and then discussing their answers to the questions. The cards included questions such as:

■ What is your favorite color? Why?

■ Which of these is better for a car: purple or green? Why?

■ What is your mother's sister called?

■ What is your favorite season? Why?

The teacher was surprised the room was not abuzz with English. In fact, the classroom was rather quiet. Students took turns reading cards aloud and then sharing their simple answers. Much to the teacher's surprise, there was very little discussion—because there was nothing to discuss.

Comments

1. I always try to imagine an activity with two native speakers. What would two native speakers say in this situation? Let's consider the first example. Following the teacher's directions, I pick up the card and read, "What is your favorite color? Why?"

   What do you think that you as a native speaker would say? I would probably say, "My favorite color is blue because I like it. Blue is a good color, so I like it. It's my favorite." Then my partner, who has to discuss this with me, says either, "Me, too. I like blue" or "Really? My favorite color is green. I just really like green a lot."

   Now imagine two non-natives with less fluency. Where is the discussion? Where is the conversation? These topics are not conversation or discussion starters. There is really very little to discuss—and it has nothing do with being a native or non-native speaker. The problem is not language proficiency; the problem is the topic.

2. In its current form, this activity would be okay for beginning or low-intermediate students. It generates speaking but not discussions. Lower-proficiency or reticent students might enjoy this as a confidence-building activity.

3. This activity uses a really good format. Having one student read the card aloud means that others have to listen, but they can also hear the response before they have to agree or disagree. The solution here is to have questions that will highlight differences of opinions. <u>Remember</u>: People don't say much when they think exactly alike.

    Better question prompts might be:

    ■ If you won the lottery today, what are the first three things that you would do?

    ■ If you could travel to any country for one week, where would you go and why?

    ■ The driving age should be raised to 25. Do you agree or disagree? Why?

    ■ Name one benefit of eating at home instead of eating out. (Each person will give one benefit.)

Unsuccessful Activity 5
Using a One-Way Task

Situation

The teacher chose a mini-mystery as his class task. He knew that his students were very bright and would appreciate solving a mystery. In fact, several had expressed interest in a recent class that they liked mysteries and detective TV shows. The teacher spent a considerable amount of time selecting a story that had language more or less at his students' proficiency level so there would not be a language barrier.

In class, he put the students in groups of three and then gave a copy of the mini-mystery to each student. He told them, "Okay, please take five minutes to read the mini-mystery individually, and then you will discuss the mystery until you can identify who the culprit is."

Around the five-minute mark, the teacher said, "Okay, work in your groups to solve the problem." There was the usual silence for the first 30 seconds. Then one group began. One boy asked, "I don't have any idea. Do you?" His second classmate looked at him and said nothing. Suddenly, the third group member said, "Wait, I know the answer. The thief was Mr. Miller because. . ."

The other students couldn't help overhearing this. They all then looked up at the teacher, ready for the discussion or perhaps the next activity.

Comments

1. This sounds like such a good activity for speaking, doesn't it? Students have a problem to solve. However, the dilemma here is that as soon as one student has the answer, she will say, "Okay, I know who the culprit is. It was the cook. The cook stole the money because he said. . . ." The other students will then say, "Yes, that's right" or just "Yes, I agree." At this point, now that one person has solved the problem, the activity is over for everyone. A good activity requires discussion; this task does not.

2. This is not a two-way activity. The teacher should have divided the story into six pieces or clues and then had the students work in groups of six. This would be similar to a Strip Story (see Activity 20, p. 181). In this way, students would have discussed the information much, much more.

   By giving each student all of the information, this was a one-way information gap, which automatically means that there is no required exchange of information. That is exactly what happened here.

Unsuccessful Activity 6
Using a Problem-Solving Task with a Difficult Solution

Situation

The teacher wanted to challenge her students, so she looked for a problem-solving activity. She did a Google™ search using terms such as *problem solving* and *brainteaser*. Eventually, she came across this well-known problem involving a wolf, a goat, and a cabbage. Because this task was designed for native speakers, the vocabulary in some of the clues was a bit tough for her students, so she rewrote the brainteaser. She prepared clues for her students so that this could be a two-way information gap activity. She then prepared copies for her students.

In class, she told the students to work in pairs. She wrote the problem on the board:

Problem

You have a small boat and need to cross the river with a goat, a wolf, and a cabbage. The boat is small, so you can take only one thing at a time.

She then gave each of the partners either an A clue or a B clue:

Clue for only Student A: If you are not with the goat, it will eat the cabbage.

Clue for only Student B: If you are not with the wolf, it will eat the goat.

The teacher then said, "Okay, I want you to work together to figure out the solution to this problem. You can share your clue with your partner, but you cannot show the paper to each other. This is a discussion activity, not a reading activity."

The teacher walked around the room as the students took turns reading or saying their clues to each other. The students began talking. "Okay, let's take the wolf first," said one student. "But then the goat will eat the cabbage." More talk ensued before students began to get quiet. The teacher tried to encourage the students to keep working, but there was a sense that this problem did not have a solution.

Comments

1. One potential weakness here is the same weakness pointed out in Unsuccessful Activity 5—that is, once one student has the solution, he or she merely announces it, and everyone else nods in agreement. Almost all of the "discussion" takes place inside each individual student's head, which is not the goal of this activity.
2. Fortunately, this activity didn't fail for that reason, but that was because the solution to this problem is just too hard. Yes, a few people can solve it, but no matter whether this problem is presented in the native language or in English, it is a very difficult logic puzzle. In the class that I observed, no one got it right. They gave up after just a few minutes because they did not see a solution. I might add that there was very little speaking going on after the initial discussion. (See page 285 for the solution to this brainteaser.)

Unsuccessful Activity 7
Using a Task with Overly Complicated Instructions

Situation

The teacher gave the students a paper with a short paragraph on it. The paragraph was supposed to be the springboard for a discussion during the last part of the class. The teacher gave these directions: "I want you to read this paragraph. Circle any words or sentences that you don't understand. Then I want you to find someone who has the same birth month as you, and you should work with that person to make sure that you have a good understanding of what the paper says. Then after that, I want you to find a new partner to discuss the topic with. This second partner should be someone that you don't usually work with. Okay? Choose a partner who doesn't sit near you in class. The two of you should write one sentence summarizing your thoughts on the topic. Then when you have your sentence, I want one of you to come to the board and write your sentence on the board in the correct space. Are there any questions?"

As an observer, my immediate question was, "Do what? I'm lost—and I haven't even heard about the actual discussion activity, just the directions."

Comments

1. These directions are too complicated. I can't even remember now what the topic of the paragraph was, so I can't discuss anything.
2. Give the directions one step at a time. When everyone has finished the first step of circling unfamiliar words and sentences, then say, "Okay, now I want you to find a partner whose birth month is the same as yours. I want everyone to stand up and find out in which month your classmates were born. For example, if you were born in April, find another student who was also born in April." Then let people have enough time to work together. Don't rush students.

Unsuccessful Activity 8
Pretending that Checking Answers Is
the Same as Discussing

Situation

The textbook had an activity about family members. Students had to fill in the blank with the correct family members. The exercise had twenty statements like these:

1. My father's father is my _____.

2. My sister's daughter is my _____.

3. My aunt's husband is my _____.

The teacher read the directions on the sheet: "Complete these statements with the correct family members label. When you have finished, work with a partner to discuss your answers." The teacher then gave the students about 10 minutes to complete the worksheet. When she was satisfied that most students had finished, she said, "Okay, now work with a partner to discuss your answers."

Students found partners quickly. In one pair, Student A read the first item, "My father's father is my grandfather," and then looked at Student B. Student B said, "Yes, grandfather," and then read the next item, "My sister's daughter is my niece." Student A agreed.

Very few students had differing answers, so there was hardly ever anything to discuss. In the few examples of disagreement that I heard, one student would say something like, "No, I think it's nephew," and after one or two additional exchanges, the problem was solved. The trouble was that this kind of discussion was very rare because most students had the correct answer already. Having students check their answers together—especially simple single-word or single-sentence answers—rarely results in meaningful or lengthy discussions.

Comments

1. This kind of activity is not speaking or discussion. There really is nothing to discuss. Most students will have the same answers since this is not an opinion question. In this task, Student A will say to Student B, "Ok, number 1. My father's father is my grandfather." Then Student B will reply, "Yes, that is my answer, too. Okay, number 2. My sister's daughter is my niece." Student A, "Yes, me, too." If there is a difference in answers, the two will correct it rather quickly since this is a factual exercise.

2. Beware of textbooks that have numerous exercises with directions that say, "When you finish, discuss your answers with a partner." Checking the answers for a grammar exercise or a vocabulary exercise—which is what this task really was—is never a discussion activity.

3. Discussion results from differences in opinion. People who think the same on an issue have less to talk about than people who disagree (a little).

4. There are several good tasks that require learners to talk about family members. See Activity 5 on p. 126. Also, perhaps you can create some sort of ranking activity (see Activity 6 on p. 131) involving family members.

Unsuccessful Activity 9
Choosing an Inappropriate Topic for the Students

Situation

The teacher of an advanced ESL class in an academic program in the United States put together a lesson on American football and the Super Bowl. He found a list of rules on the Internet. He collected some sports magazines and some newspaper clippings about the two teams that were competing in the Super Bowl. He brought in a football and two football helmets.

The teacher asked students what they knew about American football and wrote some of their comments on the board. He then put his twenty students into four groups of five students each. On the board, he wrote this task: "American football is more difficult to play than soccer." He asked them to discuss this for the next 15 minutes.

Two or three of the male students started in their groups by saying, "American football is not football. You can't use your feet, so the name is wrong. Soccer is a better sport." After these initial comments, the discussions changed topics to soccer or to sports or to what they were doing after class. The students who were talking were off topic. Some students started speaking in their native languages.

Comments

1. A topic can be a bad choice for a speaking class for several reasons. One common reason is that the topic is not of interest or relevance to the students, nor has the teacher made a good case for talking about this particular topic. My conclusion here was that the teacher was a big fan of American football, so much so in fact that he got carried away by the topic. I'm sure that he has a lot of friends that he can talk to at length about football—and who will talk hours with him.

2. A topic can be a poor choice because the students are focused on a particular goal, and the topic is not seen as meshing with that goal. These students, for example, were higher-proficiency students in an academic program. Their interest is most likely in passing the TOEFL® (Test of English as a Foreign Language) so that they can get into a university. Perhaps the teacher should have tried to make the topic more relevant by saying, "Ok,

everyone in here is working hard to pass the TOEFL®, but after you pass the TOEFL®, as I know you all will, what do you know about life at the university? Well, one thing that most universities have is a football team, and you'll need to know something about football and what happens at a university. For example, when are the games? How long are the games? Will you get free tickets as a student?" Perhaps this could have been the hook to get the students' interest. A good teacher keeps the audience—that is, the students—in mind at all times.

3. In addition to the weak topic, another problem is that the class had no real plan. The only plan I saw was that the teacher would come to class with all of this realia, introduce the topic, and then hope students talked. What were the tasks? The realia objects were good props, but the teacher had not thought things out. For example, the teacher could have brought in a soccer ball and a football and asked students to compare the two twice—once without showing them the balls and then again after showing them the balls. A discussion class is not a topic; a good discussion class has an underlying topic but it consists of a series of concrete tasks, which were clearly lacking here.

Unsuccessful Activity 10
Using Videos Incorrectly as a Speaking Task

Situation

The teacher selected an episode of the popular television show *Friends* that she thought would match her students' interests. (The students had watched videos of *Friends* before and knew the characters and overall story.) The teacher announced that the class was going to watch the video, which was approximately 23 minutes long, and then talk about the topic. She explained that Phoebe wanted to move out of the apartment, and that was the theme of this episode.

When the video was over, the teacher asked, "Okay, how was that? Does anyone have any questions? Did you understand everything? Was anything confusing?"

There was silence, which the teacher naively assumed meant that everyone had understood everything. The teacher then directed the students to work in small groups as they discussed this question: What is a good way to tell a roommate that you no longer want to live in the apartment that you share?

Comments

1. The video was too long. If these students were very advanced, then yes, they might have understood most of the language, but the vast majority of students most likely did not understand the language in the video. Instead, they got their information from a combination of some of the language and a lot of the visuals (from the video) and the body language of the characters, which represented the characters' feelings.

2. If you really want to help your students with their language—that is, their listening—then choose a smaller, more specific segment of the video and play just that segment. However, cover up the monitor so that students can only hear the video. Then play the video clip again immediately. Let students have two chances at the script. Then ask what they have understood. Write some of their ideas on the board. Write some key vocabulary or phrases on the board. Then play the video segment again. Remember that part of what you want to do is push learners' interlanguage.

3. If you don't do number 2, which means you don't teach any language per se, then why are you showing the video clip? If you want students to discuss reasons for moving out, then just write that question on the board and don't use the video.

I'm not saying that using a video is bad, but if you are going to use a video, then do something with it. Use it for a reason. Make sure that the students get some good listening practice as well as some new vocabulary from the video.

Summary

The ten examples in this chapter are offered to illustrate activities that well-intentioned teachers spent time designing and planning but that flopped. In some cases, students were left confused about what had happened. In one case, about half the students never came back to the course.

From time to time, all teachers have bad days that result in less-than-stellar classes, but good teachers recognize and admit it when a class or activity did not go well. More important, good teachers reflect on why the activity did not go well and how it will be improved the next time it is used.

6 Assessing Speaking

Good assessment is built into all good teaching. Good assessment does not just "happen." It takes careful planning as well as knowledge of the subject matter, the learner, and general testing. There are many good teachers who are not good testers. In fact, we have all had this kind of teacher at one time or another!

The first thing to remember about good assessment—regardless of the skill being assessed—is that teachers should consider assessment even as the initial class planning is started. To be sure, there most likely will be some sort of official assessment, that is, a final exam, at the last stage of the learning process, but good teachers do the initial planning of the exam as they do the initial planning of the lesson or course.

Regardless of the language skill, the number-one quality of good assessment is that it should assess a skill in the same way in which the skill was taught. If you taught a reading class for three hours each week and spent half of the time having students read to themselves and answer multiple-choice questions, then approximately half of your test (or its point value) should cover the same. (Whether spending half of your class time doing this one type of reading activity is a good plan or not is a different question. Here we are concerned with a match between teaching and testing with the assumption that the teaching—including the content and the actual presentation with practice—was good.) If the questions in class had only three choices of A, B, C, then the final exam should not suddenly contain five choices of A, B, C, D, E. If you taught a composition class in which spelling counted only 10 percent of the final essay grades throughout the term, it would be grossly unfair for spelling to suddenly count for 25 percent on the final exam because the course objectives actually emphasize spelling. (Note: The mistake here is that your teaching—with only 10 percent weight given to spelling—did not match the course objectives in the first place. The exam then should not be used out of the blue as a "gatekeeper" maneuver.)

Similarly, if students spent half of their class time interviewing other students because a major goal of the course was the ability to ask *yes-no* and information questions, then your assessment should reflect this fact. It would be wrong to omit this from the exam or to have only a handful of questions devoted to asking questions.

Revisiting Students' Speaking Needs

In Chapter 1, we considered the question *Why should we be so concerned with the teaching of conversation in an English as a Second Language (ESL) or English as a Foreign Language (EFL) classroom?* We then spent some time thinking about our students' actual language needs in terms of speaking. Why are our students taking this course? Is it a school requirement? Is it to pass some kind of proficiency exam such as TOEFL®? Is it to see if the student can perform common daily functions in an ESL setting?

The answers to the questions in this needs analysis inform teachers and curriculum writers as to how to set up a speaking course. At the same time, this should guide us toward how we should assess what is taught in this course as well. Ponder this as we briefly revisit this excerpt from the Introduction, p. 4:

> In a very general usage of the word *speaking,* we can see that speaking a language clearly entails many different aspects. It is important for all teachers of speaking or conversation to remember that the aspects deemed more important depend entirely upon the learner's ultimate purpose in learning to speak English. Thus, you need to know why your learners want to speak English. Is it for business? Business dealings with native speakers? Business dealings with native speakers face to face? Over the phone or via a computer? Is it for conversation? Conversation on the job, as with a tour leader? Is it conversation to be able to communicate at the bank or supermarket?

Clearly, learner needs drive classroom activities (i.e., your lesson plan). The format and the content of the activities drive assessment. Assessment in turn should measure how well those very learner needs have been achieved.

Three Stages of Speaking Assessment

As with any skill or content area, assessment can be done at three stages: pre-instruction, during instruction, and post-instruction. Each of these phases can provide both the teacher and the learner with a more accurate and perhaps more objective picture of the learning (and teaching) experience.

Pre-Instruction

In the pre-instruction stage, you are trying to determine how much your students already know. All teachers of all language courses need to do this stage. Good teaching is moving the learner from point X, which represents the student's initial point of knowledge, to point Z, which represents your learning objectives. Pre-instruction assessment, a sort of diagnostic test, can help you assess the initial knowledge base of your students. With one learner, it is a simple case of assessing X and then attempting to move the learner to Z, but in a class of twenty students, it is more likely that you have several students at different points, including D, G, M, and X. This initial assessment of the group and of individuals is critical in planning how much time you will have to devote to certain areas as well as identifying potentially weak and advanced students.

In a speaking class, you have several options for this pre-instruction assessment. One simple way is to talk directly to your students. You might listen to students' general fluency or even something as specific as their pronunciation of certain sounds. Based on your assessment of what you hear, you would emphasize certain areas of your course syllabus or book and perhaps omit other areas. In addition, you could also get at this information indirectly by having your students fill out a questionnaire regarding the number of years they have studied English, which areas they want to focus on in your speaking class, and perhaps whether they want to be recorded during some of the class activities. In sum, this pre-assessment is aimed more for the teacher to fine-tune the course to help the students with certain areas.

During Instruction

All good language teachers constantly evaluate their learners as the lesson is actually taking place. The most obvious feedback for the teacher is the students' performance. Are they talking to each other? Are they having trouble pronouncing certain words? Is there excessive silence from some students, which would indicate lack of fluency that is perhaps due to lack of knowledge of key phrases such as, "Could you repeat that?" or "Um, let me think about that a minute"? When they are talking, are they taking turns or are they cutting each other off? Are they making excessive grammar mistakes that hinder communication?

Based on the answer to these questions, the teacher would decide who needs more help with certain areas. Continued assessment during instruction helps the teacher know who is having problems, what kind of problems need to be addressed through repetition of this particular activity, or even when to move on from this activity. This feedback informs the teacher of the learners' progress as well as of the teacher's own progress in teaching.

One question to consider here is, "What should teachers do when they hear mistakes?" My advice here is to avoid making a correction on the spot unless you have a very good reason to do so. Most of the time, teacher correction of an error during an activity will only stifle students. It is a struggle to reach the point where some of your really shy or less confident learners will finally feel secure enough to speak up in class. When they finally do speak—and this is a victory in and of itself—the last thing you want to do is deflate this learner's emerging risk-taking. When you note that a usually silent student is speaking, go out of your way to say something good (or at least neutral) as a form of acknowledgment that everything is okay. Teacher correction is out of the question.

Even if a student is not stifled by your interruption, learners in many cases do not even notice that there has been a correction as evidenced in this rather typical example:

Teacher:	Where did you go last Saturday?
Student:	I go to the store.
Teacher:	You *went* to the store. (with emphasis on *went*)
Student:	(looking a little confused because he knows something is up) Yes. . .I. . .I go to the store. I buy many thing.

There are some learners who want immediate correction and who can understand your feedback. They know, for example, that when you say *went* in a louder, stronger tone, this means that you want them to think about what they have just said—that is, *go*, and contrast that with what you have just said in a louder voice. These good learners have a keen ear; unfortunately, this kind of learner is often the exception, not the rule. At the same time, it is equally important for you to know who these exceptional learners in your class are so that you can give them this individualized corrective feedback, which will be useful to them because it will serve as intake for them to reformulate their speaking. In essence, these good learners are able to use your feedback as a form of negotiated meaning, which they will try to incorporate in their next output. (See p. 55 for information on the research by Panova and Lyster [2002] showing that implicit corrections are often not perceived as corrections by learners and therefore do not become uptake for second language learners.)

Post-Instruction

What should you do for the average learners? If you should not correct on the spot, then what should you do? The answer is to wait until the activity is complete to provide feedback to the group. The best teaching strategy is to keep track—either mentally or on a piece of paper (if need be)—of various errors or difficulties during an activity. After you have discussed the topic or completed the activity, you might go to the board and address three issues that you noted during the class. You should never mention anyone's names or even glance in their direction. If you want to give specific feedback to a few students who you think will benefit from such feedback, then by all means, do so. However, in most cases, group feedback of three to five items can be useful to the entire group.

Let us consider a class that has just had a discussion about superstitions, a topic that usually generates a great deal of student speaking. As you turn to write on the board after the class discussion, your talk to the class might go something like this:

Teacher: Okay, that was a very interesting talk. I heard lots of
                  different superstitions that I'd never heard of before. I
                  think the most interesting one for me was that if you eat
                  twelve grapes at midnight on New Year's Eve, you will
                  have good luck.

[pause 3 seconds]

                  When I was listening to everyone's conversation tonight,
                  I heard some things that I want to talk about to help
                  your English. These are some small problems that can
                  really make your English better.
                  For example. . . [Teacher begins to write *you will have
                  lucky*] I heard some people say this. You will have lucky.

[pause] [Some students start talking to each other in a low voice.]

                  Can anyone tell me something about this sentence?

[pause]

                  There is a problem here. What is it?

[Two students vie for the floor.]

Student A: You will be lucky.
Student B: You will have luck.
Teacher: [writes both corrections on the board] Yes, there are
                  two ways to say this, but this way [points to the written
                  error and puts a dotted X through the word *lucky*] is not
                  possible.
                  Can someone make a sentence with this?
Student B: If I eat twelve grapes, I will have good luck.
Student A: If I eat the grapes, I will. . .
Student C: If you eat the twelve grapes, you will be lucky.

The lesson then continues as the teacher goes on to the second and third
errors, which may be on pronunciation and vocabulary.

Formal Assessment

In this section, we will talk about two kinds of formal assessment. One is an achievement assessment, and the other is a proficiency assessment. Both are important. Both have very different purposes. However, while teachers may need to know how to design an achievement assessment for speaking, they will rarely if ever be called upon to design a proficiency exam for speaking. Most proficiency exams will be professionally made by a publishing or testing company.

Achievement Assessment

The purpose of an achievement test is fairly obvious. This kind of test is designed to assess how much students have achieved in a specific course. In other words, how much have learners progressed (according to some sort of scale or list of objectives)?

Though novice teachers sometimes do not think about pre-instruction and during instruction assessment, all teachers are familiar with the concept of a formal post-instruction assessment. How many times have we ourselves been students in a class and then had to take a final exam in order to exit the course?

Formal post-instruction assessment may be the most common form of assessment, but it may come as a surprise to some readers that not all speaking courses feature post-assessment. When I taught at the language school in Japan, it was expected that all students would continue the next course with their group of students—if possible, with the same teacher. For this reason, we did not give much weight to a final exit test. Similarly, many conversation schools—especially those in an EFL setting—will underemphasize post-instruction assessment. (The curriculum used in my former school in Japan had a tremendous amount of overlap between levels, so levels 3, 4, and 5, for example, may have been only slightly different. Students could place into 3, 4, or 5, and students could move from 3 to 4 or from 4 to 5 even if their ability was a little weaker than that of the other students. The point is that the assessment matched the curriculum, which matched the learners' needs.)

The next logical question then is what should be tested. Again, you should test the content of the course in a manner similar to how the material was taught or practiced. In brief, an achievement test measures the course objectives, which should be based on the needs analysis that we talked about in Chapter 1. Thus, if you spent a great deal of class time having students write out and then act out dialogues, this should also be part of your final assessment.

In Chapter 1, we noted that the speaking course can be called several different course names, including speaking, conversation, oral fluency, and discussion. In the same chapter, we noted that in this course—regardless of what it is labeled—the teacher can focus on a variety of areas, including pronunciation, fluency, and language accuracy. Let us consider some possible assessments for each of these three areas.

Pronunciation

Since good pronunciation certainly contributes to good speaking, your conversation class might focus on pronunciation. Does the speaker have a marked accent that inhibits communication? Can the learner pronounce a range of sounds in English? Or are there certain sounds that the learner cannot say?

One way to assess learners' ability to pronounce certain sounds is to devise a short paragraph or a series of sentences that include sounds that you want to assess. The learner reads the material aloud. For grading purposes, the learner's reading is recorded on a cassette.

Let us consider two scenarios if you have taught a class in which you have covered the pronunciation of the –*ed* ending for regular verbs in English (i.e., /d/ versus /t/ versus /ɪd/) as well as the sounds of /b/ versus /v/ and /š/ versus /č/. Look at the sentence test and the paragraph test.

Sentence Test

Directions: Read these sentences aloud.

1. After Bob washed the dishes, he watched television for about an hour.
2. Before Victor and Ben played chess, they counted the chess pieces and placed them on the board.
3. We studied the vowels last week. Only two students really learned them well, so the teacher tested us on them again today.

Paragraph Test

Directions: Read this paragraph aloud.

Yesterday was a very busy day. I wanted to sleep late, but that was not possible. I cooked a big breakfast for myself, but I burned the toast. When I was eating, I spilled coffee on my white shirt. I changed into another shirt, put on my jacket, and walked to the office. I arrived a little late, but I enjoyed the extra exercise.

This assessment has several advantages. One of the advantages is that you can make sure that every sound you taught and practiced is assessed. If you want to assess whether the student can pronounce /k/ plus *–ed* (e.g., *cracked, baked*), you can make sure that the sentences or paragraph contain that sound several times. On the other hand, if you assessed this in a more natural arrangement by just taping the student during a conversation, you would have no way of making sure that the learner attempted to pronounce the target sounds. In the end, if the student did not produce any examples in the taped conversation, what would this mean? With this assessment, you would not be able to determine whether the student could pronounce the sound but just did not say an example, could not pronounce the sound but just did not say an example, or could not pronounce the sound and therefore (wisely) avoided saying any word that contained that sound. Another advantage is that you know exactly what the learner was trying to say (because it is there in black and white). Sometimes it is even more difficult to understand student language on a cassette when there are no visual clues for reference as there are in face-to-face conversations.

A disadvantage of this assessment is that this is reading, not speaking. Reading is more formal; people tend to enunciate more carefully. Some learners may be able to pronounce a word well until they see its spelling. (The spelling actually causes the mistaken pronunciation, not the difficulty of the sound.) In addition, if students practiced these sounds in natural speaking or conversation, it would be wrong to test this in a reading format. Students who performed well during the course in speaking practices may do worse on reading tasks. Thus, this task may not accurately assess speaking at all.

Fluency

We often hear the word *fluent* to describe a certain speaker. While this may mean that the speaker's English is correct, more often than not it refers to the ability of the speaker to deliver a communication or message at a normal speed. Thus, fluency refers to the amount of language delivered, not necessarily the accuracy. Does the speaker stop frequently to search for words? Does the speaker use words that accurately reflect his or her actual social level? (Adults want to sound as intelligent in their second language as they do in their first language.) In other words, how well does the speaker convey an intended message without an unnatural amount of hesitation or self-corrections or self-interruptions?

One way to measure fluency is to assess how much language a learner produces in a certain time period. At one of my early teaching positions, we gave an in-house test called the "John test" because the main character was named John. The John test had two parts, both of which used a series of five illustrations.

In part one of the test, learners were shown the five illustrations one at a time. They were told that the man in the picture was named John. Students were given 30 seconds to study each picture silently and then had one minute to talk about that picture. Students could say whatever they wanted. They were told that their goal was to say as much as possible in the one minute.

In the second part of the test, the five illustrations were laid out in chronological order. (In the first part of the test, the pictures were presented in random order so that there was no apparent connection between the pictures.) Learners were then told that they had one minute to use the pictures to tell the story of what happened to John yesterday. For grading purposes, the learners' language was recorded on a cassette.

For grading, two scorers listened to a student's cassette. Scorers tallied the number of t-units, which here meant any subject-verb combination. Scorers also kept track of any errors of any kind—pronunciation, grammar, vocabulary, or content (of the pictures). Students received two points for each t-unit and lost one point for each error. Thus, for the purposes of this exam, fluency was operationalized as the number of subject-verb units minus half the number of errors within a 1-minute time period.

For example, this student would receive a score of 12 because there are 9 t-units and 6 errors: 9 t-units times 2 points each = 18 points, minus 6 errors = 12 points total.

> In this picture is man. Man is name John. John has a nice face. He is a good person. I think people likes John because is good guy. John was wake up late today because he was very tired.

One advantage of this system is that it is relatively easy to gain student data. The assessment is easy for students to follow. In fact, I think many students enjoyed taking this test. Scoring this assessment is also rather easy. If you cannot understand what is on the cassette, that counts as an error. Having two scorers also made the job easier and more accurate.

A disadvantage is the question of what this assessment is actually assessing. Is a person's fluency actually definable as the number of subject-verb relationships in an utterance? In Japanese, it is more common to precede main verbs with *I think* as in "I think it's 9 AM" instead of "It's 9 AM." If a Japanese speaker used a great deal of subordination in English, he or she would be assessed as "more fluent" using this system. Another related disadvantage involves the scoring of the learners' utterances. If a learner makes more than two errors of any kind in a sentence—even if a native speaker has no problem understanding the utterance—then that learner would actually get a negative score (one t-unit is two points; three errors is three points; $2 - 3 = -1$). This is an inaccurate measure of fluency since we defined fluency as the ability to transmit a message. Thus, how can a learner receive a negative score for fluency when in fact the learner's message was communicated? In fact, a negative score never occurred while I was scoring this exam. However, the point is that it is very difficult to operationalize fluency in concrete terms.

Language Accuracy

Everyone agrees that the accuracy of learner language is important, but how important is this to overall speaking ability? To be sure, speaking accurately is important, but we have seen that obsessing over accuracy does not necessarily produce a cadre of accurate second language speakers. (As an example, I offer the availability of the paltry state of foreign language ability among U.S. students despite the most advanced technology and teaching techniques. Likewise, a further example is the relatively low level of English proficiency in certain EFL settings in spite of learners' many years of EFL instruction.) The question to ask yourself is whether your learners make so many errors— or such serious errors—that communication is hindered or even impeded.

One way to assess accuracy of spoken language is to count errors as in the example of the John test. An advantage of the John test as an accuracy assessment is that it is natural language and it is relatively easy to score. A disadvantage is that the number of errors could be related to the amount of overall language. If a person says *I goed and *I was went in a task that features many past tense verbs, the learner will have a very low score when in fact he or she missed only one item (but multiple times because the task is set in the past tense).

While this preceding test assesses speaking directly, another possibility is an indirect measure of a student's language accuracy. In this assessment, the teacher creates a cloze passage and students fill in the blanks with words that make sense. The student is not speaking, but if a speaker's ability to speak accurately correlates with a speaker's ability to complete written grammar tasks, then this indirect assessment could be valid. The ultimate question, however, is whether or not these two assessments correlate.

Direct versus Indirect Assessment

Let us consider accuracy, one of the areas just mentioned as a component in speaking. We could assess the student's ability to use grammar in speaking or on paper. We could set up an interview with the student and record the interview. The topic of the interview should be one that was covered in the course or is closely related to ones covered in the course. (*Remember:* Test what was covered in the course.) Since students spent many hours conversing with each other in this speaking course on the topic of restaurants, then it would be reasonable to observe grammar in an actual restaurant conversation that we might tape (to score later). This would be direct assessment of grammar in speaking.

However, you can imagine that it would be very laborious and time-consuming to interview each of your students. In addition, what will the other students be doing when you are interviewing this one student? Primarily due to these and other logistical concerns, grammar ability in conversation, that is, the ability to construct an utterance accurately, is often assessed in written form. This indirect assessment can be either active/production or passive/recognition.

Example of Production

Directions: Fill in the blanks to complete this conversation in a fast-food restaurant.

Clerk:	Hi, welcome _____ Billy's Burgers. _____ I help you?
Customer:	Yes, _____ a hamburger.
Clerk:	Okay, one hamburger. _____ you want cheese on that?
Customer:	No, just plain.
Clerk:	What about mayonnaise, mustard, or ketchup?
Customer:	Just a little mustard. I _____ like mayonnaise or ketchup.
Clerk:	Will there be _____ ?
Customer:	Sure, I'd like _____ french fries.

Example of Recognition

Directions: If the underlined word parts contain a mistake, circle them. Write a correction above each mistake.

Clerk: Hi, <u>welcome Billy's</u> Burgers. <u>May I</u> help you?

Customer: Yes, <u>I'd like</u> a hamburger.

Clerk: Okay, one hamburger. <u>Are you </u>want cheese on that?

Customer: No, just plain.

Clerk: What about mayonnaise, mustard, or ketchup?

Customer: Just a little mustard. I <u>no like</u> mayonnaise or ketchup.

Clerk: Will there be <u>anything else</u>?

Customer: Sure, I'd like <u>some</u> french fries.

As you can see, both of these examples assess grammatical (and other) knowledge, but the students are not speaking. In other words, the testing vehicle is not speaking. The vehicle is a more indirect way of assessing speaking.

Scoring

Scoring an indirect assessment is usually easier than scoring a direct assessment. In indirect assessment, it is easy to identify the learner's errors and you only need to calculate the points deducted for the errors. However, it is much more difficult in the case of direct assessment.

Let's consider the previous restaurant example of the student that you interviewed on tape. The directions might say, "You and I are going to have a conversation in a fast-food restaurant. I'm going to begin the conversation. You can say whatever you want. I will continue the conversation based on whatever you tell me. In this conversation, I'm going to be the clerk at Billy's Burger Place. You are a very hungry customer. This is your first time at Billy's, so you do not know the menu so well. Again, you can say whatever you want. This test is not about content. It's about your ability to carry on a conversation. Okay? Ready?"

After the test, you would need to listen to the tape to assess the student in several categories. The clearest way to assess this conversation on several aspects is to use a rubric that clearly delineates your categories, the number of points assigned to that category, and what the points within that category mean.

On the next page is an example of a rubric that could be used for speaking assessment.

The categories, the total point values for each category, and even the scale of point values listed for each rating—for example, excellent = 24–25—is completely up to you, but all of this should be based upon the course objectives, which in turn should match student needs, which in turn should match the way the course was taught. Once again, you can see that assessment is a circular, not a linear, process that must be considered from the very beginning of planning a lesson.

What are the advantages and disadvantages of direct and indirect assessment? The obvious benefit of direct testing is that you are testing the skill in a natural occurrence or use of that skill. If students know they will be tested this way, the test can have a positive washback effect on the students by encouraging them to practice that material in that natural way. An advantage of indirect assessment is that it is generally much easier to score. Listening to original student recordings is extremely time-consuming. In large classes, especially those of 50 to 75 as found in some EFL settings, direct assessment of speaking is impossible, just as direct practice of speaking is sometimes difficult. Thus, which type of test you choose can be influenced not only by the skill being assessed but also by the logistics of the teaching environment.

Speaking Assessment		Name: _____ Date: _____

Category	Your Score	Guide
Grammar 25 points		24–25 *Excellent.* Few errors; communication of ideas is clear.
		22–23 *Very good.* One or two errors, but communication is mostly clear.
		20–21 *Good.* Several errors in syntax, but main ideas are mostly clear.
		18–19 *Fair.* Noticeable errors that occasionally confuse meaning.
		12–17 *Weak.* Language is marked by errors. Listeners' attention is diverted to the errors rather than the message. Meaning is often unclear or broken.
		0–11 *Unacceptable.* Communication is impeded. Too many errors in this task for a student at this level.
Vocabulary 20 points		20 *Excellent.* Correct selection of words and idioms. Variety of vocabulary.
		18–19 *Very good.* Correct selection of words and idioms. Some variety of vocabulary.
		16–17 *Good.* Mostly correct choice of vocabulary. Meaning is clear.
		14–15 *Fair.* Noticeable vocabulary errors that occasionally confuse meaning. Reliance on simple vocabulary to communicate.
		12–13 *Weak.* Many vocabulary errors. Listeners' attention is diverted to the errors rather than the message. Meaning is often unclear or broken.
		0–11 *Unacceptable.* Too many errors in this task for a student at this level. Communication is impeded.
Fluency 30 points		29–30 *Excellent.* No hesitations at all.
		27–28 *Very good.* Hesitations in one or two places but immediately continued.
		24–26 *Good.* Occasional hesitations but recovered well.
		21–23 *Fair.* Noticeable gaps that catch listeners' attention usually followed by recovery.
		12–20 *Weak.* Several short periods of silence. Several gaps that disrupt the flow of information. Listeners' attention is diverted to the gaps rather than the message.
		0–11 *Unacceptable.* Periods of silence. Gaps without good recovery.
Pronunciation 25 points		24–25 *Excellent.* Few errors; native-like pronunciation.
		22–23 *Very good.* One or two errors, but communication is mostly clear.
		20–21 *Good.* Several pronunciation errors, but main ideas are understood without problem.
		18–19 *Fair.* Noticeable pronunciation errors that occasionally confuse meaning.
		12–17 *Weak.* Language is marked by pronunciation errors. Listeners' attention is diverted to the errors rather than the message. Meaning is often unclear.
		0–11 *Unacceptable.* Too many errors in this task for a student at this level. Communication is impeded.

Your score: _____

Comments:

Proficiency Assessment

In proficiency assessment of speaking, we are trying to determine a given student's proficiency level at a point in time. Most likely, this proficiency is being compared to some pre-established norms or targets. Of the numerous professionally prepared proficiency exams that exist, the three that will be discussed here are the TOEFL® iBT, the TSE®, and the IELTS®.

Based on the descriptions of the tasks featured in these three tests, a teacher whose students will take a particular exam should practice material in class that is similar to the content and format of the actual exam. In addition, the teacher should find out more information about how each part of the exam is scored and incorporate this information into the weekly content and exams within the course.

TOEFL®

One of the most well-known proficiency tests is the TOEFL® (Test of English as a Foreign Language). The TOEFL® is taken by thousands of students all over the world, primarily for admission into a tertiary institution in North America. The TOEFL® has undergone several major changes, and the exam now has an extensive speaking section. (The TOEFL® iBT covers reading, writing, listening, and speaking, but for the purposes of this volume, we will focus on the speaking area.)

If your students are preparing to take the TOEFL®, then your curriculum and daily class lesson plans should provide extensive practice of not only the content but also the testing format of this exam. For example, the teacher should know that the speaking section has two kinds of tasks: independent and integrated. Study the information from the website for how *The Michigan Guide to English for Academic Success and Better TOEFL® Test Scores* provides information about the iBT (TOEFL®) (www.press.umich.edu/esl/testprep/michtoefl/).

According to ETS, the tasks on the Speaking section are designed as follows:

Independent

> *Task 1:* Nonacademic topic: personal preference question.
>
> *Task 2:* Nonacademic topic: choice between two contrasting actions.

Integrated

> *Task 3:* Reading of 75–100 words; listening of 60–80 seconds and 150–180 words: Summarize about a campus situation.
>
> *Task 4:* Reading of 75–100 words; listening of 60–90 seconds and 150–220 words: Combine-convey/synthesize on an academic topic.
>
> *Task 5:* Listening of 60–90 seconds and 150–220 words; conversation involving a student and involving a problem; two solutions are presented about a campus situation: Give your opinion about solving a problem; analyze what you heard.
>
> *Task 6:* Listening of 90–120 seconds and 230–250 words; lecture explains a concept and gives two examples on an academic topic: Summarize and synthesize.

TSE®

The TSE® is the Test of Spoken English. According to ETS, the publisher of this and many other commonly used examinations, the TSE® is the most widely used assessment of spoken English in the world. Though the TOEFL® is used primarily as a measure of a learner's academic English, the TSE® is used for many purposes, including school entrance, work assignment, or general proficiency assessment.

The TSE® assesses a non-native speaker's ability to do several real things in English, including the ability to narrate a story, make a recommendation, give and then support an opinion, and persuade another person convincingly. Test-takers have to complete specific speaking tasks such as telling a story, describing a picture or chart, and answering questions about a prompt. The test is recorded and graded afterward.

The tasks on the TSE® are as follows:	
Task 1:	Look at six pictures, and tell a story about each picture.
Task 2:	Answer a question about the pictures.
Task 3:	Describe a graph.
Task 4:	Answer a question about the graph.
Task 5:	Respond to a question about an idea.
Task 6:	Respond to a question about an idea.
Task 7:	Respond to a question while playing the role of someone in a workplace.
Task 8:	Respond to a question while playing the role of someone in a workplace.
Task 9:	Respond to a question while playing the role of someone in a workplace.

For each question, you are allowed a short preparation time (e.g., 30 seconds). You then have 60 seconds to respond to the question or prompt.

Scores can range from 20 to 60 and occur in five-point increments, that is, 20, 25, 30, not 20, 22, 27. A score of 50 means that communication is generally effective and that the tasks were performed competently. Communication was generally not affected by errors (but there were errors). A score of 30 indicates that communication was poor, primarily due to errors that hindered communication.

IELTS®

IELTS® is the International English Language Testing System and is recognized worldwide for its high quality, dependability, and practicality.

The IELTS® consists of four modules: listening, reading, writing, and speaking. All test-takers take the same listening and speaking modules, but test-takers have a choice between academic or general training for the reading and writing modules. For the purposes of this book, we will look at only the speaking module.

The speaking section takes only 14 minutes (compared to 30 for listening, 60 for reading, and 60 for writing). The listening, reading, and writing sections must be done on the same day. At times, the speaking module may be done up to one week later.

The speaking section has three parts. In part one, the test-takers answer general questions about themselves, their home, their family, or other personal topics. This part lasts 4 to 5 minutes.

In part two, test-takers are given a more serious but personal topic to discuss. Both the topic and specific speaking points are given. For example, test-takers may be asked to describe a teacher who most influenced their overall education. They would be asked to comment on where and when they knew the teacher, which subject was taught, and what was special about this teacher. Test-takers are given 1 minute to think about their answers and then 1 to 2 minutes to talk about their most influential teacher.

In part three, the test-taker and tester have a discussion about more abstract topics and issues that are related to the task in part two. For example, here test-takers might be asked to talk about the value of a good teacher, what makes a good teacher, or why they would (or would not) encourage their own children to become teachers one day.

Summary

Assessing speaking is difficult for several reasons. It is difficult because of logistical reasons. If you test speaking directly, then you can only test one or a few students at a time. The test must be taped, and then the assessor must listen in order to score. It is very time-consuming.

Scoring a direct test can be difficult because of the problems inherent in what to count and how many points to assign to each component that you are counting. Does pronunciation count? If so, how do you count it? Do you take one point for each error? This could be fair to someone who has good pronunciation, but it could also be biased toward a person who spoke less and therefore had few errors. How do you count fluency? Do you count words? Should someone who says four words in "He got the answer" receive a lower score than someone who says six words in "He came up with the answer"?

Scoring an indirect test is inherently easier and more reliable (in terms of providing the same score no matter who scores it since it is more objective than a direct test). However, we have to ask ourselves how valid an indirect test of speaking is. Is editing written sentences a good assessment of a learner's ability to produce those sentences? Even if we had proof that it were sufficient, would it be a good assessment of the learner's ability not only to compose the sentence but actually say the sentence—since the assessed skill supposedly is speaking?

Finally, professional proficiency tests such as TOEFL®, TSE®, and IELTS® have their own content, formats, and scoring systems that the teacher and curriculum writer for a course should be aware of. If the students will take the TOEFL®, then the course and the assessment should lead toward the learners' goal of taking the TOEFL®. Tasks should be used to help students achieve their speaking needs, which is of course the goal of any good speaking class.

Appendix A   Ten Things You Should Know about Teaching ESL/EFL Vocabulary

1. Teach Vocabulary

Vocabulary is the most important part of a language. Without words, no meaning can be conveyed. Your students know this. If you have studied a foreign language, you know this as well.

The single most important advice about teaching any foreign language is that you should teach vocabulary. You should deal with vocabulary directly; do not assume that vocabulary growth will somehow happen on its own. In our field, there has been a tendency since the 1970s to minimize the role that vocabulary plays in understanding and speaking a language. Teachers and textbooks have downplayed direct teaching of vocabulary, instead encouraging students to guess words from context. While guessing from context may be helpful as a compensatory strategy in listening and reading, it is 100 percent impossible for learners to guess words from context when they are trying to speak. If learners don't know a word, then they can't produce it.

It is impossible within the scope of an appendix to go into vocabulary teaching in great depth, but if you remember nothing else, remember this: *Teach vocabulary.* It is extremely important in moving the students from their current English level of *i* or interlanguage to the next level of *i + 1* or even *i + 2.* Your students can already function at their current level. Your job is to give them the language and appropriate activities with feedback to move them to the next level. (See *Vocabulary Myths*, Folse [2004], for more detailed information.)

2. What Is a Word in Second Language Study?

A word can be a word in the traditional sense such as *alphabet* or *sneeze*, but a word can include more than just single words. A word can also be an **idiom,** which is a group of words that takes on a new meaning different from the meaning of the individual words. For example, *throw up* is not a combination of *throw* and *up*, and when someone says, *You've let the cat out of the bag now*, there is no cat or bag involved. A word can also be a longer phrase such as, *It has come to our attention that* (+ clause). This whole phrase means that we have just learned about something negative.

3. Which Words Should Be Taught?

The most important rationale for selecting to teach a specific word is that you believe that this word is important in meeting your students' English needs. Their needs could be employment objectives. For example, if you are teaching students who will be engaged in hotel work, they will need to know frequently used hotel room words such as *towels, soap, toilet paper, sink, remote control, ice bucket,* and *make up (the room)*. Words could also be useful for classroom or educational purposes. For example, if you are teaching a reading course in which your students must pass a final standardized exam, then you should teach vocabulary found in the course readings and on the actual exam.

It is important to know which words your students probably already know so you don't teach those words again and so you can build on students' existing knowledge. The problem of not knowing unknown words from previously studied words is common to teachers who are either new to ESL/EFL or teachers who have never taught that proficiency level. One way to improve your ability here is to study not only the current course book that you are to teach from, but also the book in the previous level (grade) and in the subsequent level (grade).

Because class time is at a premium, you don't want to dwell for a long time on words that your students can comprehend easily. You do want to spend time more efficiently on words that your students will find confusing. In an EFL setting, it behooves you to know something about the native language of your students. In an ESL setting with multiple languages, you cannot know a great deal of information about all your students' languages, but you should know something about the languages of the majority of your students. Even in an ESL setting, knowing something about one non-English language may cover more than half the students in your class.

Certain words or pairs of words in English will cause problems because a word in the L1 does not align well with the meaning of the word in English. For example, the English word *know* can be used with people or facts, but in French, you use different words: *connaître* a person and *savoir* a fact. Another example occurs with our two English words for liquids that go on top of food: *sauce* and *dressing*. Many languages use only one word for what in English requires two. A final example is with our two English words that both mean to move liquid from one place to another: *pour* (which is intentional) and *spill* (which is unintentional or accidental). In English, we make a distinction here based on whether the action was intentional or not. Some other languages have only one word that means both of these English words.

False cognates are words that look similar in two languages but have different meanings. False cognates are problematic because the learners already know the form of the word and now have to unlearn the meaning they know from their native language. Here are some examples from various languages:

English Word	False Cognate and Meaning
snack	sunaku (Japanese: a small bar or pub)
actual	actual (Spanish: current)
fair	faire (French: do or make)
page	pagi (Malay: morning)
bait	/bet/ (Arabic: house)

Some words are just confusing in English because we have two similar forms that students have a hard time separating. At the beginning levels, this confusion often results from similar sounding words. For example, beginning students—regardless of their native language—tend to confuse *chicken* and *kitchen.* At higher proficiency levels, however, this confusion is often semantic in nature. For instance, many intermediate or even advanced students confuse *economic* and *economical.*

4. Knowing a Word

What does it mean that learners **know** a word? There are many different levels of knowing a word. Knowing a word includes but is not limited to: (1) the spelling of a word, (2) the frequency of a word, (3) one meaning of a word, (4) multiple meanings of a word (e.g., *story* can be a tale, a building floor, or a lie), (5) the pronunciation of a word, (6) the collocations of a word, (7) the register of a word (e.g., *had better* is used by a higher status person to a lower status person—e.g., a teacher to a student, never vice-versa), or even (8) common errors with that word (e.g., *an economical crisis).

Knowing a word involves learning several levels of information about the word, something that is never accomplished in one single teaching of the word. I often keep in mind that learning a given word is not like a light switch that is either "on" or "off." Instead, it is more like a thermostat that goes up and down until it reaches the desired temperature.

5. Collocations

One of the most important aspects in teaching any new word is teaching its collocations. Collocations are the words that naturally (and frequently) occur with the vocabulary word. For example, *squander,* which means *to not use wisely,* is frequently used with *money, time, chance,* or *opportunity;* it is not so common with other nouns. For example, we would not usually talk about *squandering a book* even though you certainly might have some students who don't use their books wisely.

Common words collocate with many different words. For example, *take* is a common word. Collocation examples for this verb include *take your time, take the bus, take some medicine, take your temperature,* and *take a shower.* In contrast, words that are less frequent in occurrence have a much smaller range of collocations. For instance, a word such as *fight* is often followed by *with* + person, *between* + people, or *for* + objective.

6. Practicing Vocabulary: Number of Retrievals

There are many ways to practice vocabulary. The most important feature of any vocabulary practice—regardless of the actual activity—is the number of times that a student has to retrieve the meaning of the word or actually use the word in the activity. Therefore, you should choose tasks that require students to have multiple counters with your target words.

In a good ranking activity (e.g., pp. 131–133), students have to use the words repeatedly. If your target words are *sofa, computer, telephone, microwave oven, refrigerator, toaster, vase, painting, need,* and *don't need,* you could have students choose the three items that a newly married couple with a limited budget really need. In ranking these items, students are likely to mention any item more than one time. Consider this discussion about this ranking activity:

Student A:	They need a *sofa* (#1).
Student B:	No, they don't need a *sofa* (#2) because you can live without a *sofa* (#3). They need a *telephone* (#1).
Student C:	Yeah, I agree. A *telephone* (#2) is more important than a *sofa* (#3), right?
Student A:	Everyone needs to sit down after working all day. They can sit on a *sofa* (#4). For a long time, people didn't have a *telephone* (#3), but even my grandparents had a *sofa* (#5). They didn't have a *telephone* (#4).

7. Word Lists and Student Vocabulary Notebooks

Contrary to what you may have heard in your methods class, word lists are not bad. Word lists may be boring and overly simplistic at times, but there is no evidence to show that word lists are ineffective or detrimental. In fact, some students, perhaps because of educational training in their home country or simply individual learning styles, prefer to learn from lists.

Make students create and maintain their own lists of vocabulary. I require my students to have a vocabulary notebook. I encourage them to write down as many new vocabulary items as they can. I encourage them to keep this notebook as neat and organized as possible because learners are much more likely to review information that is easy to access and comprehend than information that is sloppily recorded. If learners don't frequently review from their notebook, then the action of keeping a notebook is futile. The purpose is to increase learners' retrieval of new vocabulary.

8. Use the Board

People are more likely to remember what they hear and see than what they just hear. When a new word that is worth learning (because it furthers students' English language goals) comes up in class, write it on the board. When I teach, I try to keep one area of the board set aside where I neatly write new vocabulary—including words, idioms, and phrases.

Students need you to model which words are worth learning. When you write something on the board, students are more likely to write that information down as well. When you use new, unknown vocabulary in class, students will probably not catch the new word, so they certainly can't write it down. In addition, students are counting on you to help them learn vocabulary that is appropriate for their proficiency level and that will help increase their English proficiency.

9. Short Vocabulary Drills

I usually maintain a list of new vocabulary on the board, and I frequently stop class for no more than 60 seconds to review this vocabulary. This review consists of a series of short, rapid questions about the vocabulary.

Imagine we have this list on the board after a discussion about an international war: *squander, territory, equator, colony, tiny, neutral, battle, spread, break out, isolated.* From this list, I could ask these questions: (1) Which word is the opposite of huge? (2) Which word means "in the middle of two opinions"? (3) Which word means "to begin"? (4) Which word is a line around the middle of the earth? (5) Which word comes before the words *an opportunity*? (6) Which word appears last in the dictionary? (7) Which word is hardest for you to remember? (8) Which word begins with a vowel?

These questions practice (or test) students' vocabulary knowledge on several different levels of thinking skills. Questions 1, 2, 3, and 4 practice recall of meaning. Question 5 practices collocation. Questions 6 and 8 practice form or spelling. Question 7 practices synthesis of meaning but at an individual level. You may not recognize the value of Question 7, but as students answer this question, they actually look through the list of ten words, think of the word and its meaning, and then rank the words in terms of difficulty of remembering. This action requires the learner to retrieve each word at least once and some words multiple times. Thus, the answer to Question 7 is not nearly as important as the students' mental process in reaching the answer. (However, students' answers to Question 7 are important to you as you plan which words to review more frequently in subsequent practices. The words that students answer for this question are the words that you should intentionally recycle more frequently.)

10. Test Vocabulary

Learners in a classroom will study whatever they believe might be on a future test. If you never test or include vocabulary, then learners will not focus on vocabulary. It is important for you to include vocabulary in all the quizzes and tests in your course. The format of the test is not nearly as important as the fact that students know that you are holding them accountable for learning new vocabulary.

In some conversation classes, teachers do not give examinations of any kind. In these classes, however, teachers are probably giving some kind of feedback regarding students' progress that the teacher has noted in the students' participation in class conversations. It is important for the teacher to note vocabulary in this feedback.

Appendix B   Twelve Things You Should Know about Teaching ESL/EFL Pronunciation

Note: This appendix uses the International Phonetic Alphabet (IPA), which may be new to some readers. The example words can assist readers who are not familiar with IPA.

1. Consonants

You need to know the consonant sounds that are problematic for your ESL/EFL learners. Consonant sounds differ in three distinguishing features—manner of articulation, place of articulation, and voicing. For example, in this abbreviated chart of these three characteristics for some of the English consonant sounds, you can see that /p/ and /b/ are both plosives (i.e., same manner of articulation) and made with both lips, or bilabial (place of articulation). The main difference between these two sounds is that /b/ is voiced—that is, your vocal cords vibrate when making this sound—while /p/ is voiceless. (Consult linguistics books or websites for additional information about the rest of the consonant sounds in English.)

Consonant Sound	Manner	Place	Voicing
/b/	plosive	bilabial	voiced
/p/	plosive	bilabial	voiceless
/d/	plosive	alveolar ridge	voiced
/t/	plosive	alveolar ridge	voiceless
/z/	fricative	alveolar ridge	voiced
/s/	fricative	alveolar ridge	voiceless

2. Vowels

You need to know the vowel sounds that are problematic for your ESL/ EFL learners. In most dialects of American English, there are fourteen vowel sounds. These vowel sounds differ in location within the mouth: high, middle, or low, and front, central, or back. For example, the sound /i/ as in *we* is high and front. In addition, the mouth can be rounded for some vowels (e.g., /o/) or not rounded (e.g., /i/).

Here are some examples for the fourteen vowel sounds in most dialects of American English. (Consult linguistics books or websites for additional information about vowel sounds.)

Vowel Sound	Examples
i	beat, we, need
I	sick, w<u>o</u>men
e	bay, cake, rain
ɛ	pet, said, head
æ	cat, nap
a	hot, not
u	boot, pool
o	hope, goat, no
ɔ	lawn, caught, thought
ə	cup, <u>a</u>bout, sof<u>a</u>
ʊ	put, could, book
aɪ	like, ice, mind
au	house, now, brown
ɔɪ	boy, coin

3. Your Students' Native Language Sound Inventory

Speakers of certain first languages have problems with specific sounds in English because one or both of the consonant pairs do not exist. For instance, there is no /š/ in Spanish, so Spanish speakers substitute /č/ and say *cheese* for *she's.* A less serious student error can also occur because the student's native language has the same general sound but is pronounced differently in the native language—e.g., the manner or the place of articulation is different. An example is that /t/ and /p/ in English at the beginning of words are clearly aspirated, as in *Thomas* and *Pablo,* but in Spanish the /t/ and /p/ sounds are not aspirated. (Ask a Spanish speaker and an English speaker to pronounce these two names, and you will hear the difference in the aspiration or lack thereof for these two consonant sounds.)

It is important to note that while a particular sound may be difficult for speakers of a certain L1, that same sound may be particularly difficult in a certain position within a word (but not elsewhere). For example, the sound /ŋ/ in English is easy in the middle of a word *(hanged)* or at the end of a word *(thing),* but it is difficult at the beginning of a word. (No examples exist in English though some African languages have words beginning with this sound.) Another examples occurs with /t/ in American English. Spanish speakers, for example, will have a relatively easy time with /t/ at the beginning of a word (e.g., *team* or *ten*) but a much more difficult with /t/ in the middle of a word (e.g., *water* or *wanted*) because the /t/ is not the same.

Problems for Spanish speakers learning English:
   /v/ (which they confuse with /b/)
   /š/ (which they confuse with /č/)
   /ǰ/ (which they confuse with /y/)

Problems for Japanese speakers learning English:
   /š/ (which they confuse with /s/)
   /f/ (which they confuse with /h/)

Problems for Japanese and Chinese speakers learning English:
   /r/ (which they confuse with /l/)

Problems for Arabic speakers learning English:
   /p/ (which they confuse with /b/)

Problems for Korean speakers learning English:
   /p/ (which they confuse with /f/)

Problems for French speakers learning English:
  /θ/ (e.g., _think_) or /ð/ (e.g., _this_) (which they confuse with /z/)

Problems for many different L1s learning English:
  /ae/ (which they confuse with /ah/)
  /ɪ/ (which they confuse with /i/)
  /ɛ/ (which they confuse with /e/)
  /θ/ (which they confuse with /s/ or /z/ or /d/)
  /ð/ (which they confuse with /d/)
  /ə/ (which they confuse with /ʊ/ or /o/ or /u/)
  /ɔ/ (which they confuse with /au/ or /o/ or /ə/)
  /r/ (which they may confuse with /l/ or with /h/ or with /w/)

4. Minimal Pairs

  A common technique for practicing difficult sounds involves using minimal pairs. A minimal pair is two words that differ in only one _phoneme,_ or sound.

/b/ – /p/	bear – pair	lab–lap
/v/ – /f/	veal – feel	have – half
/g/ – /k/	goat – coat	bag – back
/l/ – /r/	law – raw	feel – fear
/d/ – /t/	dead – Ted	dead – debt
/i/ – /ɪ/	eel – ill	feel – fill
/o/ – /a/	note – not	goat – got
/u/ – /ʊ/	pool – pull	fool – full
/ǰ/ – /š/	Joe – show	jeep – sheep

  With minimal pairs, it is important to use example words that not only illustrate the pronunciation contrast but are useful and relevant to your students. Some books will illustrate /θ/ and /ð/ with the words _thigh_ and _thy._ Many teachers may not want to demonstrate _thigh,_ and unless your students are studying Shakespeare or the King James Version of the Bible, *thy* is also a useless word. You may tell your adult students that these word pairs are for pronunciation practice only, but adult students will want to know what the words mean. Your adult students will be disappointed to find out that you are teaching non-conversation English in their English conversation class. Remember students' needs and try to select minimal pair examples accordingly.

5. The Amazing Range of English Vowels

Many of your students speak languages with far fewer vowel sounds than English. Spanish and Japanese, for example, do not have /æ/, /ɪ/, or the /ə/, among others. To illustrate the range of English vowels, it would be helpful to have a list of words that differ only in the vowel sound.

It is difficult to come up with 14 words that will illustrate the 14 English vowel sounds. The words should illustrate the vowel sounds and be pertinent to your students' language needs. The best list of such words that I know of involves /b/ + vowel + /t/.

Vowel Sound	Example of /b/ + vowel + /t/
i	beat
I	bit
e	bait
ɛ	bet
æ	bat
a	baht (Thai currency)
u	boot
o	boat
ɔ	bought
ə	but
ʊ	put (There is not one for /b/.)
aɪ	bite
au	bout (as in an illness: a bout of the flu)
ɔɪ	boy (There is not one with /t/ for this pattern.)

6. Pronouncing the Morpheme –*s*

In English, we use –*s* to mark plural of nouns (e.g., *cat, cats*) and to make third person singular of a verb (e.g., *I need, he needs*). This –*s* morpheme, or form, is sometimes spelled –*es*, but this variation involves spelling more than speaking.

This –*s* morpheme can be pronounced three ways in English: /s/, /z/, /ɪz/ (or /əz/). Words that end in a voiced sound are followed by /z/, words that finish in a voiceless sound are followed by /s/, and words that finish in /s/, /z/, /č/, /š/, or /ǰ/ are followed by a new syllable /ɪz/.

Ending Sound	Add This Sound	Examples
voiced /d/, /v/, /g/, /b/, /ð/, /l/, /m/, /n/, /ŋ/, /r/, all vowels	/z/	*beds, loves, bags*
voiceless /t/, /f/, /k/, /p/, /θ/	/s/	*bets, laughs, socks*
other /s/, /z/, /č/, /š/, /ǰ/	/ɪz/	*Bess's, raises, watches*

7. Pronouncing the Morpheme –*ed*

In English, we use –*ed* to mark past tense (e.g., *robbed, wrapped, needed*) and to form past participles, which can be used as verb forms or adjectives (e.g., *the book inspired the audience; the inspired actor*).

This –*ed* morpheme can be pronounced three ways in English: /t/, /d/, /ɪd/ (or /əd/). Words that end in a voiced sound are followed by /d/, words that finish in a voiceless sound are followed by /t/, and words that finish in /d/ or /t/ are followed by a new syllable /ɪd/.

Sometimes the best way to help students hear these three differences is to put an example word in a phrase in which the next word begins with a vowel. By doing this, the final ending liaises with the beginning vowel sound of the subsequent word as in these examples: *He bagged all of the cans. He backed up the car.* In the first example, *bagged all* produces the sounds of the word *doll* while *backed up* produces the sounds of the word *cup*.

Ending Sound	Add This Sound	Examples
<u>voiced</u> /z/, /v/, /g/, /b/, /ð/, /l/, /m/, /n/, /ŋ/, /r/, all vowels	/z/	*raised, loved, bagged*
<u>voiceless</u> /s/, /f/, /k/, /p/, /θ/, /č/, /š/	/s/	*voiced, laughed, backed*
<u>other</u> /d/, /t/	/ɪd/	*needed, wanted*

8. Twisters

Another common technique involves tongue twisters or phrases that focus on specific problematic sounds. If you check the Internet, you can easily find many of these useful sentences and short poems.

/s/– /š/   She sells seashells by the seashore.

/l/ - /r/   A small black bug bled bright red blood on some
              blueberry bread.

/p/   Peter Piper picked a peck of pickled peppers.

vowels: Betty Botter bought some butter,
              but she said, "The butter is bitter.
              If I put it in my batter,
              it will make my batter bitter."
              Then Betty Botter bought some better butter
              and put the better butter in her batter.
              The better butter made her bitter batter better.

9. Beyond the Phoneme: Reductions

Besides pronunciation problems at the phoneme, or single sound, level, your students may have problems with stress patterns. In many languages, stressing a syllable does not affect the surrounding syllables. In English, however, when we stress a syllable, we often reduce the surrounding syllables by substituting schwa for the vowel in that syllable.

A quick check of any dictionary will prove that schwa is one of the most common vowel sounds on any page. For example, the word *devélop* has three syllables, with the second one stressed. We pronounce the *e* in the first syllable and the *o* in the third syllable as /ə/. Our ESL students, in contrast, will often pronounce three full syllables with an /e/, /e/, and /o/. When they speak, this lack of vowel reduction to schwa produces a foreign accent. When they listen, if they hear words in longer phrases, they may take a longer time to process what they have heard since they do not associate schwa with reduced syllables yet.

Have students practice reductions in naturally occurring common phrases:

Full Phrase		Reduced Form
He's going to call you later.	=	He's gonna call you later.
I want to eat now.	=	I wanna eat now.
You have a new car, don't you?	=	You have a new car, dontya?
You have a new car, don't you?	=	You have a new car, doncha?
Where's he living?	=	Wherez e living?

10. Syllable Stress

Sometimes the stress on a certain syllable can alter the meaning of a group of phonemes. For example, *a présent* is not the same as *to presént. An óbject* is not the same as *to objéct.*

One common error in ESL/EFL English occurs when students want to use *can* in the affirmative. The modal *can* before a verb is not stressed in normal sentences. In contrast, in the negative, both the modal *can't* and the verb that follows it are stressed. Notice that in the affirmative, the subject plus *can* are pronounced as one word with stress on the first syllable: *I can* becomes *Ícan* and *She can* becomes *Shécan.*

Affirmative	Negative
Í can gó with yóu.	Í can't gó with yóu.
Shé can drive her cár.	Shé can't drive her cár there.
Shé said shé can drive her cár.	Shé said shé can't drive her cár there.

Another error is with articles and prepositions, which are rarely stressed. Notice how the content words (i.e., nouns, verbs, adjectives) are stressed while the articles and prepositions are often assimilated with their surrounding words.

ESL student: "I'm going to the meeting in the morning by bus. Can you go with me?

Native speaker: "I'm going to the meeting in the morning by bus. Can you go with me?

11. Impact of Reductions and Accenting on Student Listening

If students do not know about patterns of reduction or accenting in English, they will have a more difficult time with listening comprehension. Non-native speakers frequently misunderstand native speakers' use of *can* and *can't* in conversations. Non-natives can understand the negative form because it is stressed; however, they are often confused by the affirmative because they don't know whether the native speaker is saying yes or no. (ESL teachers often exaggerate affirmative *can*—i.e., they unnaturally stress it in class to produce comprehensible input. Unfortunately, native speakers who are not teachers do not stress this form, which of course leads to confusion for our learners.)

There are many good pronunciation books and Internet sites that can inform you about some of these patterns. The good news is that this information is very teachable, and your students will appreciate your help.

12. Correcting Errors

Only a small handful of your learners will have a "perfect" native-like accent. Your learners' goal should be to achieve an English that is totally comprehensible to English speakers. Thus, errors should be corrected when they impede communication.

Most adult learners, based on student surveys and on my own teaching experience, want to be corrected. Your job is to figure out which pronunciation errors are worth correcting and at what point. For example, Japanese speakers have a problem with /l/ and /r/. This problem is not worth much teacher or student time at the early stages. Instead, much more time should be devoted to vocabulary development. To be sure, you can bring in some minimal pair drills or other practices, but neither you nor your students should expect mastery of these two phonemes early in their English studies.

It is difficult to generalize here by saying that you should always or never do something, but I would venture to say that you should rarely correct any individual student about an individual error unless it prevents communication. Instead, after several people have spoken or given answers to a discussion task, you should go to the board to point out two or three common errors. Say something general but to the point, "I heard these phrases. [Write *Turn to the light* and *He was vely late* on the board.] Can someone tell me what the problem is?"

Good teachers know that our job is to teach, not just correct. Correcting an error involves more than just pointing out the problem. In fact, when you point out this kind of problem, most of your students will be able to identify it. They just can't produce the correct sound or stress yet.

At this point, you should be able to go to the board and write a simple minimal pair drill on the board:

1	2
light	right
late	rate
eel	ear
boring	bowling
lead	read
deal	deer

A skillful, experienced teacher can not only come up with a list of pertinent (in both phonemes and meaning) words, but also perform three or four short practice exercises with the class. For example, you might have students listen to you as you read all of Column 1, all of Column 2, and then the pairs from 1 and then 2 (e.g., *light/right, late/rate,* etc.). After this, you might have the students say the words with you in that same order. Then you might have students say the words after you in that same order. For student production without you, you could divide the room into two groups, with one group saying 1 and the other group saying 2. Then reverse the roles.

Appendix C   The Role of Grammar in Teaching ESL/EFL Speaking

As learners begin to construct utterances in English, they need three basic kinds of information: knowledge of words, or **vocabulary;** knowledge of how those words are pronounced, or **pronunciation;** and knowledge of how to put those words in a sequence that conveys the speaker's meaning, or **grammar.**

Although grammar has been at the forefront of ESL and foreign language education for decades, knowledge of grammar is not nearly as important in conversation as knowing vocabulary, including a word's pronunciation. However, this is not to say that grammar is trivial. Far from it, knowledge of grammar structures is very important in expressing ideas accurately. Insufficient vocabulary can prevent communication; insufficient grammar can interfere with communication. Learners need a solid knowledge of grammatical structures to move from their current proficiency level to a higher level.

A teacher of ESL speaking needs to know six areas regarding ESL grammar: (1) ESL grammar points, (2) how much information to teach and when to hold back information about a grammar point, (3) the necessity of errors in the language learning process, (4) which grammar errors are common according to the students' proficiency level, (5) which grammar errors are more likely according to the students' L1, and (6) how to deal with grammar errors in speaking.

1. ESL Grammar Points

You need to know ESL/EFL grammar structures. ESL/EFL grammar structures are not the same items of grammar that native speakers of English learn in school.

Perhaps you have studied Spanish (or other languages in which nouns have gender). English-speaking students of Spanish spend many frustrating hours trying to remember whether *libro* (book) and *casa* (house) are masculine or feminine. In Spanish, *libro* is masculine, so you use the definite article to say *el libro*, but *casa* is feminine, so you use a different definite article to say *la casa*. This distinction drives English-speaking adults crazy but is mastered by Spanish-speaking children as young as three or four. Thus, learning *el* and *la* is a structure for Spanish as a Second Language that is not "learned" in a classroom by Spanish-speaking adults.

By the same token, English speakers know that *another* is used with a singular noun (e.g., *another book*), *other* is used with a plural noun (e.g., *other books*), and *others* is used without a plural noun (e.g., *others*). Many ESL students, however, have a very hard time with these words and frequently say, "I have other book" or "I have others books," which are errors that a native speaker of English, even as young as three or four, would never make. Thus, "grammar" for second language learners is not the same thing as grammar for native speakers of that language.

I am including here a list of common ESL/EFL grammar points in a rather loose hierarchical level according to the proficiency level at which ESL/EFL learners usually begin to study these structures. This is not to say that learners cannot or should not learn these points in a different order. Though representative of many if not most ESL grammar or course books, this list is from *Clear Grammar*, a four-book ESL/EFL grammar series: beginner to high-beginner proficiency (*Clear Grammar 1*, Folse, 1998), high-beginner to low-intermediate proficiency (*Clear Grammar 2*, Folse, 1998), low-intermediate to intermediate proficiency (*Clear Grammar 3*, Folse, 1999); intermediate to low-advanced proficiency (*Clear Grammar 4*, Folse, 2003).

Beginner/High-Beginner Proficiency Level
present tense of *be*
present tense of regular verbs
demonstratives (*this, that, these, those*)
possessive adjectives (*my, your,* etc.)
past tense of *be*
past tense of regular and irregular verbs
wh- questions
basic word order
present progressive tense
count versus noncount
prepositions

High-Beginner/Low-Intermediate Proficiency Level
articles
be going to + VERBS
irregular past tense
how questions
adverbs of frequency
object pronouns
one and *other*
possessive
comparative and superlative
modals
problem words

Low-Intermediate to Intermediate Proficiency Level
phrasal verbs
past progressive tense
present perfect tense
adverbs of manner (*-ly / by / with*) and related terms
prepositions after verbs and adjectives
passive voice
relative clauses
infinitives and gerunds
connectors

Intermediate to Low-Advanced Proficiency Level
    past perfect tense
    word forms
    conditionals: *if* clauses and *wish*
    adverb clauses
    noun clauses
    reduction of clauses
    past modals
    subject-verb agreement

Each of these grammar points includes many subpoints. For example, for the present progressive tense, you should know that the form of this tense is composed of the present tense of the verb *be* and the present participle (i.e., *-ing* form) of a verb. The form of *be* must match the subject (e.g., *I am*, not: *I are*). You should know the spelling rules for when to double the final consonant in a verb (e.g., *hop* ➔ *hopping*) and when not to do so (e.g., *hope* ➔ *hoping; sweep* ➔ *sweeping*). You should know that the function of the present progressive is to express a current action. Present progressive often occurs in sentences with the time adverbials *now, right now, today,* or *this* _____. You should know that some verbs are not used in present progressive because they express a state rather than an action, e.g., *own, have, possess, think, want.* We do not say "I am wanting this sandwich" or "They have owning a new car." Some verbs can express both action and state; when they express action, they can be in present progressive (e.g., "I am having a good time"), but when they express state, they should be in simple present (e.g., "I have a car"). Being able to teach speaking well entails knowing not only the grammar points but also the subpoints for each grammar point.

2. Limiting How Much Information You Teach about a Grammar Point

One of the most difficult aspects of grammar to master is knowing how to tailor the amount of information to teach about a grammar point based on a student's proficiency level or current needs. Let us consider present progressive again. For beginning level students, it may suffice to teach the basic form of *be* + VERB-*ing*. It would be information overload to go much beyond that the first time you teach this grammar point.

A good example of information to withhold, especially during the initial teacher presentation, is the fact that present progressive, which by name and by definition is used for a current action, can also be used for a future time. In response to *Can you play tennis next Friday?* someone might reply, *No, I can't do that because I'm taking my kids to the beach on Friday.* Notice that the present progressive tense *I'm taking* is used for future time. This is common in conversation, but this usage would certainly be confusing to students at the beginning or even low-intermediate level. This information should be introduced later on when students are better equipped to assimilate the nuances of this aspect of this grammar point.

In a grammar class, you might be tempted to teach a great deal about each grammar point. In a speaking class, teach only what is relevant to the speaking goal and the students' proficiency level. If you want to teach students how to express their ideas in the future, you have three options: (1) *will*, (2) *be going to* + VERB, and (3) the present progressive tense. Although many students are familiar with *will*, this modal is not the most usual way to express future time. In conversation especially, *be going to* and the present progressive are the most common ways to express future time, so these two should be taught and practiced before *will*.

3. The Necessary Role of Errors in the Language Learning Process

Though many students (and some teachers) believe that errors indicate a lack of understanding, errors are a necessary part of learning a language. Without errors, there can be no growth. It is through errors that our students can sharpen their skills, test out hypotheses about the language, and eventually express their ideas accurately and appropriately.

Errors are necessary. Errors are good because errors indicate that learners are indeed trying out the language. Errors indicate that learners are attempting to stretch their interlanguage. If learners play it safely by using their limited knowledge of English to express their ideas, they will not make any mistakes, but this also means that their English will not grow as their interlanguage levels off or even fossilizes.

4. Errors by Students' Proficiency Level

Many errors are representative of a learner's proficiency level. Beginners often insert *be* in many verb phrases: **I am speak English and French.* Intermediate students are able to use many different verb tenses in their speech, but the present perfect tense continues to cause problems: **I have lived in Ohio in 2003.* Students of all levels, up to advanced even, still make numerous errors with prepositions: *Cecilia was born at Miami on June 1981.* Prepositions are, in fact, one of the most (if not <u>the</u> most) difficult ESL/EFL grammar points to master.

You will become more familiar with errors associated with certain proficiency levels as you gain experience teaching. If you are in a practice teaching setting now, you should volunteer with students from different levels to help you see which errors are more associated with certain proficiency levels.

5. Errors by Students' Native Language

One source of grammar errors is a learner's native language. Arabic, for example, has no indefinite articles, and the definite article in Arabic works somewhat differently than in English. Thus, it is not surprising that Arabic speakers say, *I have book* or *The honesty is important.* In Spanish and French, *have* is used with certain expressions that would use *be* in English, e.g., *They had hungry* or *She has twenty years old.*

The study of the differences between two languages is called contrastive analysis. While contrastive analysis can be used to explain errors, it is not so accurate at predicting errors. In Spanish, for example, negation is quite simple. You put *no* in front of any verb. The Spanish word *no* looks just like our English negatives *no* or *not.* Negation in Japanese, in contrast, involves infixes, that is, a negative form placed inside of words such as verbs and adjectives. (Yes, there is actually a negative form of adjectives, which are sometimes referred to as adjectival verbs. In Japanese, *atsui* means "hot" and *atsukunai* means "not hot.")

Based on contrastive analysis, we would predict that Japanese speakers would have a much harder time than Spanish speakers would with English negation, which is quite complex (e.g., *I am not hungry, I don't like tea, I can't sing, I didn't go*). Oddly enough, the opposite is true. After a relatively short time, Japanese learners acquire English negation and make few(er) mistakes. Spanish speakers, in contrast, continue to insert *no* before verbs even at the intermediate level (e.g., **I no have studied*). Sometimes the similarity, not the difference, between two languages can be a source of errors.

How can teachers learn about the errors that are more common among certain language groups? The more student papers you read and the more you interact with students of a certain language group, the faster you will become familiar with that group's errors. A highly recommended source of excellent information about learners' errors by native language is *Learner English: A Teacher's Guide to Interference and Other Problems* (Smith & Swan, 2001).

6. Dealing with Grammar Errors in Learners' Speech

As with most errors, you should correct grammar errors when they interfere with meaning. This also includes an error that makes the learner look less educated or less knowledgeable about his or her subject. For example, if a learner says, *I don't have no cell phone* during an interview, the meaning of the message—i.e., the lack of a cell phone—is clear; however, that learner will come across as uneducated because double negatives in English are often used by uneducated people. Therefore, this error needs to be pointed out to the learner.

During a speaking class, I would recommend a group correction in which you point out to the entire group a short list (perhaps three items) that almost everyone had problems with. You should be able to come up with a short drill based on students' errors. Your main goal is to help students be able to see the gap between what they say and what they should be saying.

Appendix D   Samples of Successful Lesson Plans

Learners in conversation classes expect to talk. They expect the teacher to have activities prepared, and they expect the teacher to be able to run the class smoothly. Classroom management problems are much less likely in a class that has been well planned. Children expect lots of fun activities that will make the class fun. Adults like fun classes, too, but they expect activities that engage them in speaking and at times overtly practice language—what they often call "grammar" or "vocabulary." Both children and adults can easily tell the difference between when a teacher has planned the class and when a teacher is just attending the class.

Every teacher has a lesson plan. Some teachers want every detail written down, including the name of the book, the page number, the number of expected minutes, and even the names of which students they should call on first. In sharp contrast, other teachers can function just as well with a small note card with four or five things written on it. What is important here is not the format of the plan; what is important is the contents of the plan.

In my early years of teaching, especially when I was doing my supervised intern (i.e., practice) teaching, I had to follow my senior teacher's format for lesson plans to the letter. I remember that template as being rather detailed and actually tedious, but it made me learn how to do a comprehensive lesson plan. At that point in my teaching career, I needed the guidance that such a detailed template required. Now, years later, my lesson plans resemble a shopping list more than the detailed format from those beginning years, but this matches my teaching style at this point in my career. For example, I know how to put students into the right size small groups with the right partners. I no longer need to write a step that says "Put students in groups," but I remember a time when I was nervous in front of my classes and felt comforted by having everything spelled out.

There are as many formats to a lesson plan as there are teachers. In general, novice teachers tend to want detailed plans, while experienced teachers tend to use less detailed, more general notes. Again, this dichotomy is certainly not set in stone.

What can a lesson plan include? At a minimum, the plan should list the activities that will be done in the class. On the other hand, a very detailed lesson plan might include any/all of the following:

✓ Teacher's name

✓ Date / Class period or time

✓ Materials needed (textbook, workbook, worksheets, cassette, video, DVD)

✓ Equipment needed (VCR, computer, DVD player, red markers, scissors)

✓ Objectives or Goals (usually two or three)

✓ Steps (a numbered list of exactly what to do in the class; the number of steps will vary)

✓ Homework (assignments to follow up on the class content; websites if available)

✓ Notes (reminders to call on a certain student, remind students about something)

The following three lesson plans were developed by two experienced teachers, Valerie Mann-Grosso and Monica Allison, who were graduate students in my ESOL Practicum course at the University of Central Florida. One teacher had a few years of experience with adult ESL and EFL. The other teacher, who had been an ESL student herself, was a third-grade teacher who had only a few ESL students in her classes. They team-taught a group of fifteen adult ESL learners from a variety of countries in a free English conversation class that met for one hour, one night a week.

Valerie and Monica wrote these lesson plans based on their knowledge of ESL/EFL, their experience teaching, and their familiarity with the students in their conversation class. I observed these three classes; everything went very smoothly. In fact, the students applauded after the class on "White Lies" (Example Lesson Plan 1, p. 255). Part of the success of these classes was due to the teachers' ability to take an idea or task and modify it to fit their own students' needs.

Good teachers constantly modify activities that they have seen in teacher preparation books and at presentations at teacher conferences. In the White Lies lesson, for example, the teachers' original idea was to have an open discussion comparing lying in different cultures. However, to make the activity more concrete, they took the scale from a ranking activity in an "ideas book" and adapted it to apply to their topic of lying and white lies. You should never reject a teaching idea without considering if perhaps at least one aspect of the activity could be useful to you.

As you look at these plans, consider which aspects seem important to you as you figure out what *your* lesson plan will look like. *Remember:* It is *your* lesson plan, so make sure that whatever format you adopt works for *you*.

Example Lesson Plan 1
(Monica Allison and Valerie Mann-Grosso)

Objectives

1. Students will become familiar with the concept of a *white lie*. Students will be able to discriminate between *white lies* and *lies*.

2. Students will compare and discuss cultural differences regarding lies and white lies.

Materials

Four sets of eight lie cards.

Procedures

1. Opening statement to attract students' attention on the topic: "What do you call it when someone does not tell the truth? Right, it's a lie. Now I'm going to tell you two situations, and you tell me if they have terrible consequences or not."

   Situation 1. Your friend got a haircut, and it doesn't look too good, but you tell her, "Wow, that's a nice haircut." (Wait for student answers.)

   Situation 2. Your friend wants a job at your company, but she doesn't have much experience. You tell your boss that your friend has a lot of good experience, and she gets the job. (Wait for student answers.)

   Can you see any difference between these two situations?

2. After the students agree on which one of the two lies is worse, write the term *white lie* on the board, and explain to the students what it means to tell a white lie. Ask students for other contrastive examples.

3. Write a scale between 1 and 5 on the board. By each number, write the corresponding words: (1) not terrible, (2) somehow bad, (3) bad, (4) very bad, (5) terrible.

4. Put students into small groups of three to four.

5. Distribute the "lie" cards, which are small cards with one line written on each. Have students read the cards aloud individually and then work as a group to rank each lie from 1 to 5.

6. After 15 minutes, bring the class together again and discuss each of the eight lie cards.

7. Time permitting, have students discuss any cultural differences regarding lies and white lies they have noticed.

Homework

Have each student write an example of a white lie that he or she has told. Explain not only the lie but when, where, to whom, and why he or she told the lie.

(Each card should be written out on a separate card.)

Lie Card #1

You told your future mother-in-law that you are a lawyer. Actually, you work at a gas station.

===

Lie Card #2

You told your supervisor that your son was sick and you needed to stay home to take care of him. Actually, your child was not sick. You just needed a day away from the office.

===

Lie Card #3

You told your tennis partner that she is improving. Actually, her game is the same as it was when you started playing more than a year ago.

===

Lie Card #4

You are home. Someone telephones for your wife, but when you are on the phone, she whispers to you that she is not home, so you tell the caller that your wife is not home.

===

Lie Card #5

You find a ring in the sink area in a restaurant restroom. You tell your friend that someone gave you the ring.

===

Lie Card #6

Your four-year-old daughter asks you if there really is a Santa Claus because her friends told her that Santa Claus did not exist. You don't want to upset her, so you tell her that Santa Claus is real. You assure her that her friends are troublemakers.

===

Lie Card #7

A friend invites you over for dinner, but she doesn't cook very well. You say that you and your husband already have dinner plans.

===

Lie Card #8

A question on a job application asks if you have ever been arrested or received a ticket. You say no, but you got a traffic ticket about five years ago.

===

Example Lesson Plan 2
(Monica Allison and Valerie Mann-Grosso)

Objectives

1. Students will improve their vocabulary of shopping-related topics.
2. Students will understand and apply knowledge of common procedures associated with warranties and procedures to return items.

Materials

Worksheet: Vocabulary Words; Worksheet: Warranty Sheet.

Procedures

1. Opening statement to attract students' attention on the topic: Let's talk about something exciting: shopping! What do women like to shop for? (Students answer: clothes, shoes.) What do men like to shop for? (Students answer: computers, cars.) Now let's brainstorm. (Teacher writes the word *shopping* on the board; students are asked to say words associated with the word *shopping*.) Make sure all students understand the words written on the board.

2. Give students the vocabulary worksheet. (Depending on time, have students do the entire sheet or maybe just part of it.) Pair each student with a partner. Ask them to provide a definition to those words in writing. (Give 5 minutes.) Teacher monitors students.

3. Next, divide the class in two groups: Group A will choose a word from the vocabulary worksheet, and Group B will have to provide the definition. The teacher writes the definition provided by students on the board.

4. Next activity: Teacher introduces the concept of warranty (e.g., what happens when you buy an item and it is defective?). Then ask one student to read the warranty sheet. Go over vocabulary items in this writing material that could be new to students. Ask another student to read the questions. Pair students and ask them to answer to the questions in writing. (Give 5 minutes.) Teachers monitor students.

5. Choose a student to take the role of the teacher. He or she will read one of the questions and choose another student to come up with the answer. Do this until all questions have been covered.

6. Ending statement: Today we have been working on improving our vocabulary knowledge on shopping, and we have learned how to read and understand a warranty policy.

Homework

Students should review the vocabulary on the worksheets.

Worksheet: Vocabulary Words

1. Damaged
2. Defects
3. Date of purchase
4. Guaranteed
5. Instruction booklet
6. Manufacturer
7. Merchandise
8. A period of time

9. Repairperson
10. To assume responsibility
11. To service
12. Warranty
13. Under warranty
14. Shipping
15. Handling
16. One-way shipping and handling

Worksheet: Warranty Sheet

This Mann, Inc. DVD Player model XYZ is guaranteed for normal household use for original manufacturing or material defects for a period of six months after date of purchase. For services, this product must be sent to a Mann, Inc. Service Center. Mann, Inc., will pay for one-way shipping and handling if the DVD player is sent to a Mann, Inc. Service Center.

Mann, Inc. assumes no responsibility if:

1. The DVD player is not used according to the instruction booklet.
2. Damage is caused by improper use of merchandise.
3. The DVD player is lost.
4. Damage occurs due to service provided by someone other than a Mann, Inc. certified technician at a Mann, Inc. Service Center.

If you have any questions regarding this warranty or product, please call our Customer Service Center at 1-800-891-MANN, or write to Mann, Inc., 3274 Allison Road, Grossoville, FL 32741.

Exercise 1

Please work with a partner to answer the questions.

1. For how long is the DVD player under warranty?
2. When does Mann, Inc., not assume responsibility?
3. Who pays for shipping and handling if the DVD player is sent to a Mann, Inc. Service Center?
4. Whom do you call or write to if you have any questions?
5. What is the exact phone number of Mann, Inc.?

Example Lesson Plan 3
(Valerie Mann-Grosso and Monica Allison)

Objectives

Students will engage in interactive activities that stimulate conversation and negotiation of meaning. Students will gain fluency with language from Plan 2.

Materials

Role of paper for each student.

Procedures

1. Remind the students of the discussion done in the previous class.
2. Give students the sheet for Exercise 2 (see p. 265). Ask students to answer and discuss the questions in pairs. Allow student to discuss for about 5 minutes; then discuss questions all together as a class.
3. Give students the Warranty sheet (from the previous class), and ask a student to read it out loud as a review.
4. Next, students will draw a paper with a scenario description—either the customer service representative (labeled with "A") or an outraged customer calling the company to complain about a product (labeled with "B").
5. Arrange pairs of desks back to back. Have an A and a B student pair up and sit back to back.
6. Explain that the pairs will participate in a phone call. One of them is the customer service representative, and the other is the customer.
7. Allow students to interact for about 15 minutes. During this time, the teacher will walk around the class monitoring the students; this serves as an informal assessment.

8. At the end, select two students to act out the scenario in front of the entire class.

9. Make a list on the board of two or three language issues that seemed to be a problem for the class. Do not single out any one student or pair.

10. To tie everything together, start a discussion comparing return policies in the students' countries and the United States.

Homework

Have students write out a dialogue between an irate customer and a stubborn customer service representative.

Exercise 2

1. Have you ever returned a product to a store or company? Why?

_____

2. Did you get a refund?

_____

3. Were you satisfied with the customer service you received from the store? Why or why not?

_____

Role Play

Use the roles on p. 167.

Appendix E   List of Classroom Materials and Websites

When I first started teaching, I didn't know what to do. I mean, yes, I had been *taught* many things, or rather, I had taken many MATESOL courses with a lot of information coming at me, but I didn't know what to use, when to use it, how to use it, etc. I knew the common sense way of using a textbook, but I wasn't very good at using a textbook for anything other than what the directions said to do. I certainly wasn't ready to venture much beyond the book. I couldn't write a successful test, and I had only one or two ways of testing. I wasn't very good at conversation classes. In fact, the idea of letting students talk in class frightened me. I could plan what I would say, but if the students did a lot of the talking, then I couldn't plan for that because I didn't know what they were going to say. In other words, I was the classic teaching program graduate—a good person with a lot of book knowledge but a limited amount of classroom real-world experience.

I had no problem admitting to others that I needed help. In fact, what I do remember vividly was that my best source of help at that time could be found in the teachers' meeting room: the other teachers. I was surrounded by many teachers who cared and who were more than willing to share their expertise. The moral: Seek out advice from your colleagues. Listen to them. Their experience counts a lot!

Besides your colleagues, you will need additional resources. This listing of resources, which is organized into books and websites, is but an overview of some of the resources available to help you teach your students.

Conversation Textbooks and Resources for Teaching Conversation

Aceituno, A. M. (2000). *Business English and conversation for the EFL-ESL classroom*. Macquarie Park, Australia: Universal Publishers.

Ashby, W. (2003). *What makes America tick? A multiskill approach to English through U.S. culture and history*. Ann Arbor: University of Michigan Press.

Baker, L. R., Most, P., & Tanka, J. (1996). *Interactions one: A listening/speaking skills book* (3rd ed.). New York: McGraw-Hill.

Baker, L. R., & Tanka, J. (1996). *Interactions two: A listening/speaking skills book* (3rd ed.). New York: McGraw-Hill.

Byrd, P. (2001). *React interact* (3rd ed.). White Plains, NY: Pearson Education ESL.

Carver, T. K., & Fotinos, S. D. (1997). *A conversation book: English in everyday life, book I* (Rev. 3rd ed.). Upper Saddle River, NJ: Prentice Hall.

Chan, M., Byrd, P., Schuemann, C., & Reid, J. (2006). *College oral communication 1*. Boston: Houghton Mifflin.

Delk, C., Byrd, P., Schuemann, C., & Reid, J. (2006). *College oral communication 3*. Boston: Houghton Mifflin.

Duffy, P. (1986). *Variations: Reading skill/oral communication for beginning students of ESL*. Upper Saddle River, NJ: Prentice Hall.

Elbaum, S. (1997). *Tell me more: An ESL conversation text*. Boston: Thomson Heinle.

England, L., & Grosse, C. U. (1995). *Speaking of business: Advanced business-tapestry*. Boston: Thomson Heinle.

Foley, B. H. (1994). *Listen to me! Beginning listening, speaking, & pronunciation* (2nd ed.). Boston: Thomson Heinle.

Foley, B. H. (1994). *Now hear this! High beginning listening, speaking, & pronunciation* (2nd ed.). Boston: Thomson Heinle.

Folse, K. (1993). *Talk a lot: Communication activities for speaking fluency.* Ann Arbor: University of Michigan Press.

Folse, K. S. (1996). *Discussion starters: Speaking fluency activities for advanced ESL/EFL students.* Ann Arbor: University of Michigan Press.

Folse, K. S. (1998). *Clear grammar 1: Activities for spoken and written communication.* Ann Arbor: University of Michigan Press.

Folse, K. S. (1998). *Clear grammar 2: Activities for spoken and written communication.* Ann Arbor: University of Michigan Press.

Folse, K. S. (1999). *Clear grammar 3: Activities for spoken and written communication.* Ann Arbor: University of Michigan Press.

Folse, K. S. (2003). *Clear grammar 4: Activities for spoken and written communication.* Ann Arbor: University of Michigan Press.

Folse, K. S., & Bologna, D. (2003). *Targeting listening & speaking: Strategies and activities for ESL/EFL students.* Ann Arbor: University of Michigan Press.

Folse, K. S., & Ivone, J. (2002). *First discussion starters: Speaking fluency activities for lower-level ESL/EFL students.* Ann Arbor: University of Michigan Press.

Folse, K. S., & Ivone, J. (2002). *More discussion starters: Activities for building speaking fluency.* Ann Arbor: University of Michigan Press.

Fragiadakis, H. K. (1998). *All clear! Intro: Speaking, listening, expressions and pronunciation in context.* Boston: Thomson Heinle.

Gabler, B., & Scholnick, N. F. (1995). *Listen-in': Listening/speaking attack strategies for students of ESL.* New York: St Martins Press.

Gelin, M. T. (2000). *Taking turns: A pair-based text for beginning ESL.* Ann Arbor: University of Michigan Press.

Hahn, L. D., & Dickerson, W. B. (1999). *Speechcraft: Discourse pronunciation for advanced learners.* Ann Arbor: University of Michigan Press.

Hahn, L. D., & Dickerson, W. B. (1999). *Speechcraft: Workbook for academic discourse.* Ann Arbor: University of Michigan Press.

Hanreddy, J., & Whalley, E. (1996). *Mosaic one: A listening/speaking skills book* (3rd ed.). New York: McGraw-Hill.

Hanreddy, J., & Whalley, E. (1996). *Mosaic two: A listening/speaking skills book* (3rd ed.). New York: McGraw-Hill.

Hess, N., & Pollard, L. (2000). *Now you're talking! An interactive fluency workbook.* White Plains, NY: Pearson Education ESL.

Heyer, S. (2005). *Just joking: Stories for listening and discussion.* White Plains, NY: Pearson Education ESL.

Jones, L., & Kimbrough, V. (1987). *Great ideas student's book.* New York: Cambridge University Press.

Jones, L., & Kimbrough, V. (1987). *Great ideas teacher's manual.* New York: Cambridge University Press.

Jones, L., & von Baeyer, C. (1983). *Functions of American English teacher's manual.* New York: Cambridge University Press.

Jones, L., & von Baeyer, C. (1983). *Functions of American English student's book.* New York: Cambridge University Press.

Jones, L. (2001). *Let's talk 1. Student's book.* New York: Cambridge University Press.

Jones, S., Byrd, P., Schuemann, C., & Reid, J. (2006). *College oral communication 4.* Boston: Houghton Mifflin.

Keller, D. P. (1986). *Interactions two: A speaking activities book.* New York: McGraw-Hill.

Keller, D. P., & Thrush, E. A. (1987). *Interactions one: A speaking activities book.* New York: McGraw-Hill.

King, K. B. (1997). *Taking sides: A speaking text for advanced and intermediate students.* Ann Arbor: University of Michigan Press.

Klippel, F. (1985). *Keep talking: Communicative fluency activities for language teaching.* New York: Cambridge University Press.

Kozyrev, J. (2002). *Talk it over! Listening, speaking, and pronunciation, 3* (2nd ed.). Boston: Houghton Mifflin.

Kozyrev, J. (2002). *Talk it up! Listening, speaking, and pronunciation, 1* (2nd ed.). Boston: Houghton Mifflin.

Kozyrev, J., & Baker, M. (2001). *Talk it through! Listening, speaking, and pronunciation.* Boston: Houghton Mifflin.

Madden, C. G., & Rohlck, T. N. (1997). *Discussion & interaction in the academic community.* Ann Arbor: University of Michigan Press.

Maher, J. C. (1992). *International medical communication in English.* Ann Arbor: University of Michigan Press.

Matthews, C. (1994). *Speaking solutions.* White Plains, NY: Pearson Education ESL.

Matuck, A., & Vali, Y. I. (1998). *Gotcha! Speaking and listening activities for intermediate learners.* Carlsbad, CA: Dominie Press, Inc.

Molinsky, S. J., & Bliss, B. (1993). *Day by day: English for employment communication.* Upper Saddle River, NJ: Prentice Hall.

Molinsky, S. J., & Bliss, B. (2000). *Side by side: Student book 1* (3rd ed.). White Plains, NY: Pearson Education ESL.

Molinsky, S. J., & Bliss, B. (2001). *Side by side: Student book 2.* White Plains, NY: Pearson Education ESL.

Morley, J. (1979). *Improving spoken English: An intensive personalized program in perception, pronunciation, practice in context.* Ann Arbor: University of Michigan Press.

Moshin, D. (2002). *Building blocks of English: A conversational approach to fluency.* Burlingame, CA: Alta Book Center Publishers.

Nunan, D. (2001). *Expressions 1—Meaningful English communication. Student text.* Boston: Thomson Heinle.

Nunan, D. (2001). *Expressions 2—Meaningful English communication. Student text.* Boston: Thomson Heinle.

Nunan, D. (2001). *Expressions 3—Meaningful English communication. Student text.* Boston: Thomson Heinle.

Nunan, D., & Beatty, K. (2002). *Expressions intro—Meaningful English communication. Student text.* Boston: Thomson Heinle.

Nunan, D., & Beatty, K. (2002). *Expressions intro—Meaningful English communication. Teacher's annotated edition.* Boston: Thomson Heinle.

Olson, K. (2001). *Something to talk about: A reproducible conversation resource for teachers and tutors.* Ann Arbor: University of Michigan Press.

Painter, R. (2002). *Conversation starters for intermediate ESL students.* Champaign, IL: Imprint Books.

Penrod, G. A. (1993). *Touchy situations: A conversation text for ESL students.* Wake Forest, NC: Delta Publishing Company.

Porter, P. A. (1992). *Communicating effectively in English: Oral communication for non-native speakers* (2nd ed.). Boston: Thomson Heinle.

Quann, S., & Satin, D. (2000). *Learning computers, speaking English: Cooperative activities for learning English and basic word processing.* Ann Arbor: University of Michigan Press.

Reinhart, S. M., & Fisher, I. (2000). *Speaking & social interaction* (2nd ed.) Ann Arbor: University of Michigan Press.

Richards, J. C., Bycina, D., & Wisniewska, I. (2005). *Person to person: communicative speaking and listening skills* (3rd ed.). New York: Oxford University Press.

Roemer, A., Byrd, P., Schuemann, C., & Reid, J. (2006). *College oral communication 2.* Boston: Houghton Mifflin.

Rooks, G. M. (1988). *The non-stop discussion workbook* (2nd ed.). Boston: Thomson Heinle.

Rooks, G. M. (1990). *Can't stop talking* (2nd ed.). Boston: Thomson Heinle.

Rooks, G. M. (1994). *Let's start talking.* Boston: Thomson Heinle.

Schoenberg, I. E. (2004). *Speaking of values. Conversation and listening.* White Plains, NY: Pearson Education ESL.

Schoenberg, I. E. (2005). *Topics from A to Z. Book 1.* White Plains, NY: Pearson Education ESL.

Schoenberg, I. E. (2005). *Topics from A to Z. Book 2*. White Plains, NY: Pearson Education ESL.

Smith, B., & Swan, M. (2001). *Learner English: A teacher's guide to interference and other problems*. Cambridge: Cambridge University Press.

Spaventa, L. (2004). *Improvisations for creative language practice*. Brattleboro, VT: Pro Lingua Associates.

Stafford-Yilmaz, L. (1998). *A to zany: Community activities for students of English*. Ann Arbor: University of Michigan Press.

Stempleski, S., Rice, A., & Falsetti, J. (1986). *Getting together: An ESL conversation book*. Boston: Thomson Heinle.

Tillitt, B., & Bruder, M. N. (1985). *Speaking naturally*. New York: Cambridge University Press.

Tillitt, B., & Bruder, M. N. (1985). *Speaking naturally. Student's book*. New York: Cambridge University Press.

Ur, P. (Ed.) (1981). *Discussions that work: Task-centered fluency practice*. New York: Cambridge University Press.

Vai, M. (1998). *The heart of the matter: High-intermediate listening, speaking, and critical thinking*. Boston: Thomson Heinle.

Wall, A. P. (1998). *Say it naturally 1: Verbal strategies for authentic communication* (2nd ed.). Boston: Thomson Heinle.

Wall, A. P. (1998). *Say it naturally 2: Verbal strategies for authentic communication* (2nd ed.). Boston: Thomson Heinle.

Webster, M., & DeFilippo, J. (1999). *So to speak 1, Integrating speaking, listening, and pronunciation*. Boston: Houghton Mifflin.

Webster, M., & DeFilippo, J. (1999). *So to speak 2, integrating speaking, listening, and pronunciation*. Boston: Houghton Mifflin.

Westfall, M. (1998). *Greetings! Culture and speaking skills for intermediate students of English*. Ann Arbor: University of Michigan Press.

Westfall, M., & McCarthy, J. (2004). *Great debates: Language and culture skills for ESL students*. Ann Arbor: University of Michigan Press.

Wright, A., Betteridge, D., Buckby, M., & Ur, P. (1984). *Games for language learning*. New York: Cambridge University Press.

Yorkey, R. (2002). *Talk-a-tivities: Problem solving and puzzles for pairs*. Burlingame, CA: Alta Book Center Publishers.

Yorkey, R. (2004). *Springboards: Communication starters*. Burlingame, CA: Alta Book Center Publishers.

Zelman, N. E. (1986). *Conversation inspirations for ESL (supplementary materials handbook)*. Brattleboro, VT: Pro Lingua Associates.

Websites

Title	Web Address
Activities for ESL Students	http://a4esl.org/
Boggles World: Jobs, Worksheets, Lesson Plans and Flashcards for the ESL and EFL Teacher	http://bogglesworld.com/lessons/archive.htm
Breaking News English. com: Ready-to-Use EFL/ESL Lesson Plans & Podcast, Current Events Lesson Plans	www.breakingnewsenglish.com/
Churchill House School of English Language	www.churchillhouse.com/english/downloads.html
Dave's ESL Café	www.eslcafe.com
The Educator's Reference Desk	www.eduref.org/cgi-bin/lessons.cgi/Foreign_Language/English_Second_Language
EFL4U Teaching the World English	www.efl4u.com/
EnglishClub.com	www.englishclub.com
English Daily	www.englishdaily626.com/
English-4U	www.english-4u.com/
English Language Teaching Web	www.eltweb.com/liason/Lesson_Plans_and_Exercises/
English-to-go	www.english-to-go.com/
ESLBASE for ESL Teachers and Employers	www.eslbase.com/
The ESL Center	http://members.aol.com/eslkathy/esl.htm
ESL Flow.com	www.eslflow.com/
ESL Go.com	www.eslgo.com/resources/sa.html
ESL Junction	www.esljunction.com/
ESL Lesson Plans and Resources	www.csun.edu/~hcedu013/eslplans.html
esl-lounge.com	www.esl-lounge.com
ESL Monkeys: English as a Second Language Resources	www.eslmonkeys.com/teacher/lessonplans.html

ESL TESOL Lesson Plans	http://esl.about.com/bllessonplans.htm
Interesting Things for ESL Students	www.ManyThings.org
The Internet TESL Journal for Teachers of English as a Second Language	http://iteslj.org/
John and Sarah's TEFL Pitstop	www.lingolex.com/jstefl.htm
Karin's ESL Partyland for ESL Students and Teachers	www.eslpartyland.com/default.htm
Language Arts Mini-Lessons Elementary (K–5)	http://youth.net/cec/ceclang/ceclang-elem.html
Lesson Plans	www.teachnet.com/lesson/
Lesson Plans Page.com	www.lessonplanspage.com/
Lesson Plans: 39 Content-Based ESL Lesson Plans for Beginning through Intermediate Students	www.everythingesl.net/lessons/
The Linguistic Funland	www.tesol.net/tesl.html
MES-English.com: MES Resources for ESL/EFL Teachers	www.mes-english.com/
NW Regional Educational Laboratory: Language Arts Lesson Plans	www.nwrel.org/sky/mat.asp?ID=3&search=2&m=23&d=6
One Stop English–Solutions for English Teaching	www.onestopenglish.com/
One World, One People ESL Lessons	http://members.aol.com/Jakajk/ESLLessons.html
Randall's ESL Cyber Listening Lab	http://esl-lab.com/
Sites for Teachers	www.sitesforteachers.com/
Southern Methodist University ESL Conversation Buddy Program	www.smu.edu/esl/ConversationBuddy.html

Taiwan Teacher	http://geocities.com/Athens/Delphi/1979/index.html
Teacher's Desk	www.teachersdesk.com/lessons/lessons_esl.htm
Teachers.net Lesson Bank	http://teachers.net/lessons/
Teaching English	www.teachingenglish.org.uk/try/plans.shtml
Teaching English as a Foreign Language	www.tefl.net/index.htm
Technology: The Art and Science of Teaching with Technology	www.teach-nology.com/teachers/lesson_plans/esl/
UsingEnglish.com ESL Teacher Lesson Plans & Worksheets	www.usingenglish.com/lesson-plans.html

References

Barkhuisen, G. (1998). Discovering learners' perceptions of ESL classroom teaching/learning activities in a South African context. *TESOL Quarterly, 32,* 85–107.

Biber, D., Johansson, S., Leech, G., Conrad, S., & Finegan, E. (1999). *The Longman grammar of spoken and written English.* London: Longman.

Brown, H. D. (2000). *Principles of language learning and teaching.* New York: Longman.

Corder, S. P. (1967). The significance of learners' errors. *International Review of Applied Linguistics, 5,* 160–170.

Corder, S. P. (1981). The significance of learners' errors. In *Error analysis and interlanguage* (pp. 1–13). Oxford: Oxford University Press.

Dolly, M. (1990). Adult ESL students' management of dialogue journal conversation. *TESOL Quarterly, 24,* 317–231.

Doughty, C., & Pica, T. (1986). "Information gap" tasks: Do they facilitate second language acquisition? *TESOL Quarterly, 20,* 305–325.

Duff, P. (1986). Another look at interlanguage talk: Taking task to task. In R. Day (Ed.), *Talking to learn* (pp. 147–181). Rowley, MA: Newbury House.

Elley, W. B. (1989). Vocabulary acquisition from listening to stories. *Reading Research Quarterly, 24,* 174–187.

Ellis, R. (1991). Grammar teaching—practice or consciousness-raising. In R. Ellis, *Second language acquisition and second language pedagogy.* Clevedon, UK: Multilingual Matters.

Ellis, R., & He, X. (1999). The roles of modified input and output in the incidental acquisition of word meanings. *Studies in Second Language Acquisition, 21,* 285–301.

Ernst, G. (1994). "Talking circle": Conversation and negotiation in the ESL classroom. *TESOL Quarterly, 28,* 293–322.

Folse, K. (1993). *Talk a lot: Communication activities for speaking fluency.* Ann Arbor: University of Michigan Press.

Folse, K. S. (1996). *Discussion starters: Speaking fluency activities for advanced ESL/EFL students.* Ann Arbor: University of Michigan Press.

Folse, K. S. (2003). Applying second language research results in the design of more effective ESL discussion activities. *CATESOL Journal, 15,* 101–111.

Folse, K. S. (2004). *Vocabulary myths: Applying second language research to classroom teaching.* Ann Arbor: University of Michigan Press.

Folse, K. S. (2006). The effect of type of written exercise on L2 vocabulary retention. *TESOL Quarterly, 40*(20).

Folse, K. S., & Bologna, D. (2003). *Targeting listening and speaking: Strategies and activities for ESL/EFL students.* Ann Arbor: University of Michigan Press.

Folse, K. S., & Ivone, J. (2002). *First discussion starters: Speaking fluency activities for lower-level ESL/EFL students.* Ann Arbor: University of Michigan Press.

Folse, K. S., & Ivone, J. (2002). *More discussion starters: Activities for building speaking fluency.* Ann Arbor: The University of Michigan Press.

Fotos, S. (1993). Consciousness-raising and noticing through focus on form: Grammar task performance versus formal instruction. *Applied Linguistics, 14,* 385–407.

Fotos, S., & Ellis, R. (1991). Communicating about grammar: A task-based approach. *TESOL Quarterly, 25,* 205–628.

Green, J. (1993). Student attitudes toward communicative and non-communicative activities: Do enjoyment and effectiveness go together? *Modern Language Journal, 77,* 1–9.

Gregg, K. (1984). Krashen's monitor and Occam's razor. *Applied Linguistics, 5,* 79–100.

Hulstijn, J., & Laufer, B. (2001). Some empirical evidence for the involvement load hypothesis in vocabulary acquisition. *Language Learning, 51,* 539–558.

Joe, A. (1998). What effect do text-based tasks promoting generation have on incidental vocabulary acquisition? *Applied Linguistics, 19,* 357–377.

Krashen, S. (1985). *The input hypothesis: Issues and implications.* London: Longman.

Lazaraton, A. (2001). Teaching oral skills. In M. Celce-Murcia (Ed.), *Teaching English as a foreign language.* Boston: Heinle & Heinle.

Liu, D. (2003). The most frequently used spoken American English idioms: A corpus analysis and its implications. *TESOL Quarterly, 37,* 671–700.

Long, M. (1989). *Task, group, and task-group interactions.* Paper presented at RELC Seminar, Singapore.

Lyster, R., & Ranta, L. (1997). Corrective feedback and learner uptake: Negotiation of form in communicative classrooms. *Studies in Second Language Acquisition, 19,* 37–66.

Mackey, A. (1999). Input, interaction, and second language development. *Studies in Second Language Acquisition, 21,* 557–587.

Mackey, A., & Philip, J. (1998). Conversational interaction and second language development: Recasts, responses, and red herrings? *The Modern Language Journal, 82,* 338–356.

Mulling, S. (1997). *Getting Them to Talk: Communicative activities for the ESOL Classroom.* (ERIC Document Reproduction Service No. ED409731)

Nakahama, Y., Tyler, A., & Van Lier, L. (2001). Negotiation of meaning in conversational and information gap activities: A comparative discourse analysis. *TESOL Quarterly, 35,* 377–405.

Newton, J. (1991). *Negotiation: Negotiating what?* Paper presented at SEAMEO Conference of Language Acquisition and the Second/Foreign Language Classroom, RELC Singapore.

Nunan, D. (1996). Towards autonomous learning: Some theoretical, empirical and practical issues. In R. Pemberton, E. Li, & H. Pierson, H. (Eds.), *Taking control— Autonomy in language learning* (pp. 13–26). Hong Kong: Hong Kong University Press.

Oliver, R. (1998). Negotiation of meaning in child interactions. *The Modern Language Journal, 82,* 372–386.

Oliver, R. (2000). Age differences in negotiation and feedback in classroom and pair-work. *Language Learning, 50,* 119–151.

Panova, I., & Lyster, R. (2002). Patterns of corrective feedback and uptake in an adult ESL classroom. *TESOL Quarterly, 36,* 573–595.

Peirce, B. (1995). Social identity, investment, and language learning. *TESOL Quarterly, 29,* 9–31.

Perez, B. (1996). Instructional conversations as opportunities for English language acquisition for culturally and linguistically diverse students. *Language Arts, 73,* 173–181.

Pica, T. (1996a). The essential role of negotiation in the communicative classroom. *JALT Journal, 18,* 241–268.

Pica, T. (1996b). Do second language learners need negotiation? *International Review of Applied Linguistics, 34,* 1–21.

Pica, T., & Doughty, C. (1985a). Input interaction in the communicative language classroom: A comparison of teacher fronted and group activities. In S. Gass & C. Madden (Eds.), *Input in Second Language Acquisition* (pp. 115–132). Rowley, MA: Newbury House.

Pica, T., & Doughty, C. (1985b). The role of group work in classroom second language acquisition. *Studies in Second Language Acquisition, 7,* 233–248.

Pica, T., Holliday, L., Lewis, N., & Morgenthaler, L. (1989). Comprehensible output as an outcome of linguistic demands on the learner. *Studies in Second Language Acquisition, 11,* 63–90.

Pica, T., Kanagy, R., & Falodun, J. (1993). Choosing and using communication tasks for second language instruction and research. In G. Crookes & S. Gass (Eds.), *Tasks and language learning: Integrating theory and practice* (pp. 9–34). Clevedon, UK: Multilingual Matters.

Pica, T., Lincoln-Porter, F., Paninos, D, & Linnell, J. (1996). Language learners' interaction: How does it address the input, output, and feedback needs of L2 learners? *TESOL Quarterly, 30,* 59–84.

Pica, T., & Long, M. (1986). The linguistic and conversational performance of experienced and inexperienced teachers. In R. Day (Ed.), *Talking to learn* (pp. 85–98). Rowley, MA: Newbury House.

Polio, C., & Gass, S. (1998). The role of interaction on native speaker comprehension of nonnative speaker speech. *The Modern Language Journal, 82,* 308–319.

Porter, P. (1986). How learners talk to each other: Input and interaction in task-centered discussions. In R. Day (Ed.), *Talking to learn* (pp. 200–222). Rowley, MA: Newbury House.

Richards, J. (2001). *Curriculum development in language teaching.* New York: Cambridge University Press.

Selinker, L. (1972). Interlanguage. *International Review of Applied Linguistics, 10,* 209–231.

Sharwood Smith, M. (1981). Consciousness-raising and the second language learner. *Applied Linguistics, 2,* 159–169.

Simpson, R., & Mendis, D. (2003). A corpus-based study of idioms in academic speech. *TESOL Quarterly, 37,* 419–441.

Storch, N. (1999). Are two heads better than one? Pair work and grammatical accuracy. *System, 27,* 363–374.

Swain, M. (1985). Communicative competence: Some roles of comprehensible input and comprehensible output in its development. In S. Gass & C. Madden (Eds.), *Input in second language acquisition.* Rowley, MA: Newbury House.

Swain, M. (1995). Three functions of output in second language learning. In G. Cook & B. Seidlehofer (Eds.), *For H. G. Widdowson: Principles and practice in the study of language.* Oxford: Oxford University Press.

Swain, M. (2005). The output hypothesis: Theory and research. In E. Hinkel (Ed.), *Handbook on research in second language teaching and learning* (pp. 471–484). Mahwah, NJ: Lawrence Erlbaum.

Swain, M., & Lapkin, S. (1995). Problems in output and the cognitive processes they generate: A step towards second language learning. *Applied Linguistics, 16,* 371–391.

Williams, J. (2001). Classroom conversations: Opportunities to learn for ESL students in mainstream classrooms. *The Reading Teacher, 54,* 750–757.

Yorio, C. (1986). Consumerism in second language learning and teaching. *Canadian Modern Language Review, 42,* 668–687.

Index

Answers to Crossword Puzzle, page 157

¹A	P	²R	I	³L		⁴M	⁵A	⁶R	
		U		I		⁷O	N	E	
⁸L	I	N	C	O	L	N		⁹S	
E				N			¹⁰T	E	A
¹¹A	B	¹²B	R				E		T
P		E			¹³J		N		U
	¹⁴O	F		¹⁵A	F	T	E	R	
¹⁶K	N	O	¹⁷W		N		H		D
	¹⁸R	E		¹⁹I				A	
²⁰W	E	D	N	E	S	D	A	Y	

Answers to Brainteaser, page 198

- Load the goat in the boat, cross the river, unload the goat.
- Go back across the river, load the cabbage, take it to the other side of the river, and unload it.
- Load the goat, take it to the other side of the river, and unload it.
- Load the wolf, take it to the other side of the river, unload it.
- Go back across the river for the goat.